MW00780806

SUPREME
ALPHA MALE
BIBLE
The 1ne

EMPATH & PSYCHIC ABILITIES POWER.

SUCCESS MINDSET

PSYCHOLOGY • CONFIDENCE.

WIN FRIENDS & INFLUENCE PEOPLE.

HYPNOSIS • BODY LANGUAGE

ATOMIC HABITS.

DATING: THE SECRET.

Sean Wayne

CONTENTS

INTRODUCTION

Trusting someone is one of the most important traits to master if you want to be successful in life. While you have decided to bet on yourself, the majority of Men out there will continue their boring lives, controlled by their emotions, like weak little leaves in the wind. In fact, some guys won't graduate from little children to Alpha Males until they master their emotions and become truly confident. Modern society, however, has seen a shift in what it means to be male, and it is not necessarily for the better. Look around any public space, and evaluate the Men you see.

We all want to be Alpha Men— strong, confident, and healthy. Sadly, what you'll see are scores of deconditioned Men lacking energy and trust. As a result, they suffer for the rest of their lives: home, work, and society. We all know, deep down, we can be better, but pride and ego often prevent us from doing anything about it. No matter how much a Man wishes to improve himself, the amount of misinformation on how to be a Man is so overwhelming that it stunts his progress even more. Man, provider, leader – the masculine half of our species has many terms to define it, but one of the most popular is the very misconstrued idiom "the Alpha Male." The term Alpha Male simply means "one who leads," but it has become synonymous with arrogant, macho, manly Man.

So, instead of a Man of compassion and integrity, one who knows who he is and carries himself accordingly, we see an inwardly insecure Man who feels the need for one-upmanship and a dick-swinging bravado. The difference between these two contrasting pictures of Man is easy to see. Which one do you want to be?

If you want to be the original Alpha Male – one who radiates true masculine energy, is in shape, full of subtle trust in himself, happy, healthy, and comfortable in his own skin, then this book is for you.

In this book, you'll learn how to master the art of trust, which will make you the top Alpha Male in your social, or even your professional, circle. You're just a few steps away from becoming a success in whatever you do and whatever social and professional circle you are in.

MEET SEAN WAYNE

Sean Wayne is a self-made Man, graduate of International Relations and Diplomatic Science. He knows exactly what he's talking about because of his intense studies and skills in relationships of all kinds. He is an authority in personality development because to him, work, well-being, wealth, and love relationships are not just an exact science, but also a noble art. Helping people achieve the next level of being a Man matters deeply to him because what you're about to learn has helped plenty of Men gain the confidence to go after what they want. **Sean** is the perfect person to be writing this book as—thanks to his father's experience as a noted psychiatrist and his own psychophysical skills—he has become a talent, and later guru, of psychological manipulation, persuasion, and therefore... of relationship.

His goal behind writing is simply to transform anyone from any background, social upbringing, and personal beliefs into a 100% alpha male, left, right and center. And what better way to do this than getting into the psychology, habits, verbal and non-verbal language, charisma, self-esteem, vision, and a lot of tenacity of the Men who have it all, and presented by a Man who is an authority when it comes to being passionate and enthusiastic about the hows and the whys on how even you can be an ALPHA MALE. No bullshit, no snake oil; just pure, hard facts that you may never have realized until you picked up this book.

Above all else, the goal of **Sean Wayne** while letting you in on this Bible full of secrets and strategies is simply to let you reach the pinnacle of your potential as a Man. His love for the topic and willingness to share it with anyone who can benefit from this for the better is a testament to just how much he wishes for everyone to resolve their deep-seated pains and inadequacies, and have the opportunity to finally achieve the absolute pleasure they could only dream of. Living the reality of a real ALPHA MALE.

CHAPTER ONE

THE 3 KINDS OF MEN: BETA MALE "NICE GUYS," JERKS & ALPHA MALES

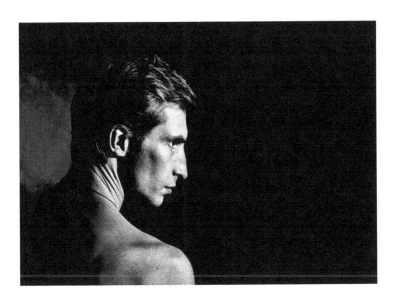

GROWING UP, my mom, aunts, and other older ladies always told me I needed to be a nice guy to get a girlfriend. I would have to buy a girl flowers regularly, give her presents, and take her out to eat. "Wow," I thought, "I'm going to have to have a great job, so I can spend all that money!" So I internalized their counsel, sadly. I strived to be the good guy all through high school and college, the one that girls supposedly wanted. Girls would always say how much they enjoyed what I did, but a kiss on the cheek was the most action I ever got.

Once I got to college, though, the advice I started getting changed. Suddenly, it was the common understanding that you needed to act like an asshole rather than a nice guy to be successful with women. I tried this suggestion out too, and noticed that some people reacted to me more when I was behaving like a jerk. I didn't get the praise I expected though. I got to have my first sexual relationship, but it was with a head case of low self-esteem. And I still had issues with a lot of girls choosing other guys over me.

So, I took a nice hard look at the guys who were successful with women, those who weren't, and those in between. I realized that there are three types of Men: nice guys or Beta Males, jerks, and Alpha Males. And make no mistake, for women, there's certainly a pecking order and nice guys are at the bottom of the pile, even though they might make up the majority of the male population.

The Nice Guy Or Beta Male

Nice guys are Men who are essentially begging for love. They are the ones turning up with flowers at a woman's house, taking her to fancy restaurants, and buying her Filet Mignon with fine wine. They are also the ones that end up feeling disappointed when they bring her home because she doesn't even invite them in. And even through all the hell of it, he doesn't learn anything – he goes back to using the same methods with the very next woman he meets.

The ironic thing is that some women think that nice guys are manipulative. It's quite clear to the woman why a guy is doing so many nice things for her: "They're just after one thing!" Nonetheless, she thinks he might have good relationship potential, so she puts him on the back burner and eventually maybe even has sex with him. But boy, she will make him wait for a long time! Some women set a minimum of three dates, which is like winning the lottery for the nice guy, and many other women make guys wait months before they "get lucky." And when sex arrives, it's a huge event, and the woman is making a big deal out of it. Hopefully, though, the guy doesn't have a high sex drive because he can't get sex whenever he likes. Sex happens only if she is in the mood, and this is a fact he'll need to accept. So why don't nice guys win? The issue with the nice guy is that while women already see him as dishonest, they also see him as dull. The nice guy talks about rational things, like foreign policy or how a car engine works. Often, he brags about himself and how much money he makes, suggesting he can provide for a woman. "How boring," she thinks.

Committing to rational discourse and trying to impress a woman with your smarts and earning potential is a mistake that 99 percent of guys make. It destroys the woman's desire for you because it expresses need and low self-worth. If you weren't needing her endorsement, you wouldn't try to impress her. If you were a high-value (Alpha Male) instead, she would be the one wanting your approval.

The other problem is that women who associate with guys during the mating ritual absolutely loathe rational and boring conversation. It takes her out of her trance! But don't misunderstand me. You shouldn't pretend to be an idiot around girls. In reality, women find Men who are experts on something to be very attractive. So, what you need to do is make sure that you talk about interesting things within your area of expertise, not mind-numbing material.

In fact, if you haven't already done this, you should start becoming an expert in something right away. It doesn't matter what: Immovable property, rock music, *South Park* trivia, faith, history, the possibilities are endless. A Man with expertise in a particular field is instantly an Alpha Male when it comes to that field. Just be sure to captivate her with the information you have in common. Don't bore her. As the song goes, girls just want to have fun and the sweet, boring guy isn't fun. Go to places where singles meet and check out the couples you see. If a girl looks lonely or is talking on her cell phone endlessly, then she is most definitely there with her boyfriend. That's because her boyfriend is a good-looking guy who's no fun to hang out with and doesn't excite her.

But remember: A Man asking a woman for her acceptance and sexual attention is doing it out of desperation and misery. Looking to lay hot chicks? Then keep this in mind first and foremost: the fastest and easiest way to kill any desire that a woman may begin to feel for you is to feel insecure about yourself, or to be in need, or to seek approval. When you are desperate to please, you end up coming on too hard or too early. When you act clingy it looks like begging. There's an old saying about banks: they want to loan you money only when you're already loaded. If you really need the money, then you can forget it.

The Problem With Being Her "Friend"

Have you ever had a girl who is a friend that you chased around as the months went by, hoping she would eventually fall for you? Lots of guys, particularly the shyer ones, do this. These guys end up being very pathetic. They listen carefully as their female friends tell them about the real Men in their lives jerking them around.

Believe me, that is where I was. The low point arrived when one of my female friends, who I had a massive crush on, asked me to hang out at her apartment with her. "Superb!" I thought, "am I dreaming?" This was the moment I was waiting for, right? I followed her plan like a nice guy while we sat in her living room, including spending a good two hours carefully going over every single word that her neighbor next door (a druggie bartender) told her that day at lunch. "He was laughing and he called me crazy. Do you think he loves me?" I did my best - I told her that I thought he was a jerk and she could do better. I gave her all the justifiable, logical reasons why this was true. She told me that she agreed with me. Girls always agree that the "wrong guy" is wrong, but, of course, they forget it and have sex with them anyway. Just like she did.

If there were any fairness in this world, women would eventually come around to liking the nice guys. Truth to be told, they do sometimes, but usually when they are older. By this point, they have generally already had children with some idiot who bailed on them and the children, and the thought of settling down with a weak-willed Man who will hang around and take in a steady paycheck is beginning to have an appeal. Women simply don't like spineless people. And when you behave like a nice guy, follow the agenda of the woman, and defer decision-making to her, she does not value you.

Good guys want the woman to choose where to sleep and when they have sex. They have no idea that this thoughtfulness pulls them down immediately into the lifelong friend zone. And that's why the nice guy doesn't get laid. As I said, women don't always like to be the ones in control of sex. You must take that responsibility as the Man and lead the way. This is what many women want you to do, and trust me, when you do, they love it!

Avoiding The Beta Male Mindset

Nice guys do sometimes appear to be passive-aggressive, as well as being too indecisive. Women are often passive-aggressive themselves, so when this particular characteristic is displayed in a Man, they are turned off. What does it mean to be passive-aggressive? It is being passive until you are driven too far, and then instantly becoming aggressive. Have you ever had a woman who was expecting you to read her mind, and then acts crazy when you read it wrong? This is passive-aggressiveness.

The nice guy constantly gives in and does whatever the woman wants instead of finding the middle ground between passive and aggressive, which is assertive. When the woman finds the nice guy's antics unappealing, she eventually leaves him for someone else, and the nice guy will lament about how he "did it all for her." And this is where the problem lies. Nice guys also have jealousy issues, born from their insecurity. They are too outwardly dependent - the woman is the source of all their happiness. You see, the feelings of jealousy that many Beta Males feel regarding women come from a vulnerable place. So, if you feel this way about a girl, suck it up and let those feelings go.

When a girl feels a guy is insecure, it's like he is telling her, "Yeah, I feel inferior to those other dudes you're hanging out with." Showing that lack of self-confidence makes the girl not feel less confident about you too. She begins to wonder if the grass is greener in other pastures.

I know it's hard not to feel jealous, but look at it this way: if you thought you were the best, and you could attract hot babes and get laid easily, would you care if your girl went off talking to some other guys? Not at all, this would be her loss! So here's a fresh way of thinking I want you to adopt: "I'm growing into a high-value Alpha Male." Keep repeating this to yourself as an affirmation throughout the day. We'll talk more about affirmations in a later chapter.

By the way, you might still be wondering what to do if your girl is talking to other dudes. The very worst thing you can do is attempt to try to stop her. This makes it so she, not you, has the higher value. Instead, the best way to react in these situations is to say, "Have a good time!" with a tone of total indifference when she says she will go hang out with some other Man. Let her see that you're not one bit worried. In the meantime, you are also talking to other people. This turns the tables so she's the one who is now worried about whether you're going to leave her for the competition. This sets you out to have a higher value.

Another way to avoid getting upset at the actions of a woman is not to take individual women seriously or give a great deal of concern about what they think. Getting overly concerned with the thoughts and feelings of a woman is a waste of time, for the bottom line is that you can not control what a woman thinks or feels. You can only control your reactions. Rather than taking women too seriously (which gives them power over you, making you vulnerable and unattractive), just treat them as a common source of fun and enjoyment in your life. That's it.

Have a spine with women instead of being a pushover. The next time you're with a woman, try saying "no" to her. Saying "no" to women can sound harsh. But do it gently, like this – Her: "Let's go rent a movie." You: "No, not yet. Let's go in about an hour." In saying no, you are establishing your authority and setting yourself up as a challenge for the female. When she sees you as a challenge, instead of being bored, she will be intrigued by you. When you say YES to everything your wife suggests, she will soon say NO to you in the bedroom. Most of all, what you need to know is that women resent every kind of need. The Alpha Male is attractive to women because his happiness comes from within, so she has no responsibility for his emotional state to stress her out.

Let me stress one thing here: Women are central to your inner state. You have to value yourself first for them to see you as lovable. You have to be optimistic about your future and go for the thing you wish for. There are a lot of nice guys out there who feel anxious around women, and as a result, put themselves down. That's why nice guys finish last when it comes to love.

The Jerk

The dick, or jerk, is on a middle level, above the nice guy. Some assholes appeal to women more than nice guys because they aren't dull assholes. Although the asshole and his girlfriend create an emotional rollercoaster of drama, at least the girl gets the ride's emotional highlights along with those low points. He can make her cry, in other words, but he also makes her laugh. And the doubts that she has provide some level of suspense in her life.

Here's what you need to get about people: women need to tap into their desires instead of their rationale if they are to be sexually turned on. The good guy makes the horrible mistake of appealing to a woman's rationality, whereas the one good thing a jerk does is try to appeal to her feelings. Jerks get laid because they are so persistent - they get woman turned on and then go for the lay. They're sexually aggressive, unlike the sexually passive nice guys. While the jerk produces negative emotions in women, they often feel that at least they produce emotions, as opposed to the nice guy, who bores them.

It's not all perfect for the jerks though. The kinds of women who go for jerks are mostly head cases with low self-esteem, depression, and other emotional problems. These women also act odd and insecure when it comes to relationships, so in any case, they're not really the kind of women a well-adjusted Man would want to go for.

The good news is that there is still a higher level of Man. This is what is called the Alpha Male. An Alpha Male causes positive emotions in women and nol negatives ones.

The Alpha Male

What is an Alpha Male? If the term confuses you, then allow me to give you the simple understanding of what an Alpha Male truly is. The concept of an Alpha Male is something most people misunderstand. Many assume that external factors lead to being an Alpha Male. To some people, an Alpha Male is:

- the Man that receives attention from all the ladies.
- a Man with a great job and happy family.
- a celebrity.
- a CEO.
- the Man with a great body and a six pack.

In other words, if a Man has a certain status, position, physical trait, or ability to communicate, then he becomes an alpha Man. Well, he may have certain traits of an alpha Man, but if these traits are used to cover up an inner beta male, he is not necessarily an alpha. In other words, to be truly an alpha Man, you need to have the self-confidence and belief that makes you one. There are all those traits within you. You just have to discover them and take them out. The process of becoming an Alpha Male starts with a strong mind. Don't just look at Men you admire and try to replicate their behaviors. Find your own reason for achieving the status of an Alpha Male. You'll only succeed if you have a strong sense of who you want to be, and why you want to do so.

True alphas have strong reputations. This doesn't mean that you need to be overly agreeable in an attempt to get everyone to like you. Instead, trust in your own beliefs. An Alpha Male should be able to maintain absolute confidence in himself, regardless of what other people think or say. If you maintain a strong mind and hold firm to your personal values, you'll end up filling your life with people who admire and appreciate you for who you are. Strong networks of friends and allies can only be developed by being true to yourself.

The Inner Alpha Wrap-Up

Not every guy is the complete opposite of an Alpha Male, but that doesn't mean there aren't areas for him to work on. That's what this book is for: to help any Man who feels like something is missing in his life. It will help you to identify just what that missing piece is, and will drive home a long-term solution that will change your life for the better.

Of course, we all have bad days, bad weeks, and even bad months. However, if you're aware of these things and actively working to improve yourself, you'll be putting your best foot forward each day, no matter where you're at in your own personal journey. We must always endeavor to move forward and be better Men. The act of maintaining this attitude towards each and every day is what makes Men great leaders, partners, friends, and--of course--alphas. If you stay sharp, keep in control, and remain fit and healthy, you'll create a great life, while inspiring others to do the same.

You might feel skeptical about this. Getting in shape and eating well certainly don't seem like world-changing habits--but that's exactly what they are. What our world needs is a new breed of Man, a combination of modern assets and the primal instincts of our ancestors. Training and eating well will help you develop your strength and confidence, and will lead you to do great things both big and small. In order to achieve this, your head must be in the right place, and you need to be able to put concentrated time and effort into who you are and what you want to become. Think about what you want out of each individual day. Ask yourself what ultimately drives you, and what truly makes you happy.

Remember: thoughts lead to actions, actions become habits, and habits define you who are. With this in mind, there's nothing holding you back from beginning your ascent to the status of Alpha Male.

Next comes the biggest factor – your nutrition. Getting this wrong can be a health, waistline, and libido killer. Having a big gut and finding it hard to walk up a few flights of stairs is really only the start of a number of issues affecting health, including low sex drive, diabetes, heart disease, depression, and low confidence. It's easy to see how so many can get it wrong. Mass advertising, lax government policies, celebrity fads, and know-it-all nutritionists present conflicting messages. It can be too much to even contemplate, let alone master. However, it's really quite simple. When performed on a regular basis, healthy nutrition can be your best form of medicine that helps to create the awesome body that your mirror will reflect. Not to mention, healthy nutrition will shape a healthy, confident, and vibrant guy who loves waking up each day.

Once you understand healthy nutrition, you should write your own weekly meal plan. After that, check the plans we provided, as well as the included bonus material for more details and information. For the most part, you can follow the plans laid out in this book. Pay attention to the food you eat and how your body reacts to it and let this be your guide. Once you've followed the guidelines and you're feeling awesome and starting to look like the kind of Man you want to be, then you can start getting specific. In this instance, turn to the back of the book to see how you can contact Mike if you have questions or would like guidance.

It's easy to see how exercise and training can become confusing for some people. While this part of your daily life is not affected by the same level of propaganda as food is, there are still mixed messages. However, exercise (and getting to a point where you look good) involves hard work, people commonly look for an easy option or a quick fix. This can lead to stagnation, frustration, injury, weight gain, and a feeling of losing heart about training entirely. This often results in giving up until you reach the breaking point again and feel you need to do something or you'll keep getting worse.

Perhaps you're in danger of not having that realization. That's where the good news comes in. Training isn't that complicated; in fact it's really basic. You just have to work hard. There are many programs and approaches, but if you stick to these principles and combine staying active with the other steps in this process, you'll be well on your way to becoming a ripped and athletic Alpha Male. Again, go through your key points. Check the information in your bonus material if you want to learn more and then start using the available programs. Too many guys over-think training and try to get everything a certain way, constantly searching for the "perfect" program that will finally get them in shape. Don't fall for this. Keep it simple and train as if you're an athlete and your paycheck depends on it. Do keep in mind that, no matter who you are, where you live, or how old you are, you can train hard and get in shape.

Living a balanced life sometimes seems impossible. Some people say they'll get a more balanced life when they retire. However, this approach will always prevent you from reaching it. Many Men today struggle with the concept of balance. We spend too many hours at the office and not enough doing the things we enjoy with the people we enjoy. What's worse, we don't get nearly enough quality sleep. The week can't go fast enough and the weekend comes and goes. This pattern of high stress, little enjoyment, and poor sleep results in a hormonal imbalance that, left to its own devices, can give rise to metabolic diseases or worse. Living like this means that you're heading to a bad place.

One of the best tools for feeling amazing every day is managing stress by getting enough quality sleep. Many people miss this point and this is why there are so many stressed out, fat, and hormonally disbalanced Men everywhere. Like everything else, it doesn't have to be that way. It's easy to put some actions in place to ensure that you get enough sleep, less stress, and more enjoyment out of your day. Start by always enforcing a positive frame of mind in yourself. Once you set goals that are based on your core values, you'll start heading in the right direction each day. From there, focus on sleep and nutrition and ensure that you are always balanced in all that you do. If this seems like a nice idea, but you feel that it isn't practical, you need to sit down and get a hold of your priorities. Go back to your core values and find out what matters most to you. If all you care about is to make lots of money and die rich, so be it. However, if you want to be healthy, well-adjusted, and able to spend time with your loved ones doing things that give life meaning and make you smile, reconsider your priorities and take control of your life. After all, this is what we're talking about – Alpha Males have control of their lives and they love how they live.

The final step in your journey to unleash your inner alpha is to master the finer points, the icing on the cake and the polish that makes the shoe shine. This is an area that is lost on a lot of Men. If you don't understand the consequences of your choices and how you come across to others as a Man, you'll miss out on many moments in life that matter. No doubt, confidence will come from getting in shape but it also comes from your actions. You have to actively seek activities that improve your confidence levels and exude confidence. We're not talking about arrogance, self-importance, or selfishness. We're talking about subtle confidence that includes self-worth and looking after yourself. We're also talking about being able to do the things that a Man should do. There's a missing link in our development as Men because of a lack of traditional rite of passage; this can arguably cause a women-dominated world without the proper tools to function as a Man. Conversely, we can have far too much masculine energy that causes us to act based on ego and macho bravado. Our primal and animal instincts are to garner respect and be desirable to encourage potential mates who want to mate with us. These instincts can be defeated as a result of our lifestyles. It is up to you to walk proudly and assert your confidence and dominance. This is what being an alpha Man means and it is exactly where the finer points of being an Alpha Male are relevant.

Once you've started to initiate some of these steps, you'll see your confidence grow, your situation improve, and your life change for the better. This isn't due to the universe aligning for you, but because you're starting to develop a clear view about yourself and becoming a better Man. You'll be doing things for yourself. You'll be doing things for others. You'll be hustling all the time to improve and be an awesome guy and become an alpha legend. Once you nail this stuff, you can begin fine-tuning your progress with the help of a life coach.

To become an alpha legend, a leader, and a magnet for people and good luck, you have to be dedicated to these changes. Don't wait or deviate from the path or you'll miss opportunities. Get to a point where you're happy and stay the course. If need be, you can always iron out wrinkles as you go. If you're staying the course, you're staying productive, which means that you're moving forward. This is the hustle you need to get into. To improve any part of your life, from sleep to weight loss to attracting the right mate, you have to hustle and work your butt off. No one will do this for you– you have to take ownership of your own life and your own fate. You're now actively working to build your muscles and become strong. Similarly, train your hustle muscles. Always look to increase your hustle. Stop obsessing over the things that don't matter and just get going. Get out of your comfort zone, stretch yourself, and evolve. You should always make your own luck, remember?

This whole process is about recognizing the potential within you. This is about patience, practice, progress, and being dedicated. This is about having maturity when it's needed and the power of laughter when it's not. This is about your mission to become a better Man and positively affect the world and the people around you every day. This is about hustle and hard work. This is about building a better version of yourself – a great body, a great character, and a great life. This is about waking up happy and rested in the morning and discovering a passion for life that pushes you to get better and better.

Alpha Males are the pioneers of society - people look up to them. The Alpha Male is a leader. He is self-confident, socially dominant, outgoing, friendly, has high self-esteem, ando has his shit together. He can joke and be fun. The Beta male is annoyed when a woman says something rude to them, while the Alpha Male laughs about it because he thinks girls are like his teasing younger sisters. And when a woman later feels remorseful for her mockery and discovers that the Alpha Male didn't make a big deal out of it, she gives him big points for that.

Many of the social interactions we participate in have the subtext of domination and control. Studies of social circumstances show that influential people mark their territories in numerous nonverbal ways, such as taking up space with their bodies, using a louder voice, manipulating interactions and using strong eye contact.

Those around the Alpha Male appear to be drawn to their world because they feel comfortable and fascinated with them. Since the alpha Male is not needy, he does not feel possessive or jealous about women. He does not smother women by placing them on a pedestal either. He knows that any woman will be fortunate to have him, and if any woman doesn't go for him, that's her loss, not his. The Beta male, meanwhile, is anxious, has low social status, and is generally an apprentice rather than a frontrunner. He feels secretly resentful of successful people, has low self-esteem, and is clingy and insecure toward women. Which one do you want to be?

CHAPTER TWO

WHAT DOES IT MEAN TO BE AN ALPHA MALE?

WHAT EXACTLY IS AN ALPHA MALE? If the term confuses you, allow me to give you a simple explanation of what an Alpha Male truly is. The concept of an alpha Male is something most people misunderstand. Many assume that an alpha Male is defined by external factors. To some people, an alpha Male is:

- the Man that receives the attention from all women
- the Man with a great job and a happy family
- the celebrity
- the CEO
- the Man with the best body, including a six-pack

In other words, if a Man has a certain status, position, physical traits, or ability to communicate, then he becomes an Alpha. Well, he may have certain traits of an Alpha Male, but if these traits are used to cover up an inner beta male, he is not necessarily an Alpha. In other words, to be truly an alpha Male, you need to have self-confidence and believe in who you are. All these traits are within us all. You just have to discover them and nurture and grow them.

Most importantly, becoming Alpha originates from having a strong mind -- a mind that most people dream about having. Becoming Alpha is about finding your reason for being Alpha. Whatever you imagine doing, you've got to have a strong enough reason for doing it.

True Alphas have a good reputation. But having a good reputation doesn't mean you have to agree with every Tom, Dick, and Harry. Reputation comes when you trust what you believe or what you value. Most importantly, there is the willingness to never dismiss the things you believe in, regardless of what people say. That goes hand in hand with being strong-minded. Look closely around you. You'll realize the people you've surrounded yourself with respect you. Here's the ultimate definition of an Alpha Male based on my research: A Man with a strong mind, a strong reputation, and a strong network of friends that can support him.

The Simplest Secret To Being Dominant

When it comes to enticing women, dominance is key. If you can master a dominant attitude and use it to take charge of your relationship with women, you'll be much more likely to end up in a sexual relationship.

One way to exercise dominance is through "framing" of reality. For example, say a woman generates some meaningless drama and paints it as a big deal. If you go along with her, you're being pulled into her frame of reality, thereby reducing yourself to beta male status. If, on the other hand, you choose to reframe her drama as funny and trivial, you're bringing her into your frame, which establishes you as the dominant force in the interaction. Most people would let themselves be sucked into the woman's frame by having a long conversation or fight about the supposed source of drama. But if the matter at hand isn't truly important, you should be able to shrug it off. If you gently agree with her and move on, you can then change the subject to something interesting and mutually beneficial.

Remember that your belief system is what matters most. If you keep up internal affirmations such as "I'm a good catch" and "I'm the reward, not her," the woman is guaranteed to buy into that paradigm as well.

Women don't like putting themselves on a pedestal. Dehumanization works both ways: idolizing a woman can be just as harmful as looking down on her. Not only does it prevent you from making a meaningful, human connection; it also puts you in a position of neediness and inferiority.

Think about your experiences with needy people in your life. Chances are that you found them stifling and they seized every possible opportunity to gain your attention. They constantly asked for help and companionship and they were insecure in themselves and therefore unable to enjoy anything on their own. The psychological effect of clinginess is repulsive rather than attractive. Do you want to seem like that kind of person to the woman you've chosen to pursue?

All of us fall victim to clingy or vulnerable thoughts at one time or another. Try to be on the lookout for thoughts such as these:

> *"If I lose this girl, I'm not going to have sex for months."*
> *"I really wish that this girl would like me."*
> *"What do I need to do to make myself more appealing to this girl?"*

Ironically, when you try too hard to make someone like you, it has the opposite effect. A safer, healthier way to reframe your desires is by putting *yourself* on a pedestal. You are a winner, and your actions should make it clear that you're well aware of that.

Here's a quick example of how a beta male suffering from the above self-doubts might approach a common situation: asking a girl out to lunch.

BETA MALE: May I please have the privilege of escorting you to lunch? It can be my treat. Where do you wish to go?

WOMAN: Thank you! How about El Supero Expensivo Ritzo?

The two will go to lunch, but the woman will only view him as a nice guy and a good friend. He isn't going to get laid because his attitude is passive and needy rather than confident and alluring. Beyond that, his wallet is going to be significantly lighter. A lot of Men complain about the amount of money that they spend on women, failing to recognize the fact that the cash they spend is entirely within their own control. When you nervously offer something like a lunch date, you're showing the woman that you would be honored by her presence, and therefore that you're willing to pay any amount of money in order to obtain it. In choosing an expensive restaurant, she doesn't think that she's taking advantage of you--in fact, she sees it as doing you a favor, since she's agreeing to your offer to take her out in the first place.

Now let's take a look at how an Alpha Male would handle the same exchange.

ALPHA MALE: I'm going to have some lunch at my favorite place, El Cheapo Restaurant. (*then, almost as an afterthought:*) You're a fun person--come eat with me.

The guy in this example is confident in himself and his decisions. He wants lunch, he knows where he wants to get it, and he would enjoy a woman's companionship--but his plans won't change based on whether or not she chooses to come with him. She's being invited to come because she's fun, not because he's desperately trying to please her. This serves as a sharp contrast to the first situation, in which the Man was clearly putting the woman on a pedestal.

You might have noticed that "come eat with me" is an order, not a request. This is because an Alpha Male doesn't fear putting his balls on the line by *telling* rather than *asking*. Don't act tough or bossy, though--make sure to soften your words by using them in a playful manner. She and you both know that you aren't actually commanding her to come with you, but it's still important to display confidence.

Finally, take note of how the second example doesn't portray lunch as a romantic date, but rather a fun outing. This helps steer the woman away from putting her relationship with you in the same category as past ex-boyfriends. If it does take a romantic and sexual turn, that will be fun and exciting rather than boring and predictable.

All women are logically immoral under the right conditions. When you embrace that mentality, you become a good catch. You don't need a woman to confirm and support you as a strong person; instead of validating you, she should feel that she needs to actively pursue you out of her own desire.

In summary, as a sexy Alpha Male, you will:

- Make women come into your life, rather than forcing your way into theirs.
- Take the lead role when it comes to dating and sex, since women tend to be passive in those areas.
- Stir women up emotionally.
- Be a guy who's aware of his own high value, so that women feel compelled to win your love.
- Don't take women--or anything else in life--too seriously.
- Have your own values, be assertive, and speak for yourself.
- Remember that a woman's approval is never required!

If you prioritize all of these things, women will be tripping over themselves in their eagerness to be with you!

The Two Main Types of Alpha Males

The first type of Alpha Male is reserved for any animal that lives in the wild. In this case, being an Alpha comes into play as a kind of "survival of the fittest." "Kind of" is used in this context because even within the wild kingdom of animals, there is a kind of unspoken code that they all follow. This code is that aggression and violence are expressed only when necessary – when the need for food or to defend oneself calls for it.

The exception to this rule, though, is the expression of male aggression and violence to determine who has the right to mate and/or lead the group. Here, you'll see that most Alpha Males are the younger, more mature, larger, and stronger Males of any given family species. This holds true whether the animal is a carnivore, herbivore, or omnivore. The older, slower, weaker, and possibly smaller animals are bumped out of the Alpha position.

The second type relates to the human-animal that lives and interacts in modern society rather than in some prehistoric times. Here, we find that Men are engaged in a contest to fight for their food and possessions. Within this contest, there are two types of Men – the ones who add to society and are fruitful members of their family, community, nation, etc., and the Men who have the confidence to dare to be who they really are without folding or bending to others.

In other words, when determining whether or not a Man is an Alpha, ask yourself: Does he claim his personal territory (in all things), or is he constantly subjecting himself to those who invade such space without a fight?

The True Traits of an Alpha Male

But a real Alpha Male is more than just physically strong and charming. In fact, being an Alpha Male doesn't just come down to physical appearance, it's about qualities and personality. If you wish to become a true Alpha in your group, team, or community, it's not just about how you look, but about how you act and behave. Here are the personality traits and key skills you need to develop to become an Alpha Male:

- **Confidence:** Confidence is number one on this list, but many people don't understand what confidence really is. Many people associate confidence with being an asshole or cocky. This is far from the truth. These are a bully's tools for making yourself feel better about yourself – i.e. self-validation or validation by your peers. An asshole is a bully who desperately tries to convince everyone around him (and himself) that he's a hard guy or "dominant." "Players" are often associated with being very confident and charismatic Men, but that's not necessarily true.Thinking very little of women (other than as sex objects), enough to lie and manipulate them deliberately, is neither an expression of trust and confidence nor a charming quality. An Alpha male knows exactly how to tread the fine line between trust and arrogance. That's what makes them stand out from the crowd.

- **Leadership:** This is a trait that is commonly associated with being an Alpha Male. The importance of leadership in most societies is so significant that even military divisions use it as an assessment to find out who is the Alpha of any group. The clue is that only a real Alpha Male will assume a leadership role to which all others willingly submit and become his subordinates.

- **Charm and charisma:** Being charming or charismatic are two other traits associated with the

Alpha Male. This is mostly due to two different reasons:

• Charming and charismatic Men are outgoing and perceived as interesting, or the life of the party.

• They're confident because they're attractive on their own.

Yes, being a people person is an attractive trait and, in fact, it naturally attracts people to an individual with attentive ears and attitudes, but it is not a necessary trait to be considered an Alpha. Not all Alpha Males are frontrunners, or rather not all Alpha Males feel the need to be in a leadership role.

Charm and charisma are more related to one's ability to express oneself naturally and to not really care what others think, all the while taking into account the emotions, ideas, and beliefs of others. This is not to be confused with the fear of expressing oneself fully or backing down from one's position. An Alpha also carries a strong sense of trust with them by creating positive solutions to obstacles they may encounter in whatever endeavor they engage in.

• **Assertiveness:** One more thing that's often going to be seen as Alpha Male is assertiveness. This means he's someone who dares to go after what he wants or do what needs to be done – a personality that is confident and powerful. An Alpha Male will clearly state what he wants to everyone, including to the women who want his attention. Whether it's in the form of opinions or desires, assertive Alpha Males will have to defend their position from time to time; there will always be someone who challenges his Alpha Male position.

- **Positive body language:** Alpha Males tend to exhibit the type of body language that gets the message across about who they are. For example, they will always make and keep eye contact in all circumstances. The way they walk exudes confidence. Smiling is another positive piece of body language they display. When the situation presents itself, an Alpha Male will smile. Finally, their voice has an authoritative tone. This doesn't mean that they have the power to order someone around, it just means they have a strong voice that allows them to be heard without having to yell.

- **Humility:** A true Alpha Male expresses himself with humility, yet can declare his strengths when required. A truly self-assured Man feels no need to force others to recognize his presence and is content to sit quietly to the side. He feels no need to initiate elaborate gestures, movements, or verbal signals, to distinguish himself from others. He knows that being his true self is enough.

- **Consideration for others:** The human Alpha Male will always bear in mind how his actions, words, or thoughts affect others. For instance, when passing through an entrance, he may hold the door open for the next person following behind, regardless of their perceived gender. Another example is that the Alpha Male, when passing others in a narrow passage (without giving up his own personal space), will politely shift his body. He takes into account that all choices and actions he makes can have a direct or indirect impact on others, and thus, acts to minimize negative impressions on people. An Alpha Male will never change lanes while driving without first seeing if the lane is clear and he has sufficient space to do so safely. An Alpha Male's never going to engage in a "chest-puffing contest" with another male just to defend his ego.

- **Honesty:** Being an alpha Male is not only about being trustworthy, but also about expressing oneself genuinely and not talking for the sake of talking. There is a purpose that underlines all they do, yet it allows for moments of pure playful fun. An Alpha Male does everything in a way that fully expresses the self, without allowing the Entity of the Ego to pollute things. He has nothing to prove because he has true general self-confidence. Therefore, he will not shout to be heard, nor will he express this need for attention by listening intrusively to music (forcing everyone else to recognize his presence). Finally, he certainly doesn't dress a certain way just because that style is considered popular.

- **Responsibility:** The Alpha Male takes responsibility for his expressed actions, decisions, and words, and assumes that responsibility. This also means confessing and surrendering to the consequences of his mistakes. It means acknowledging that he made a mistake and apologizing when necessary. This acceptance transcends and moves into a form of expression beyond just taking responsibility in conventional ways. The Alpha Male naturally and effortlessly expresses his willingness to take responsibility for his actions.

- **Maturity:** This one may seem to be too far out there, but what I mean by maturity is that the Alpha Male has developed a sense of when things are right and when they're wrong. There's always a time and place for anything and everything we do in life. A true Alpha Male knows when to play around, when to be serious, when to be aggressive, when to put himself in charge, and when to be sexually playful.

- **Respect:** The Alpha Male is naturally respectful of those he comes into contact with, but will not respect those who show no respect for him or others. Here is when the human Alpha Male might decide to be like the Type 1 animal Alpha Male and shut down the problem inside the pack (put them back in their place, so to speak). This doesn't always mean using physical methods. The Alpha Male may choose to use verbal projection and sometimes even his spiritual presence alone.

- **Steadfastness:** This is an interesting trait associated with an Alpha Male, which is somewhat related to the Type 1 Alpha Male. The Alpha Male will "be on their own " when in their "territory," or when it comes to their beliefs. But this is not about ego. He will just stand by his position whenever he feels strongly about something. However, he will also take back any statement made by mistake and apologize for any misspoken words. The true Alpha Male does not feel the need to impose himself in the personal space of others just to prove how tough he is. Remember, he doesn't need validation.

- **Determination:** Another key feature of Alpha Males is that they are very decisive. They know what they want and take action to get it. They do not spend hours flip-flopping over stupid shit, here and there. Most guys spend too much time worrying about things and never pull the trigger when it comes to action. That's not what Alpha Males do. Alpha Males are decisive. They know what they want, they create a plan to get it and they act on it.

- **Dominance:** An additional significant feature of Alpha Males is that they are influential. This is not in a risky way where they sense the need to dominate everybody, but they are nonetheless dominant by their very nature. They're natural leaders; they're on top of the totem pole. They're ready to stand up for those they love and care about. You have to spend some time learning how to be dominant if you want to be an Alpha Male. Many of us have mental roadblocks we need to overcome first. Dominance, however, is important. Dominance means that in any situation you always come out on top – and that's exactly what Alpha Males do.

- **Purpose:** Another solid indicator that an individual is an Alpha Male is their very clear masculine purpose. Most guys mess up this part. Your goals should actually come before everything else. Your goals should come before women. There are no exceptions. When a Man puts his wife before his purpose, he deprives his authentic self from the world. When he's putting his purpose before everything else, he can accomplish great things – in fact, it's the only way you can ever do great things.

- **Courage:** You have to be ready to take risks in life. You have to be willing to follow your fear and do what you need to do. This is exactly what Alpha Males are doing. They don't have any second thoughts about taking risks, even though they might sound scary. The only way to achieve anything worthwhile in life is by taking risks. If you're not willing to do so then in Henry David Thoreau's words, you'll live a quiet life of despair. Having courage is one of the basic features of Alpha Males, because nothing worthwhile is accomplished without it.

- **Calmness:** Calmness is another key Alpha-male trait, particularly when under pressure. Alpha Males are aware that they're on top, so they don't need to prove anything. Have you ever seen those guys trying to start fights? Some Men are always looking to prove themselves in some way. That's not Alpha, it's Beta. Beta Males are the ones who feel the need to prove themselves and put others down. Again, true Alpha Males don't care about what others think because they know they're always on top.

- **Comfortable with losing and failure:** Losing and failing should never make you happy, but it happens. You must understand why you have struggled or lost, so you can make adjustments and improvements to stop losing and start winning. Don't feel comfortable losing, but if it does happen, be resourceful. Find out why, and find the lesson in the experience to aspire to be a winner in the future.

- **A beginner's mind:** There's always something you can learn. Always be mindful of every encounter. A very important quality of cultivating a beginner's mind is letting go of the ego. Once you do this, you won't feel entitled to anything anymore, and your only motivations become to learn and grow. When personal growth becomes an individual's goal in life, they are filled with humility. And if you are having problems achieving personal growth, it is okay to get help. Ask and you will receive.

- **Not needing validation from others:** What makes an Alpha Male special is that he doesn't need to seek approval from others to make himself feel better. He doesn't seek validation from people around him, but at the same time, he doesn't have a sense of superiority (like a jerk has). He's not looking at others for how to live his life – he's making his own laws and doesn't care if somebody disagrees. He will consider and respect the views of others, but he will never be motivated by them.

- **Not comparing himself to others:** Many guys need to compare themselves to others, but not an Alpha Male. This is not because he thinks he's better than others, but because comparing and judging others based on their looks, values, social status, or ideas doesn't even cross his mind. Whenever an Alpha Male comes across a new woman, he's not going to put her on a pedestal. A beautiful woman has no greater value to him than an average-looking one. He believes all human beings are equal.

- **Optimistic with a good sense of humor:** Humor plays an important part in attraction, and an Alpha Male can make people laugh around him. However, he's not trying to be the funniest guy around. He is not cracking jokes relentlessly in the hopes of getting others to chuckle. The reason he attracts women is because, in practice, he has a positive attitude and knows how to be self-amusing. An Alpha Male will make fun of a moment, as he finds it humorous, and others will also be amused and respond to it.

- **No problem dealing with tension:** An Alpha Male is a Man who keeps his cool in the toughest circumstances. He stays calm and level-headed when others have problems dealing with tension. He can adapt to any situation and remain totally comfortable and centered. This is particularly important when meeting women, as women are going to ruthlessly test a Man to see how he responds. Since an Alpha doesn't even break a sweat, he's going to be seen as hot.

- **Authentic:** Whatever an Alpha Male does, it's real. His actions and interactions mirror who he is. He does not need to make use of tricks or deception to make others think of him as someone he is not. To pretend to be another person doesn't even cross his mind. If you ever meet an Alpha Male, you will recognize him right away by the way he carries himself.

- **Self-assurance:** Certainty is vital to a Man who has essential decisions to make. The concept of an Alpha, in itself, is someone who is very confident and has no questions regarding his choices. Nobody, except himself, will change his mind on the things that he thinks are real. This does not mean, however, that he is hard-headed and denies when he's in the wrong. Whenever he is in the wrong, he is very modest and has no trouble admitting it to himself and others.

- **Gentle and protective:** It is only natural that a leader should be protective and gentle towards his own kind. Looking at the animal kingdom, you will notice the Alpha animal protecting its pack. When danger arises, an Alpha wolf will protect its kind. If a non-pack member walks near an area controlled by the leaders, then subordinate pack members sound off alarms, and the Alpha may launch an attack.

Being protective means not only protecting others but also helping others and solving their problems together. When someone comes to him for help, an Alpha Male is always ready to help and never runs away. In addition to that, an Alpha Male is a gentleman who cares for his clan, especially the feMales. Therefore, he practices being a gentleman.

Common Confusion About Alpha Males

Whenever there is talk of an Alpha Male's attitude, some people think he's a guy who shows his superiority over others by being the group's loudest and most violent person - someone who continuously needs to be in the middle of awareness to feel validated. A Man who's so desperate for attention that he'd do anything to make himself stand out, even if it means fighting with others.

But the guy I just described isn't an Alpha Male in any way. He is a jerk. The reason some people confuse these two types of guys is because the jerk has some Alpha Male characteristics. He is optimistic and volatile (a massive turn-on for women), but he lacks maturity and is typically too self-centered to be considered an Alpha.

He's just an immature boy compared to the Alpha Male and has to put down other people to feed his massive ego. So the next time you come across a jerk, don't try to mark him as an Alpha Male.

The Truth About Becoming Alpha

As you can see, becoming an Alpha Male comes down to devloping many traits. Do not take such examples as rules when you're trying to become one. Look at them more like instructions on how to become a satisfied Man. If you try to force yourself to act in any rigid way, you'll just slow your progress.

To become an Alpha Male, you don't need to seek perfection. The Alpha Male does not have any fantasies about being perfect nor does he aspire to be so. He only knows how to play to his strengths, mitigate his weaknesses, and strive tirelessly to become a better Man. And so should you!

Building Self-Confidence Above All Else

We say it takes years to build self-confidence, and just a few rude or hurtful words to kill it. Most people are shy and aware of how others will perceive them. That's why most people are motivated to please others or to be someone they themselves would look up to. There are some innately optimistic, highly charismatic Men. Perhaps you could easily identify these individuals when you were in school. They might have been talented, good-looking, excellent speakers, or a combination of these qualities. They were very involved in their social groups, and over time, they continued to build their self-confidence.

Unfortunately for people who are naturally shy and self-conscious, the reverse is true. There are also those who, especially in school, are not yet in touch with their true talents and abilities during the early stages of their social life. Unfortunately, this is usually the time when they need to show off the most to gain self-esteem. In addition, their capacity to develop self-confidence is hampered dramatically, ultimately making them Betas in their adult lives. These people often tend to shy away from public-speaking engagements, and generally take fewer opportunities.

All in all, this is the most significant Beta Male issue – they rely too much on their social image, and as a result, their self-confidence suffers. Betas limit themselves, take less responsibility, become less socially active and completely lose confidence in being the celebrity they are meant to be. This is why you need to embrace self-motivation and reject the idea of letting others form your perception of yourself. In other words, you should free yourself from the external picture and concentrate on your self-image first. Know that once you become an Alpha, you can enjoy a brand new social image.

Being Self-Disciplined

This book will teach you techniques to achieve the necessary self-discipline you'll need to use your strengths and weaknesses in your favor. For now, you will focus on stopping yourself from thinking about your social profile. It may sound counterintuitive, but remember that you need to have an honest opinion of yourself, based on self-respect, instead of seeking recognition and ego boosters from other people. In other words, don't rely on others to create a positive self-image.

Prevent yourself from bragging to your peers at all, particularly about the progress you'll make throughout the rest of this book. By the end of the month, give them a nice treat by showing them the new you. If you're especially active in social media, you can just try to limit your posts and updates to the essentials. Be humble and see how rewarding it is to do the right thing, without letting others know.

You should congratulate yourself before you start you finally realized the need to be an Alpha. Each person eventually gets tired of being a Beta,but not all dare to take the first step. This is the first trait you need to be a male Alpha – and you have it.

Realizing you need to be an Alpha isn't all the changes in attitude you'll need to make to be successful in this endeavor. Trusting yourself is extremely important if you want to succeed. It is also one of the utmost significant Alpha Male traits. However, the majority of Betas ignore this. And there's a good chance you haven't grown your self-confidence to the fullest if you don't consider yourself an Alpha, but how do you know for sure that you're not an Alpha Male?

Signs That You Are Not An Alpha Male

Now that you know all the important traits of being an Alpha Male, it's important to also understand the signs to look for in yourself and others that may determine that you are not an Alpha Male:

- **You complain too much:** Have you ever met this type of Man? He is the type that complains about everything on the planet. The sort that will tell you how the economy is in the toilet, the IRS is stealing our money and most of his friends suck. Men like this hardly have any stable relationships. Do you know why? Because most women get fed up with their whining. Besides, if these Men only whine and complain, how will they solve their family's problems? A Man who complains isn't an Alpha. When an Alpha Male has a problem, he finds the solution. Period. If the economy is bad, he looks for ways to improve his financial situation. He stays calm and comes up with a solid way out. This attitude is better than spending the rest of your day whining and not doing anything about it. True Alphas never grumble.

- **You have low self-esteem:** Obviously. Have you ever seen a Man constantly having to read his girlfriend's texts and messages every time she leaves the room? The Man who walks up in the middle of the night to go through his girl's texts, or to check if his girl has other male friends she talks to. This is an indication of low self-esteem. It means you think other Males are better than you, and they're going to take away your girl. Another example is when a Man feels a woman would be better off without him, or a Man who begins to see that he is not a particular woman's type, based on his personality and physical features. True Alphas muster up their confidence and believe they have something unique about them that the world loves. You're not a true Alpha if you don't value yourself.

- **You like to gossip:** Gossiping is a female trait. Men with a mission and focus seldom have time to gossip because they are engaged in achieving their goals. Similarly, Men who gossip don't know their time's best use and probably don't have any plans for their future. True Alphas keep their minds busy with their ideas and friends that can help them to scale their vision and mission. Stop belittling people if you want to be an Alpha, even if you're treated badly!

- **You handle crises poorly:** What do you think makes a Man? How he reacts to a crisis. If you've lived long enough in this world, you've encountered different crises, from relationships and politics to schools and friendship; the difference between an Alpha and a Beta is how each one handles them. Beta people are known to react to every crisis they encounter. True Alphas acknowledge the urge to change in a time of crisis. An average Man panics in response to crises. An Alpha Male works towards solving the crises.

- **You bully people:** Let's get one thing straight: Alphas don't fear fighting when it's needed. But this

SUPREME ALPHA MALE BIBLE. THE 1NE.

doesn't mean they should be bullying everybody around them. Bullying people does not make you an Alpha. It makes you look animal-like. Alphas focus on challenging people at an intellectual level, rather than bullying them. The days that Alphas were considered bullies are long gone.

- **You play blame games:** The first thing that Betas do when things go wrong is to blame other people or circumstances. They blame their parents for not giving them a better education. They blame their friends. They blame their teachers for not giving them a perfect grade. If you wish to become an Alpha, take on responsibilities yourself. Believe that "shit" happens and it could be because of you. Alpha Males are the guys who will accept 100 percent responsibility. Your life will only change when f you stop accusing others and shoulder the responsibility of your actions.

- **You lie:** Always ask yourself: Why are people lying to each others? People lie because they want two things:

  - Protection

  - Admiration

A child lies to avoid being scolded by her father. Due to admiration, a young Man will steal. True Alphas stands for truth and will tell the truth. They tell the truth no matter how hard it is. As an Alpha Male, you want to be that kind of person.

- **You aren't a gentleman:** True Alphas are the ones who will open the door for a woman, carry her bag, etc. If you're the type of guy who expects the lady to pay the bill after having a date with you, then you're not a gentleman. Gentlemen aren't financially broke and they have money to spend on their wardrobe. You have to be a gentleman if you want to be a true Alpha. A true gentleman will always be mindful of his manners and grooming habits. He will carefully choose and keep his home and will have a high standard of living.

- **You act before thinking:** Emotion rules the world and it is the reason most Men make bad choices. Frustration and depression cause people to make bad decisions. People who are not Alpha Males will either respond positively or negatively to emotion. Train yourself from now on to think before you act. How? Simple, try to write down what you are about to do before making any decision. That's the only way to gain insight on which decision you should make.

- **You don't handle fear well**: Fear is something we all have, including Alphas. What sets true Alphas apart from Betas is how they handle fear. Fear in your life will always be there, whether you want to start a new business or start something new. You will always be afraid. Most people who live in fear never actually take the first step in accomplishing anything. Fear can come in many different ways: fear of starting a business, fear of networking, fear of offending others, and fear of making bad choices. There is fear. It is something we cannot deny. But true Alphas are intrepid. With die-hard courage, they approach everything so it will work no matter what.

- **You have a victim mentality:** Don't play the victim or have the mentality of "why me" when things don't go right. Don't miss out. Take control of your life. The fact is that life is not always going to be perfect. There are ups and downs. Life is happening and things are happening. But never get so weak that it will ruin your day, your week or your life for a long period of time. Allow things to roll off your shoulders, and continue to move forward. The longer you act like a victim or feel sorry for yourself, the longer it takes to accomplish what you want in your life. Spend your energy becoming a stronger person and spending less time like the universe is against you (it's not).

- **You procrastinate:** Time is your most precious resource. Why? Because you'll get old one day and look and feel tired. And then, you will die. And I don't think you will actually comprehend this until you experience this with someone close to you, or you begin to get older. Don't let time pass you by. The more you wait to achieve something, the longer it takes to get successful or reach whatever goal you have. The more you wait to achieve something, the less likely it is that it will happen. Just get going. Stop making excuses.

- **You underestimate yourself:** Don't sell yourself short. Know the value of yourself. Do not take jobs that don't pay you enough (unless it's a stepping stone to things bigger – never settle). Don't be scared to let people know about your accomplishments and achievements (do it humbly). Be proud of what you have accomplished throughout your life. When you undervalue yourself, you'll feel like people are taking advantage of you and not showing you the respect that you deserve. You have worked hard to be the person that you are. Be proud, and let others know about it. As I have already said, never settle. You deserve the best.

Okay, So What Next?

Are you willing to be an Alpha Male, and master the art of trust? Then evade the above traits. Be the fearless Man that ladies long for. Try to change your behavior, if you have any of the above traits.

Women can tell if you are drowning in fear. Always trust your values and abilities, for they are what makes a Man an Alpha.

CHAPTER THREE

GETTING READY TO GROW & BUILD A CONFIDENT MINDSET

YOU ARE NOT YET an Alpha Male, and it will take a whole lot of personal development to get to that level. You'll have to focus on every aspect of yourself, from your attitude to your work ethic, and trust in yourself.

The first thing you need to understand, in order to become an Alpha Male, is why you aren't one yet.

What's Gone Wrong?

We all know that we like women and that we want women, but that's pretty much as far as we've gotten. We're honking our car horns and yelling at girls on the street, rather than pursuing them in a way that will make us attractive to them. Why do Men do these things? Why do we behave so poorly? Men have bigger waistlines than ever, soaring rates of disease, and worrying statistics when it comes to divorce, job satisfaction, depression, and suicide. We aren't developing or improving, we know that no matter how poorly we act, we tend to end up with women anyway. Everywhere you look, beautiful women are accompanied by Men. Do you think that these are special Men? Are they gifted? Highly unusual? One of a kind?

The truth is that the majority of Men are facing a few main issues:

- They are physically deconditioned, causing their hormones to function suboptimally. This leads to being overweight, unfit, weak, and inflexible, with poor posture, poor sleep problems, and various illnesses and diseases.
- They have low confidence and self-worth.
- They are undersexed--either due to lowered libido, a lack of sexual opportunities, or both.

Why is this happening? Why do we have low self worth? Why is depression and general dissatisfaction with life so rampant? Why are we not enjoying a great and healthy sex life? We're in bad shape. For the most part, we're simply eating the wrong foods, not doing enough exercise or the right kind of exercise, living over stressed lives, not getting enough quality sleep and having our priorities all mixed up. These elements work as a whole and when one or more is affected, the others are too, leading to a sense of unbalance. Left unchecked, this unbalance can and will present itself as a physical, emotional and/or spiritual dysfunction.

Here's a typical scenario: You're spending too much time at work and not enough quality time doing things you enjoy. This starts to cause higher levels of stress, which are usually handled very poorly and encroach on the time you do get away from work. Sleep suffers dramatically and this vicious cycle becomes a downward spiral. This can result in losing motivation at home and any real control in your life. Fear can start to take over as a dominant motivator of your actions--the fear of losing motivation at home, in your social situations, and in your work environment. This feeds on itself and becomes huge.

A fear of rejection from partners or potential partners is also a real prospect. This all leads to a perceived loss of control which in turn leads to an actual real loss of control. This is less than ideal for Men when we want to be in charge of our lives and our days.

The good news is that we can change. However, there's a downside to that. There is a lot of information out there about what to do when you feel stressed, depressed, and unmotivated. It's confusing, overwhelming, and often conflicting information. It can really feel like a kick in the teeth instead of the help we're needing at this point. We can lose further confidence and end back on our downward spiral. Now the weight keeps piling on, the confidence continues to drop, we struggle to emotionally or intelligently articulate this to ourselves, let alone others, and soon we remember that we haven't had sex in months and we're getting depressed. It's hard to build the self-esteem and the sense of comfort we need at this point. The society we live in and its trappings of wealth and possessions are also factors that make us feel worse instead of better.

This is alarming particularly when we witness soft Men everywhere nowadays. No, I'm not saying you should be a brute to get ahead. Males, however, should have an ingrained toughness, a masculine physique, and the steadfastness to withstand life's blows. This is what is seriously missing today when yesteryear's Men. Let's look at another thing. Not every guy in great shape is an Alpha Male. There are jerks who are ripped everywhere, but they are not well-rounded Men. To unleash your alpha, you must be mentally and physically strong.

Finding out what happens can be a chicken and egg situation. Do we have low esteem because we couldn't find the time, motivation, or energy to do anything about it? Are we unhealthy because we deal with too much stress and not enough quality sleep or are we tired and stressed because we're unhealthy, out of shape, and are constantly busy?

Where the Problems Lie

How many Men do you know who second-guess themselves on a daily basis? Sentences such as, "Yeah, honey, whatever you want," are commonplace from a guy who is essentially being dominated by his partner. He lacks the gumption to take the lead of a situation and own it.

How many Men rave about how happy they are in their lives? These days, the answer is very few. The media only serves to worsen the situation. So many Men are in a long-standing rut, doing the same thing every day, with intermittent happiness and no true, deep-set satisfaction.

This misery and ignorance are sending today's Men on an unpleasant journey to an early grave. It also increases a lack of confidence and self-sufficiency, leading to long-term unhappiness and depression, as well as physical consequences such as obesity, diabetes, heart conditions, and loss of fertility.

Decoding The Personality of an Alpha Male

The first thing we think about when we hear the term "Alpha Male," is a super good-looking guy who is macho, muscular, charming, and heroic. This may sometimes be true, but a real Alpha Male is more than just physically strong and charming. It is not enough to be in shape. You also need the intellect and the right qualities. And this is exactly what we will be talking about in this chapter. Below are an Alpha Male's top qualities. If you wish to become a true alpha in your group, team, or community, it's not just about how you look, but mostly about how you act. Here are the traits that you need to develop to become an Alpha Male:

Have Confidence

An Alpha Male is always confident. You need to portray yourself as a confident person, no matter how you dress or how you look. A lot of people have the wrong idea about confidence. Being self-assured as an Alpha Male doesn't mean that you should act cocky or arrogant. Instead, you should present yourself as someone upon whom others can depend. More than anything else, confidence signals reliability. As a team leader, for example, when a problem occurs, you should be able to give your team the confidence that you are reliable. Look at all the world's great leaders, they display a high level of trust even when things don't work in their way. This is not to say you're supposed to be a cheerleader for others, but rather to be confident in what you want, where you're heading, and in yourself.

For example, if you go shopping with a friend, you shouldn't have to ask their opinion on a shirt that you want to buy. A self-assured Alpha Male knows what he wants without seeking somebody else's approval. Trust in yourself, and be confident in your choices without depending on other perspectives.

Be Competitive and Take on Challenges

Competitiveness is an important trait of an Alpha Male, who doesn't shy away from challenges and competition. An Alpha Male loves it when he can solve a difficult and challenging problem, and shows curiosity in the process of doing so. Everyone wants to win and no one wants to lose. An Alpha Male intentionally chooses things that are challenging to do rather than looking for an easy way out. Look at Arnold Schwarzenegger. He is at his best when someone tells him that something is impossible and no one has ever done it. This is because Alpha Males love to be the first to do something. So, ask yourself, do you love challenges? If you've never challenged yourself, you don't know your limitations. The only way to know your own abilities is to always challenge yourself and how far you can go. And that's also a great way to improve your skills and abilities.

Take sports, for example. If you're not competitive and you don't like challenges, you can't win the game. The same holds true for your life. You have to be willing to take up challenges and to compete to get what you want.

Develop Solid Communication Skills

You don't need to be a communication master to be able to deliver a speech like an experienced speaker. Alpha Males, however, have strong communication skills and they effortlessly deliver their message to their audience. Body language also includes this confidence. The way you stand, the way you walk, eye contact, and your gestures are extremely important because they portray your level of confidence. Alpha Males have a strong body language, so you can tell from the way they talk and how they walk that they're on the ball. Work on developing this skill.

Being a good communicator doesn't only mean that you talk well, it also means that you're not afraid to make your point. While interaction is a huge topic and it takes time to master, you can always start by developing the basics, such as speaking a little louder and more firmly, showing confidence in your speech, making eye contact with the person you are talking to, and standing up and walking straight. Give a strong and solid handshake when you meet someone for the first time. Give a good impression to others and dress appropriately.

Be Decisive and Courageous

You'll need to work on your courage and your decision-making skills. For instance, many people have a hard time deciding what to do over the weekend or even what to eat for dinner on any given day. As an Alpha Male, you're supposed to be decisive and understand what you want. You shouldn't spend an hour thinking about what to have for dinner. Just make the choice and stand by it.

Decision-making is the first part. What's more important is to stand by what you've decided. Once you have decided on some-thing, stand by what you have decided unless you know you have made the wrong decision. Stop changing your mind like you're changing your clothes every day. An Alpha Male clearly knows what he wants, makes a clear decision, and stands by what he had decided. Whether it is on the job or at home, Alpha

Males are proactive. They are looking around, judging the situation, and then making a clear decision and remaining firm to that. If you wish to be one of the Alpha Males, learn how to cultivate confidence and take responsibility for your decision.

Be Physically Fit

While many people think that being fit is all it takes to be an Alpha Male, that's not true. A true charismatic leader doesn't need to be physically strong; he just has to be physically fit. Obviously, you're not going to expect an Alpha Male to be unhealthy, nor are you expecting him to be unfit. Not everybody can have a body like Dwayne Johnson, but the key is to make sure you're healthy and physically fit. You don't have to have Schwarzenegger's body but you have to be in good shape. Therefore, commit yourself to exercising and maintaining your overall health.

Prominent athletes like Cristiano Ronaldo and Roger Federer, for example, are extremely fit, yet they don't have muscular bodies like Dwayne "The Rock" Johnson. It all depends on your know-how. Most athletes aren't building muscle, but they are physically fit and strong to perform well in their fields. You can't be a great leader and drive your pack to success if you're always feeling sick, tired, and exhausted. Maintain your fitness level, and always work on your energy levels.

Show Strong Determination

While you don't necessarily need to be physically strong, you need to be strong in what you do. Alpha Males are extremely determined in their lifelong quests and missions. It is because of their determination that they become an Alpha Male. Look at Thomas Edison, he was successful in achieving his goal because he was determined to. He knew what he wanted, and even when the entire world told him that it was impossible, he did it until he proved them all wrong. It's not an easy task to become an Alpha male. Sometimes, people will go against you and reject your ideas, but you have to be determined to keep moving forward and believe in yourself.

You will see that all Alpha Males share a common feature, which is sheer determination. Their determination is making them press on and work on their goals and dreams, ultimately making them the great people they are today. They become an Alpha Male for not wanting to give up. You will finally succeed and people will admire you if you refuse to quit and you march determinedly on.

Show the Qualities of a Leader

Thinking that an Alpha Male is a leader is only natural. In a pack of wolves, you'll notice a leader that stands out within it. Alpha Males have their own ideas, beliefs, and vision. And people are naturally drawn to them and want to follow them because of these qualities. Mahatma Gandhi is one of the very best examples of leadership. Gandhi was the person who led India to becoming independent. Because of his bold vision, he succeeded in influencing others and drew a huge following that led him and the people of India to a successful movement for independence.

This is not to say that alpha Men are aggressive. An Alpha Man is someone who's kind and gentle and who's going to sit back and watch everybody do their own thing. But make no mistake, an Alpha Male is going to stand up and fight for his and his friends' rights. A true front-runner takes care of his comrades, and when necessary, takes bold action.

Be Charismatic and Radiate Aura

Another powerful personality trait that an Alpha Male displays is that he is charismatic and radiates an aura from within. You'll know when you look at him that he is an alpha. He looks charismatic, can attract attention, and stands out from the crowd.

When an Alpha Male enters a room, it creates a stir. Whether it's due to their unique way of dressing, their strong and solid body language, or their powerful auras, Alpha Males are always capable of commanding the attention and respect of those around them. If this sounds difficult, that's because it is; nobody makes the transition from beta to alpha overnight. With the right application of time and effort, though, you can adopt any and all of these characteristics. For starters, think about your body language at all times. Stand up straight, walk confidently, and maintain businesslike mannerisms.

Earn the Respect of Others

Don't take this to mean that you should demand respect. It is earned, not demanded. When you demonstrate and improve yourself, people will automatically give you respect. You don't have to go out and beg for respect. Be your best at what you do, and people will naturally respect you and your accomplishments.

Being the best refers to being true to yourself and working hard to achieve success. Look at all the celebrities and professional athletes that people respect because they are the best at what they do. Why do you think Lionel Messi, despite being small, is able to gain the respect of his fans all over the world? It's because he is the best at what he does.

Be Gentle and Protective

It is only natural that a leader should be protective and gentle towards his people. Looking at the animal kingdom you will notice the alpha animal protecting its pack. When danger arises, an alpha wolf will protect its pack. If a non-pack member walks too close to an area controlled by the leader of the pack, subordinate pack members sound off alarms. The alpha may launch an attack as a response.

Protecting also includes helping others solve their problems. When someone comes to him for help, an Alpha Male should always be ready to help his friends and never run away. In addition to that, an Alpha Male is also a gentleman who cares for his clan and especially the women in it.

But beyond these things, the most important realization you'll ever have as you strive to take your place as an Alpha Male is that there's no "end" to your work. You'll have to embrace the fact that you're never going to reach the end of your journey.

Why? Because an Alpha Male is all about growth and improvement. He is laser-focused on his goals, and he will take the fastest route to get there, which means developing himself and constantly adapting to the changes.

Personal growth and improvement relates to every part of an Alpha Male's life, from his interests and career to his relationships. No part of you is perfect right now, and it is probably never going to be, but it's your job to keep developing every part of your character so you continually reach higher heights and achievements.

You'll have to start thinking about yourself as an ongoing project. From this moment on, you have to think in terms of steady growth and improvement, right up to the moment you take your last breath. You need to prime yourself to never accept anything that is "good enough" again and always look for something better.

This is a different mindset than the one most people have. It certainly a different mindset from the one you've had until now. Most people see themselves as fully developed human beings who either fit the needs of a particular situation or don't. They either give in to the throes of depression or find something or someone else to blame when they can't accomplish something.

That's why you'll hear so many excuses thrown around, like:

- It just wasn't in my comfort zone.
- I could have done it if I had the right tools.
- It wasn't my fault; I just didn't have enough training.
- I'm not clever/attractive/good enough to reach my goals.
- It was totally his fault, I should have been placed with a better team.

This is nonsense. If you have ever used any of these excuses (or anything similar to these excuses), it's time for a reality check. In this world, few situations can't be changed and improved simply by examining our role in the situation. If you are unable to climb a wall, that is not the wall's responsibility. If you work on your upper body strength for a while before you give it another go, you can probably turn things around and get over that wall. If you can't find a job, there's no point in blaming the managers who don't even know you exist – it's up to you to become the right person for the role you're hoping to play.

An Alpha Male knows these things and embraces the simple idea that there is no challenge that can't be overcome with a bit of personal improvement – or by finding a way to change the status quo otherwise. It is time to stop thinking of failure like the end of the world. Instead, you must begin to see failure as an opportunity to learn something new, to grow as a person, and to find a new path to success. Didn't pass the test? Then you have to figure out why you failed, whether it was too little time spent studying, or not dedicating enough effort into the task, or something else altogether. Didn't get picked for the team? Then it's time to find out what your fellow sportsmen saw as your weaknesses and work on them until they become your strengths. Prove them wrong - this is what an Alpha Male would do.

What I'm trying to tell you here is that your male Alpha self is never going to be perfect. And that is not a bad thing. The idea of being an Alpha Male is not to be Prince Charming, with shining armor and an empire of devoted subjects. No. Being an Alpha is about being the kind of guy who can recognize his flaws and deficiencies, figure out what he needs to do to be better –and then go ahead and do just that.

At some point in your life, school or college introduced you to the notion of "lifelong education.". They meant you were supposed to keep reading books even when no one made you, and they were right in more ways than they realized. What they probably didn't tell you, however, is that learning cannot be passive and reading a book is not enough. You need to go out into the world and find knowledge.

The takeaway from this chapter is that you should never shy away from new things, nor decide you can't do something before you even try to do it. If you're not yet ready to take on a challenge, it's your job to get ready. I can't do that for you, I can just keep hammering it into your head: You are in charge of your own growth, you are the only one who can get it done. If you start forgetting this, come back to this chapter and remember it– otherwise, you will slip back to the sad little version of yourself that you wanted to get away from to begin with.

Regular Men get stuck in a rut because they're not prepared to put in the amount of time, effort, and mental strength it takes to step up to the next level. Alpha Males acknowledge that striving for impossible goals could be their only way to grow and improve. An Alpha Male takes that challenge between his teeth and holds on until he is overcome.

Improvement Tips

Write down a list of challenges that really scare you – from climbing a mountain to meeting new people. Discard the excuse you've always used to convince yourself that what you want is beyond your reach – and now figure out how things need to change so that you can actually overcome your fears. Choose one thing from that list, then go out and tackle it – keep trying until you overcome the fears that prevent you from achieving your goal. Once the fear is gone, move on to the next item, and then the next, and the next. Keep on doing it, updating your lists along the way. The challenges never stop coming and you should never stop trying to overcome them.

Next time you fail at something, pay attention to your gut reac- tion. Listen to yourself and the excuses that you are making. Discard them completely and replace these thoughts with a new one: "This is just a stumbling block along the way, and my job here is to work out how to overcome it." Push yourself to triumph over failure in the best possible way – by moving forward. Never back down.

Find your weaknesses. What aspects of yourself hold you back the most? Are you uncomfortable speaking in public, and avoid speaking up during meetings at work? Or are you too easily distracted and struggle to complete your tasks on time? Things won't change overnight, recognizing the areas where you need to improve is half the battle. When you become conscious of your inadequacies, it makes you more likely to try to conquer them.

Change for the better. It doesn't matter what it is – pick one aspect of your life, big or small, that you're not happy with right now. You may be stuck in a dead-end job, or you can't bear looking at the terrible view outside your window. Create what you want to change and then make a plan for achieving that changet. Stay up on that plan, never wavering, until you have seen it through.

Give yourself goals. Never sit just back and let life come to you – Alpha Males go out and get what they want. You have to create your own opportunities in life, and to do that, you need to know what you actually want. You can do this for every aspect of your life, from your relationships to your bank account, your career and aspirations. Never set your sights low – Alpha Males strive much higher than the Average Joe ever will, and they do so with full confidence that they will be able to reach that far. Once you have an overall goal, break it down further so you'll know what steps you'll need to take along the journey to achieve it. Let's say you want to be elected Mayor of your town –Think about who you need to know, what you need to do and how you can win votes

Continue breaking this down until you have a list of tasks to follow and you know exactly when and how to complete every item of that list. Few of us are born with laser focus, but an Alpha Male is not afraid to have a plan of action to guide him and keep him motivated along the way.

Let go of the unimportant. Look at your weekly schedule. How much time do you spend on things that will help you improve, and how much time do you spend just playing around? Success won't come to you on its own, so you'll need to make time go find it. Unless you own a time machine (and if you do, I'm pretty sure I would already know your name), the only way to do that is to eliminate from your life the things that don't matter and won't help you develop. Why not work out, make a dinner date with a colleague, or learn something new instead of playing video games tonight?

Certain Alpha Males may naturally possess these traits, but others need to use practice, self-awareness, and determination to manifest them. Most Men don't start off as mighty Alpha Males. In general, they naturally possess just a few of the traits, and then gradually increase their level of understanding to master the rest.

Some Men never transcend their own natural-born Alpha Male status levels. These Men may succeed in inadequate social circles, but they experience frustration when they are confronted with more competitive environments and Alpha Males who have actually spent time honing their abilities.

Really, there is no excuse for not learning and improving yourself. If you want to be more successful at work, with women, with friends, and in every part of your life, the best thing you can do is start training yourself to be the ultimate Alpha Male.

Achieving the Alpha Male mentality is something you never fully master. In fact, it's not that different from martial arts. You can train your whole life and you can still learn something new every day! But the best way to start is to simply do it. Start educating and applying every new lesson to your life. With training and self-awareness, you can become the powerful, significant, fruitful Alpha Male you've always fantasized about becoming.

In just a few years we've seen Men going from pudgy, shy, awkward, angry Omega Males to powerful, attractive, suave, well-loved Alpha Males, but you have to take the journey seriously. And you have to be prepared to admit that you have to change who you are as a person in order to succeed.

Getting Started With Mindset

My biggest challenge has been changing people's mindsets. Mindsets play weird tricks upon us. We see things the way our mind tell our eyes to see them. This is why it is impossible to have a 100% unbiased view of the world. Our experiences growing up have shaped much of what we believe in, how we see things, and our perceptions of what reality is. Don't expect, for example, a person who grew up in abject poverty and with regular sexual and emotional abuse to believe in the "goodness" of life – at least not in the near future, and certainly not until that person chooses to change their view of the world.

This brings me to another influential and equally important factor when it comes to your mindsets: thoughts. For example, you may not have grown up in a socially and economically challenging neighborhood, but because you saw a rich friend become bankrupt in a short period of time, you tend to always worry how easy it is to lose everything in the blink of an eye.

The more you think about it,the more convinced you become that this will happen to you, and when you begin to believe your mind will look for ways to bring your belief to pass.

You may have no control over many things that happen to you – being fired from your job, growing up in a poor family, and losing your business because of an economic downturn – but you can control your thoughts. In fact, your subconscious mind, which essentially controls most of your behavior, cannot tell the difference between what is a real experience in your mind and what you are creating. It just accepts whatever you put into it, and modifies your behavior accordingly to make it happen. The decision is yours. Will you continue to hold on to misconceptions about who you are by letting society and your past experiences shape your self-confidence, or will you do something about it? If you want to start doing something about it, here are some of the wrong mindsets that need to be eliminated before the right ones can grow.

Perfection

Perfection is one of the misconceptions that may cause you to feel a lack of confidence. Sadly, many people believe that only those who are perfect can be good enough. While it is hard to be confident after you've made mistakes, this doesn't mean that you don't have the right to be confident despite your imperfections. Perfectionism is always a sure-fire recipe to suck the confidence out of you. Why? Because no one is perfect. If you're only going to feel confident when you're perfect, I've got really bad news for you. You will never become confident this way.

Confident Alpha Males, like Michael Jordan and Novak Djokovic, aren't perfect at all! If you remember (or Google it), at one point Michael Jordan failed to make the cut of the varsity team of his school. He has missed free throws and open jump shots many times in his career, too. Did these mistakes hinder his belief in himself and his abilities? No. In fact,these mistakes drove him to improve further on what is arguably his generation's best set of basketball skills. Consider Novak Djokovic, the current top-seeded Men's tennis player in the world. He didn't win all of his matches. He has missed shots as well, and continues to do so every now and then. He is number one but he is not perfect. He isn't perfect, but his confidence in his ability to play against and beat the best athletes in his sport is not affected by his imperfections.

Mindsets Are Permanent - Wrong!

Many people believe in fate. They believe their destinies were determined long ago. These are the people who use excuses like:

- This is how God made me.
- I grew up in an unfortunate family and I'll probably die in one as well.
- This is who I am and I can't do anything about it!
- Once shy, always shy!

These statements reflect the belief that everything in our lives is permanent and cannot be changed. Why is this harmful? Obviously, this kind of thinking doesn't give you hope for a better future, i.e. you can be confident and become Alpha in reality! Without such hope, you wouldn't do the things you need to do to become a confident Man.

If this is the root of your mindset, you will consistently reject anything that requires effort to change yourself for the better. You can try to deny your true mindset for a few days, weeks, and even months, but eventually you will have to accept the truth: You are hopeless.

Achievements = Confidence

While it is true that accomplishments can make a shy person confident, or a slightly confident Man much more confident, it doesn't mean you have to reach them first to become confident. In fact, the reason many great Men were able to achieve their accomplishments was because they first believed in themselves. Any achievement that requires no self-confidence is either accidental or circumstantial, at best. It's like a shy Man who saved a drowning child. He receives so much adulation and praise from the public after his heroic feat, and that might make him feel confident for a while, but such confidence is purely circumstantial and will most likely be a short-lived one. It will probably disappear after the initial euphoria about his heroics has died down.

Look again at people like LeBron James or Kobe Bryant, two of the greatest basketball stars ever, who went pro straight out of high school. They had so much confidence in themselves that they risked going straight to the NBA, the toughest basketball league in the world, right after graduation. Their confidence led to great and lasting accomplishments: Championship trophies, MVP awards, etc..

So do not dwell on the idea that you need to accomplish everything before you become confident. First, you need to have confidence in yourself before you can even hope to achieve anything meaningful or significant.

How To Change Your Mindset

There are many different ways of eradicating misconceptions, some are easy and free while others are complicated and expensive. Here are some practical ways that you can eradicate the wrong mindsets that keep you from becoming confident and turning into an Alpha.

- **Hunger for the beast:** One of the greatest ways to defeat a difficult enemy, is to starve it to death. Any living thing will die without enough food and drink. Mindsets are similar: stop feeding them and they will die. Do you feed your mindset? If so, in what ways? One way we feed harmful mindsets is by allowing them to repeat unhealthy ideas in our mind.

If you're always thinking about why you can't be confident, and how you're not confident, you are allowing these thoughts to grow and take over in your mind. You need to stop yourself from doing this the moment you realize it starts. Remember: The less you think about your misconceptions, the more you'll starve them to death. And with work, you can starve them enough over time to be able to destroy them.

- **Self-interrogation:** One of the best ways to gradually eradicate wrong mindsets is by challenging them – and one of the best ways to do so is to question their validity and benefit regularly. Think of it as a court hearing, where the defense attorney –you– is merely trying to establish reasonable doubt against the prosecuting attorney's charges –the wrong mindset– and thereby destroy any legal claims or powers that it may hold over you. Let me be more specific. For example, let's take the rationality of these misconceptions. One way of establishing reasonable doubt is by questioning these misconceptions in terms of both validity and benefits. Some questions you may ask yourself regularly about your mindset are:

1. How real is this? What about my friend Hubert who once believed there was no God? If mindsets are permanent, then why is he now a minister in a local church?

2. Do I really believe that the way I think and feel about myself can't be beneficial to me? Will I really be able to live life to the fullest, which is really what I want, if I continue to believe that this is so? If it is true that first I have to achieve something significant before I feel confident about myself, then what should I do about my best friend George? He's not exactly well-off, hasn't gone to college, nor is James Dean's reincarnation, but how is it that he is confident enough that he can approach random beautiful women everywhere and get their numbers effortlessly?

3. If I quit my current belief that I need to achieve success before I become confident about myself, would my life become better? If I continue to hold on to that screwed-up belief, could I live life to the fullest?

Do this often and over time, you will find yourself slowly getting rid of your misconceptions about confidence, and will eventually root them out enough to plant new seeds of confidence.

- **Birds of a Feather Flock Together:** Consider hanging out with confident people if you feel the first two approaches are too burdensome for you. There is such a thing as spirit transferring, and simply by hanging out with people infected with trust, you may

be able to catch enough of the trust virus to uproot
your old, wrong mindsets.

Remember that experience is the best teacher, and of course, the best experience is personal. But the experiences of other people can also be very good teachers, which can help you eradicate major wrong mindsets. To put it another way, actions speak louder than words. When you hang out with truly confident people, you put yourself in a position to see the foolishness of your lack of self-confidence, and gradually condition your mind to uproot it.

Easy Alpha Male Exercise For Building Confidence

When you find yourself in circumstances beyond your control, you can help get yourself out of it by creating a list of what or who you blame for not getting what you want in life. Go now and make this list. Did you make it? Amazing. Here are a few things it probably includes:

1. Many people, like your parents, who did a bad job raising you, or your boss who now holds you back. The people who made fun of you in high school and made you feel bad. Some people taught you to be irrationally afraid of strangers and you feel nervous today.
2. Your circumstances. You were born into poverty, your dad beat you, you went to a bad public school and missed out on many other people's educational opportunities.
3. Your biology. Your profile is asymmetrical, you are short, and so on.

I'm not trying to downplay your problems. The point is that too often in life, due to circumstances beyond our control, we become immobilized. Then, we are unable to create change. We cannot change the way our parents raised us, so it's a waste of time to be angry about that today. No matter how upset you are, what happened can't be changed. Looking at your blame list, can you see any real reason why you should be so convinced that because of the actions of the people on that list, you can't do anything to improve your life? Why would you give them that power?

Study after study has found that simply thinking that we are in charge of our situation will have a major impact on our behavior. The more we believe we are a victim of our circumstances, the more likely we are to give up. You will become a more optimistic person when you start moving towards the belief that you have total control over your own life, which psychologists call an internal locus of psychological influence. You have the will to improve the issues where you are weak at the moment. For starters, if you're hideous, hit the gym, boost your diet, and focus on your garments and grooming.

You'll also be taking responsibility to empower yourself. You will understand that as you become more determined to improve yourself, and persist in going for the things you wish for (such as sex), you will increase your chances of getting them. The more you believe you have control over your life, the better the chances of getting what you want.

Your Thoughts

You think constantly. Most of our perceptions originate from our feelings, which come from our thoughts. The good news is that, as thinking beings, we can control our emotions, and therefore our feelings. We may opt for positive or negative thoughts (and therefore, a feeling) depending on the circumstances. The bad news is that having negative thoughts is often easier, so we need to work to stay optimistic.

For instance, suppose you are attending a speed-dating event where each of the women checks "no" by your name to suggest they don't want to see you again. A negative view of that would be to think that you are worthless, so of course people wouldn't want to talk to you. So what about all those other guys who looked a lot better than you? Perhaps if you had stayed home and played Halo 2, it would have been a better evening.

A positive view would be to understand that you wrinkled your forehead with every girl and bent too far forward, showing you were anxious and striving too hard for acceptance. Correct those two major errors in the body language, and you will give a better impression of yourself next time. What you think of yourself becomes part of your self-image and your life. If you are hopeful, then you will be attracted to good people and good things. So if you want to be a successful Man, you need to start thinking positively. Reminiscing on the past can produce many negative thoughts. You have definitely screwed up before – we all have. The trick is to let go of the past.

I need to make sure you understand this: The only place the past still exists is in your head. Learn from your past mistakes, then put them to rest, and don't worry about them any more. Seek to do away with negative thoughts. Identify the roots of negativity in your life, and stop letting them affect you. I personally avoid certain people, albums, and TV shows. For example, I avoid the news since it's so full of negativity. (Don't feel like you need to be a news junkie. If the world's over, somebody's going to tell you!).

Developing A Positive Mindset

It's all up to you and your behavior.

"Why would I be attractive to any female?" You wonder. "I'm too short." You enter the classroom and you sit in your usual place. You remember the girl who sat in front of you and turned around and said, "Do you have a piece of paper? "Yeah," you say, and you give her a piece of paper. Then, you don't talk to her for the rest of the class. You think back to that girl that night, dreaming of her as you lie in bed alone, thinking what a loser you are.

What you didn't understand was that the girl made an extra effort to talk to you. Perhaps she didn't really need a piece of paper. She could just have asked someone else for it. But she asked you, maybe as an excuse because she was interested in talking to you. Maybe she sent you a clear message, but you had no idea what she meant. You have to believe that something is possible for it to happen to you. If you believe in my example, then you'll be open to women coming into your life. But if you don't believe that's a possibility, then you're going to block it internally, even when it's blatant.

Waiting for something to happen to you is a waste of opportunities. Identify and let go of negative thoughts as they crop up. Let the positive thoughts and feelings flow as you suppress the negative thoughts. Choose to be self-confident and happy, no matter what external circumstances you're facing. Be satisfied with yourself, and know that no matter what happens, you'll be happy. Your confidence comes from within, and every day you must work on improving yourself because that's central to who you are.

Here are some ways to build a more positive attitude:

1. Constantly see yourself as the person that you want to be. Imagine how you would act and how happy you'd feel if you were the ideal version of yourself. Visualize how much money you'd make, the house you'd live in, and the body you'd have. Avoid negative influences in your life, including friends who like to make cynical remarks.

2. When you remember the past, think only of your achievements. Recognize that any mistakes that you made are only temporary and the result of bad luck more than anything else. Assume success (but don't get attached to this idea). Think of yourself as a confident Man, and believe that as you're every woman's dream lover, you will eventually find the success you want. Look at yourself in the mirror, and smile while you admire what an attractive Man looks like.

3. Start to notice your thoughts. Remember: your thoughts influence you, so you can have any visualization you want. When you believe in your reality, use your visualizations to pump you up instead of shutting yourself down. Albert Einstein once said, "Your thought is your preview of the possible attractions of life."

4. Make promises. I've had a lot of success changing my attitudes just by changing the way I talk to myself. A lot of this success comes from making statements. Affirmations are things you repeat over and over before you believe them. You are constantly making remarks to yourself as you go throughout your day. Pay attention to what these statements tell you about yourself. You may be sabotaging yourself by

incessantly repeating negative comments throughout the day, such as:

- "I'm such a loser."
- "I'm not good at talking to attractive women."
- "I'm sad."
- "I'm in a bad mood."
- "I'm lazy."
- "I'm stuck in a dead-end job and can't do anything about it."

The more you think about these, the more you unconsciously reinforce these notions, and the more ingrained they become in your mind. The more you repeat an argument to yourself, the more you imagine it and believe it, the more convinced you become that it's true. When you engage in negative self-talk, your problems and insecurities will pile up.

However, the good thing is that you can start to make positive affirmations. You can program these into your mind by repeating new beliefs to yourself over and over again. For example, take the sentence, "I'm becoming more extroverted." First, your mind will lift its BS meter and try to block it because it's a radically new concept. After all, you've spent years convincing yourself you're introverted.

Then one day, after several weeks of doing your affirmations many times a day, you're doing something you'd never have done a month before – maybe you're waiting to check out at the grocery store and suddenly decide to make the others in line laugh with some light banter. We will discuss affirmations more in Chapter 5, as well as how to make them, but believe me when I tell you: They can be life-changing.

The Right Crowd

Hanging out with the right crowd not only helps uproot old and wrong mindsets, but it also helps replace them with the right ones. I want to share a bit of my own experience, so you can really see how important your mindset is. I used to be shy. The last thing I wanted in this world was to speak in front of a crowd – I would have rather died. Whether the crowd was as large as just two people didn't matter. "Death before speaking in public," was my motto.

Because we learn by imitation, I was able to imitate the way confident people spoke in public, and eventually gained the confidence to overcome my fear of speaking in public. I was able to gain confidence to overcome my shyness and speak in public by hanging out with confident public speakers. As I saw and heard them, I began to believe that it was not impossible at all – that public speaking was something well within my reach. As a result, self-confidence built up within me, until I became the leader of the group. Now, I am comfortable and confident speaking in front of large crowds.

Other Alpha Males can transform you into a confident Alpha Male too simply by hanging out with them. So if you know someone who fits the bill, hang out with these people more often and as frequently as possible. The more time you spend with such Men, the faster you will be turned into the Alpha Man you want to be.

Excellence, Not Perfection

Remember: Perfection is one of the greatest trust-busters of all time. The extreme opposite of perfection is not poor quality, is excellence. Excellence is simply giving the best of yourself in life and work. Whether it's with your schoolwork, office work, sports performance, or just dressing well, excellence is not only achievable, but a great way to boost your trust.

The key to excellence is to make the most of what you've got. Excellence doesn't mean donating $1,000 a month to charity when you're just making $1,100 a month. If you can afford up to $300 for monthly donations based on your circumstances, giving out $300 is excellent. Buying a $2,000 suit when all you can afford is a $300 one is just stupid. Excellence means going for the best $300 suit you can find.

When it comes to quality, I would like to think of excellence as "no-holds-barred." Just as underground fighters give it their all when it comes to beating the hell out of the other guy at matches, so it should be with you when it comes to fighting for the things that matter most to you.

Continuous Improvement

When it comes to excellence, what's excellent now can only become average in a few years, or even months. It's not unusual in today's ever-changing world to find that the very expensive smartphone you bought just three months ago has become obsolete by the next month.

We're not talking about gadgets here, of course. We are talking about you and the skills you will develop in the upcoming months, and the impact these will have in your life. We are talking about how developing new skills can build up your confidence, and how increasing your confidence can lead you towards excellence. Let's start by talking about marketing.

Social media marketing has become a force to be reckoned with when it comes to business, and as such, the demand for highly competent social media or internet marketers has gone up considerably. More importantly, increasing numbers of people are catching up to this demand and are honing their skills as social media marketers.

If you're a marketing professional, you must know that Facebook, Twitter, and Instagram are very budget-friendly and effective social marketing tools. If not, your career is in deep trouble. A marketing professional – or any professional, for that matter – who doesn't keep up with the new trends in his field risks losing his job or his customers to younger, more aggressive, and social media savvy marketing professionals. Apart from being familiar with social media sites, you would also need to be up-to-date with the latest developments in social media and how to use these to your advantage. In marketing, as in any other field, you need to catch the wave early and position yourself well. You have to stay on top of your game. Otherwise, you'll lose. Remember, being on top of your game is a great source of natural confidence, and if you don't spend your time constantly developing personally and professionally, you run the risk of being left behind. Continuous personal and professional growth, on the other hand, is a highly effective tool to become and remain confident.

Personally, I believe reading is the best source of continuous personal and professional growth. Books, either in traditional form or ebooks, give me access to some of the most brilliant minds in their fields. Another benefit of reading is that I can read to myself whenever it is most convenient to me, for as long as I like to. Next to reading, my second choice for personal development is attending seminars. The only reason they're second on my list is because they can take dedicated time. Otherwise, I would have placed them at the top of the list.

Finally, I can grow personally and professionally by hanging out with people who are very good at what I want to learn. Since more is caught than taught, when it comes to learning, witnessing firsthand the things we want to learn makes for a strong learning experience

Getting Ready To Grow

You are not yet an Alpha Male and it will take a whole lot of personal development to get to that level. You'll have to focus on every aspect of yourself, from your attitude to your work ethics and trust in yourself. But beyond these things, the most important realization you'll ever have as you strive to take your place as an Alpha Male is that there's no "end point" to work towards here—you'll have to embrace the fact that you're never going to reach the end of this particular journey. Once you become an Alpha Male, there's always more work to be done.

Why? For what? Because an Alpha Male's all about growth and improvement, even if he's already doing pretty good. He has a laser focus on what he wants to accomplish and he will take the fastest route to get there, which means developing himself and constantly adapting himself to be the best he can be.

It refers to every part of his life, from his interests and career to his relationships. There's no part of you that's perfect right now, and there's probably never going to be - but it's your job to keep developing every aspect of your character so you're continually hitting higher heights and making more achievements.

You'll have to start thinking about yourself as an ongoing work of art. From this moment on, you have to think in terms of steady growth and improvement right up to the moment when you take your last breath. You need to prime yourself to never accept anything that is "good enough" again and always look for something better. You're not going to be done until the time you're finished. Everything, literally everything, until that moment will be a learning experience.

It is a different mindset to the one with which most people work. This mindset, which you have certainly worked up to now, needs to continue. You have not reached a point where you cannot grow anymore and you're not fully formed. If you don't accept this mindset, you can either give in to the throes of depression or find something or someone else to blame when you cannot accomplish something.

That's why you'll hear people make so many excuses, like:

- It just wasn't in my comfort zone.
- I could have done it if only I had the right tools.
- It wasn't my fault; I just didn't have enough training.
- I'm not clever / attractive / good enough to speak / talented enough.
- It was totally his fault; I should have been put in a better team.

In fact, this is nonsense. If you use these excuses or know people who do, it's time to wake up and stop hanging out with them. In this life, there is little that cannot be changed when you put your mind to it. If you are unable to climb a wall, that is not the wall's fault. Hit the gym, get stronger arms and muscles, and you will be able to climb the wall just fine. If you can't find a job, there's no point in blaming the hiring department who knows little to nothing about you–it's up to you to learn the right skills for the job you want.

An Alpha Male knows these things and embraces the simple idea that there is no challenge that cannot be overcome by either changing himself or the circumstances he's in. Stop seeing failure as the end of the world. Instead, look at it as the opportunity to learn something new, to grow as a person, and to find a new path to success.

You didn't pass the test? Then you have to work out what went wrong. Maybe you didn't study enough or procrastinated about getting the work done. Your dream team didn't pick you? Maybe you didn't train properly or you were using the wrong techniques to get into shape. You can always turn it around and do it better. That's what being alpha means.

When we talk about being alpha, we don't mean that you're going to be perfect and an embodiment of perfection. And that's okay. The idea of being an Alpha Male is not to be a fantasy prince with a sparkle in his eye and an empire at his feet. It's about being the kind of guy who can recognize his flaws and what he's lacking, define what he wants to do to become better, and then take all the needed actions to do just that.

Your school or college presumably spoke to you about the notion of "lifelong education" when you were enrolled. They meant that you were supposed to keep reading books even when no one makes you do it and they were right in more ways than they realized. What they probably didn't tell you, though, is that you don't get to learn from books. You need to be a lifelong learner in real life as well, and that means not being afraid to go out there and gather the experience you need.

The takeaway from this chapter is that you should never shy away from new things, nor decide you're done before you even try to do anything. If you're not yet ready to do something, it's your job to get ready. I can't do that for you. The best I can do is to keep drumming it into your head so it will be done. If you start forgetting this, come back to this chapter. If you forget about your goals and give up, you've slipped away from the best opportunity in your life to be the best person you can be.

Beta Men get stuck in a rut because they're not prepared to put in the amount of time, effort, and mental strain that it takes to step up to the next level. Alpha Males acknowledge that striving for even the seemingly impossible could be their only way to grow and improve. The challenge won't go away but strength and conviction will get an Alpha Man through it.

Improvement Tips

Write down a list of challenges that really scare you, from climbing a mountain to meeting new people. Also write down the excuse you've always used to convince yourself that they're beyond your reach. Then, figure out how things can be changed so that you can do all these challenges. Choose one thing from that list, then go out and tackle it. Keep at it until you have overcome it. Move on to your next challenge and follow the same process. Don't stop because challenges won't magically disappear from your life.

Analyze your gut reaction next time you fail at something. Listen to the excuses that you are making for yourself. Discard them completely and replace the mindset that came with them with a new one: "This is just a stumbling block along the way, and my job here is to work out how to overcome it." Push yourself to overcome the failure in the best possible way by going forward and never backing down.

Find your weaknesses. What aspects of yourself hold you back the most? When you're working, can you push through a difficult project continuously or do you get easily distracted and procrastinate? You can't change things overnight but it's winning half the battle to recognize where you need to improve. This can make you conscious of your inadequacies and more likely to try to move past them when they rear their ugly heads to hamper your development.

Make a difference for the better. It doesn't matter what it is. Pick one aspect of your life, big or small, that you're not all that pleased with right now. You may be stuck in a dead-end job or you can't bear the view you see from your window each morning. Discover what you want to change and then make a plan for doing it. Stick with that plan and never waver, until you have seen it through.

Develop goals for yourself. Never sit back and let life come to you. Alpha Males go out and get what they want. You have to create your own life opportunities and to do that you need to know what you actually want. In every aspect of your life, from your relations to your bank balance, career, and aspirations, you can do that. Never set your sights low. Alpha Males strive much higher than the average Joe ever will and they do so with the full confidence that they will be able to reach that far. Once you have an overall goal, break it down further so you'll know what steps you'll need to take along the journey to achieve it. Let's say your goal is to be elected mayor of your small town. Who do you need to contact, who will run your campaign, and how will you convince your fellow citizens to vote for you?

Continue breaking your goals down until you have a task list to follow and you know exactly when and how to get every item done. We are not born with laser focus, but an Alpha Male is not afraid to guide and organize himself so as to keep motivated along the way.

Let go of trivial matters. Right now, look at your weekly schedule. How much time do you spend on things that will help you improve, and how much time do you just spend playing around? Success won't come to you so you'll need to make time for it. Unless you own a time machine (and if you do, I'm pretty sure I would already know your name), the only way to do that is to cut out things that don't matter and won't help you move forward. Why not work out, make a dinner date with a colleague, or learn something new instead of playing video games tonight?

Certain Alpha Males may be proactive by nature. But others need to learn how to use practice, self-awareness, and determination to encourage these traits in themselves. Most Men don't start off as Alpha Males. In general, they naturally embody just a few of these traits and then gradually increase their level of understanding to master the rest.

Some Men also cannot become Alpha Males. These Men may still succeed in modest social circles, but they experience frustration when they are confronted with more competitive environments and with Alpha Males who have actually spent time "honing" their abilities.

Really, there is no excuse for not being dedicated to learning and improving yourself. To be more successful at work, with women, with friends, and in all of your endeavors the thing you have to do is to start training yourself to be the ultimate Alpha Male.

It is a lifelong pursuit, since the male alpha mentality is something you never fully get to master. In fact it's not that different from martial arts. You can train your whole life and you can still learn something new every day! But the best way to start is to simply do it. Start educating and applying each of these new things in your life. With training and self-awareness, you can definitely become a powerful, significant, and capable Alpha Male, just like you've always fantasized to become.

In just a few years we've seen Men going from unhealthy, shy, awkward, or angry beta Males to powerful, attractive, capable, and well-loved Alpha Males. But you have to take the journey seriously. and you have to be prepared to admit you have to change who you are as a person if you want to succeed.

The Most Important Power Attitude You Can Have

If you're like most guys, you're thinking of women as a reward for working hard and living well. It is a tradition that goes back through history. In the Middle Ages, the lovely maiden at the end of a Man's long, arduous journey was the reward for the gallant knight. I used to think so, too. And it led me to believe that I would have to get the finest car, have the highest-paid job, and spend tons of money on women to make them like me.

Looking back, the hell of it was that this approach did not have much luck with the girls. "Yeah, if I just keep working hard and being a good guy who knows just how to buy the right kinds of flowers," I thought, "women will like me." After all, any time you ask a woman for advice, that's what they're telling you to do.

The truth, however, is that women can give awful advice! Just like Men, women have a vast range of experiences and perspectives, and they're just as liable to be wrong about something as you are. Even worse, most women are likely to advise you to be more passive and subservient, rather than the opposite. If you follow their words, you'll end up as an easily controlled beta male rather than an intense, sexually confident alpha.

As a college sophomore, I had an enormous crush on a roommate of mine. In an attempt to make her like me, I did all of the things that other women suggested: I left the toilet seat down, I bought her CDs, I fixed things in our apartment. I even cleaned up after her whenever she left a mess. She told me that I was a sweet guy, but we never had sex. She didn't find me appealing because I was trying too hard to be "nice." And being nice without being confident is the ultimate beta behavior.

So I made friends with a guy during my junior year who seemed like the opposite of what I imagined a successful guy should be like. He didn't spend money on girls, he didn't jump enthusiastically to join girls who asked him to go shopping with them, and he didn't try to impress girls with his car or career ambitions.

Yet this guy had women constantly falling for him, fawning over him, flirting with him, and having sex with him. What he did was to express Alpha Male qualities that made women attracted to him on a primal level, I later realized. The wholehearted conviction that he was a good catch was in everything about him and how he handled himself. It was his mentality of power from which his success came. He:

- Would only have sex with women whom he thought were worthy because of his assumption that he was a good catch.
- Would only be affectionate towards women who won their right for his affection.
- Would only be interested in what women said if they said something relevant, rather than chatting away mindlessly.

You can only be desirable to another person once you make yourself the catch. Human nature dictates that people see higher value in what they have to work for, rather than not.

This is basic supply and demand: whatever is in short supply commands a higher price than average. For example, as I write this book, there's a recorded market shortage of Splenda sweetener. The company that makes it is trying to build a new factory because its existing factory is incapable of meeting demand. So now, thanks to news stories about this fact, people who would never have used Splenda in the first place buy up the stuff and cause a shortage of it.

You should take advantage of this as an Alpha Male, and increase your "catchiness" by using these three techniques:

1. Don't be accessible to a woman if she's not worth your time. If you do this, you'll avoid being friend-zoned or putting up with women who are not really interested in you sexually or in a relationship.

2. Don't immediately return phone calls. You are a busy Man as an Alpha Male and women need to accept that. If possible, always hang up first as well, not because you're trying to be rude or are interrupted by another call, but because you're genuinely busy.

3. Don't go on dates when you have better things to do. Dating doesn't enrich your life or make you a catch for women. When you're unavailable at times, they will see you as more worthwhile than if you're always at their beck and call. Also, guide your dating decisions based on how your date acts when you turn her down. Don't compromise for someone who acts childishly when things don't go her way.

You live the life you want, as an Alpha Male, free from needing someone else's approval. Unfortunately, most people don't live the life they want for precisely that reason, i.e. they're afraid of getting disapproval. So, move away from things you don't need and only do what you want. You are a Man of great importance who deserves to be treated right.

Creating Your Own Reality

Life is what it is. You can read about other people's lives and experiences online and in books. Many religious sites, for instance, speak about God as if it is clear that He exists, whereas atheists would say that it is nonsense. Read on and you will find compelling arguments for both opinions! How can that be, considering that both sides cannot be correct? This happens because each person experiences life differently.

Is it bad to hurt someone? Like say, break their leg? You are probably thinking, "Damn right, it's terrible." But imagine you were a British soldier in 1914 and breaking your enemy's leg prevented you from becoming cannon fodder on the Western Front. That would be the least you can do to defend yourself. So, here's the thing: you need to find your own version of the truth. Truth is objective, but personal truth is not. It is open to interpretation. Say it's a rainy day outside. If you want to go to a picnic, you'll probably be annoyed. However, if you're a farmer and it hasn't rained in months, you'd be ecstatic. Even natural disasters aren't catastrophic for everyone.

You thus have the ability to see the world as you wish. You can get your own perspective on things and frame them as it suits you better. An individual with a poor grasp on reality is drawn into the expectations of the world by other people. A person with a clear grasp on reality is unaffected by the opinions of other people and attracts others into their world instead.

Let's say you're going to a nightclub and can't find a parking space. That will annoy a beta male who lets external factors affect him. But you can phrase it in such a way as not to get annoyed. Since parking is so hard to find, it means that lots of people are out and about. This means that you'll be able to meet more people. Getting stuck in a traffic jam? That's all right if you have a chance to take a rest, relax, meditate, and perhaps listen to some soothing music. Don't let anger take over when things don't go your way. Take advantage of the situation any way you can.

Now, let's look at how you frame yourself. This frame will be the basis of your success as an Alpha Male.

Easy Alpha Male Workout – Fixing your belief about yourself with women.

You need to internalize the fact that women are fortunate to have you. Ponder the questions below and write down your answers. This exercise can be simple, but it is necessary because if you have not yet fully internalized the Alpha Male mindset, redirecting your thinking patterns is key. Plus, it's always helpful to find some stuff that you can re-read later when you need to relive your journey.

1. If you bring a woman into your life, how can you make her happy?

2. Imagine you've got little time as a busy Man for others' attempts to grab your attention. What rules do you have to decide who gets your attention?

3. What are some fun things you like to do that are usually pursuits for women as well? (Women need feelings to become sexually responsive, and they love emotionally relevant things like talking to friends on the phone. The best way to kill a woman's mood for sex is to talk about boring things like corporate balance sheets.)

4. What are the things that a woman would find attractive in you? What about some things you're going to be working on that would make you attractive?

5. What are the things you would expect from a woman to consider dating her?

Come up with your own responses, but note that there are certain things women need, such as great sex, fun, positive emotions, and common hobbies. While you're thinking about what makes you attractive to women, you also need to think about what you're getting out of the deal. For me, a lack of interest in sex, dishonesty, childish drama, and being obese and unhealthy are deal breakers.

Only you know what you're put off by and what attracts you in a woman. I encourage you to answer the questions above before moving on.

Now that you've completed the exercise above, you know more about yourself and your needs. You're on your way to knowing how amazing you are, to put it differently. You've discovered your value and what you bring to the table. If your interests aren't understood by a woman, then it is her loss not yours.

I like bringing an example of a luxury car at this point, like a Lamborghini. This illustrates your importance in the relationship. Depending on who you ask, a Lamborghini has no inherent value or it is the most important part of someone's life.

For example, Lamborghini dealers are strongly of the opinion that their vehicles are of great value. As a consequence, they're not letting you test drive one of their cars right off the street, unlike Ford or Dodge dealers.

When you take control of your thoughts and mindset and follow your dreams, you will realize that you are becoming genuinely happy in a way you have felt before. Your inherent value is such that you'll never need to worry about attracting women. You just need to be yourself. This is the best way to not only feel good about yourself, but also to follow a strategy that has been shown to work many times throughout history.

This strategy is as follows:

1) Be spontaneous when you're in company. Do not make plans, only stay focused on what comes naturally.

2) Hold the prevailing structure in all of your dealings.

3) Maintain and prioritize your own frame of reality, rather than letting yourself conform to the woman's expectations.

If you follow these three simple points, you'll find that your wildest fantasies come true. You'll be able to make any woman interested in you just by looking into her eyes!

Be true to yourself and share that truth with women. Be romantic, pursue sex, and, above all else, remember that your goal is to be happy and enjoy your life. This guide will provide you with everything you need to become an Alpha Male. All that's left to do is apply your knowledge.

CHAPTER FOUR

DEVELOPING UNSHAKEABLE CONFIDENCE

ALPHA MALES ARE the type of self-confident and assured guys that are driven not only by testosterone, but fueled by their desire to succeed in life and fulfill their purpose. They are full of integrity, and they are competitive. They do not allow others to tell them what to do or to discourage them from pursuing their dreams. They are confident in themselves and their actions, and others can see that. They can easily interact with others socially, and girls flock to their magnetic personalities.

The single most unattractive trait to women is neediness. You can have six-pack abs and a seven-figure salary, but if you are a needy guy, she will find you sexually repulsive. This is why every weekend, both single millionaires and broke guys sleep with another girl. While the wealth and physical appearance of a Man matters to some extent, their attractiveness pales when compared to one thing and only one thing: Confidence.

Confidence is the single most attractive trait for women. Confidence shows that you are a masculine Man who is capable of catching big buffalo and protecting it (and any offspring) from saber-tooth tigers.

Insecurity and neediness prove just the opposite. If you are needy and insecure, you come off as a frail, submissive guy who will not give her the best chance to survive the harsh evolutionary conditions in which our ancestors lived, and therefore, will not give her the best chance to pass on her genes.

Some of these steps may feel quite natural to you, while others are going to take work. Rest assured that each step is relevant. Concentrate on one or two steps at a time, and put real, calculated effort into your life. It takes time for that to happen. But within just a few short weeks, you should begin to notice a difference in your thought patterns and perceptions. Just remember to continue to work and practice. All of this will ultimately pay off!

Step 1. Continue to Practice Self-Awareness

Be honest with yourself about who you are and who you want to be. Self-honesty is a huge part of this journey.

Which are your weaknesses? What qualities do you have? Don't sugarcoat responses. Figure where you can begin to improve yourself and start doing the work. For every Alpha Male, self-reflection is extremely important. The story of a Man who was lost, confused, and self-defeated is at the start of every powerful Alpha Male story. If you want to get better, you must learn to see yourself for who you really are. Be honest about your failings. The first step to getting better is to admit you've got a problem! Are you penniless? Offensive? Self-deprecating? If so, you'll need to eliminate those habits and replace them with healthier equivalents.

Step 2. Stop Complaining

True alpha Men never complain. They see what it takes to achieve a goal and they do it. If something is wrong, then they will change it. They do not talk about it and keep going. So stop complaining today. If you catch yourself whining, remember that powerful Alphas don't complain about the problems facing the world. They are taking action to fix it! When you run into obstacles, look at them as opportunities. See each trial as an opportunity to learn and to grow. Sure, it's no fun going through tough times. But you will find that if you just stop complaining, put your mind to the grind, and work to get through it, you will be miles ahead of the curve.

Step 3. Stop Making Excuses

You have to be stable in your choices and actions as an Alpha Male. No more excuses. If you have to start running each morning, do so. No apologies. If you don't wish to go to that dinner party, decline the invitation, and say you don't want to go. No apologies. There's no excuse for your behavior. You pick your fate. Now is the time to stop letting other people's opinions control your life. So Alpha Males call things by their names. If you didn't make it because you were lazy, then admit you were lazy. At least then you are going to be lazy and honest, rather than lazy and in denial! Still, get what needs to be done at the end of the day done. Don't let excuses run your life.

Step 4. Find Your Purpose and Pursue It

Alpha Males don't march to someone else's drum. They decide and pursue what they want out of life. Stop being wishy-washy.

Stop being unsure of what you want. If you need to get away and meditate on what you want for your life, do that. Find out what your life purpose is, and follow through. True Alpha Males find their reason for living and pursue it with relentless tenacity. On the other hand, wishy-washy Men never achieve Alpha Male status.

If you see a good opportunity, consider it. If you want it, know it then and there. Either commit or let go. Do not play games half-way. You are either all in or all out. A true Alpha Male puts his purpose above everything else. It is very, very important to define what the purpose of your life is. You'll always struggle to find meaning and direction if you neglect this step.

Step 5. Face Your Fears

Maybe you have to do things that scare you on your journey. Asking for a raise, quitting your job, getting closer to a beautiful woman, standing up when someone is trying to push you around, or setting healthy boundaries in your relationship. All these things can be scary. But it's very important to find your strength and face your fears head on.

An Alpha Male learns to deal calmly and strategically with his fears. That, however, takes practice. Start now by not shying away from scary situations. Instead, seek them out and face them. One of the reasons the world has so few Alpha Males is because most of the Men are cowards. There is no place for fear in the Alpha Male's heart. Banish fear from your heart or you will be defeated by your weaknesses.

Step 6. Start Believing In Yourself

A true Alpha Male doesn't need anyone's approval. Why? Because he already holds himself to a high standard and consistently reaches that standard by doing all he can to be exceptional. So start by looking into the mirror today, and give yourself a pep talk. Tell yourself that you are the Man, and stop holding back your fear of rejection. If you can begin to believe in yourself, then you will begin to give off that unmistakable Alpha Male aura. Girls love it. Bosses love it. When you walk through a room, people will be parting like the Red Sea. You must become the kind of Man who is 100 percent comfortable and at peace with himself. You don't need anyone's approval. You believe in yourself and that's all that matters.

Step 7. Become Self-Reliant

Individual strength and independence are hallmarks of successful Alpha Males. That type of Man is not relying on other folks to make his way in life. He makes his own money, pays his own way, and accepts no charity to keep himself afloat. For example, if you want to become an Alpha male but your parents pay for your apartment, the first step you need to take is to stop depending on them financially. Pay your own way. If you can't afford it because you don't make enough money, start working overtime or find a better-paying job. A true Alpha Male always relies entirely on himself for his survival. This also holds true in an emotional sense. You need to stop depending on other people for your emotional wellbeing. Do you need to go on and on to your girlfriend about how awesome you are to reassure yourself that she loves you? This is not self-confidence. This is dependency, and if you really want to be an Alpha Male, this is not the way to live.

Step 8. Start Getting In Shape

One thing that many people forget nowadays is their body. You don't have to look like Thor to attract gorgeous women. But you must put constant effort into your body, health, and state of mind. Start hitting the gym. Start getting rid of your belly fat. Get rid of your body's extra flab, and start building leaner muscle. If you're too lazy to go to the gym, you probably don't have what it takes to be a true Alpha Male. Clean up your diet too. Stop sipping soda. Stop eating junk food. Eat healthy food that nourishes your body and helps you perform at at your peak. You don't have to be a bodybuilder of world-class athlete to look and feel good. You can achieve significant improvements in 20 minutes, 30 minutes, or an hour a day. Anything will help!

Step 9. Be A Man Of Your Word

A true Man of the world will keep his word forever. If you commit to something, stick with it. If you say you will do it, stick with it. Let your word be your pledge, and stop agreeing to things you don't want to do.

Many Men are flaccid and wishy-washy. Those characteristics are super unattractive and they only earn you disrespect. You can always count on a true Man of his word, and he will earn the respect of his peers and rivals for that. So be a Man of integrity. Do what you're supposed to do. Never render empty threats. Always be eager to back your words up with action and be careful of what you say, so that your words don't betray the fact that you're just a talker and not a walker.

Step 10. Don't Be Afraid Of Failure

A powerful Alpha Male will take calculated risks without fear of failure. He understands that failure happens, but he also knows that the greatest failures carry the greatest lessons with them. Besides, he is wise enough in his choices and confident enough not to be daunted by the possibility of setbacks. An Alpha Male can, and sometimes will, struggle, but he will succeed far more often. Why is he successful? Because he tries. A lot of Men are far too anxious to even try. This is what separates the Alpha from the rest of the pack. That's why the Alpha will have more wealth, more resources, and more success than beta or omega Males.

Step 11. Seek Challenges In Combat

Much of the Alpha Male mentality of power comes from human evolution. When we were cavemen, we had to fight every single day for our life. Human beings had to be prepared to fight whatever predator tried to kill and eat them, or they would not survive. The result was that Alphas climbed to the top of the food chain. They had more women, more resources, more warriors. People know that these Men were mighty leaders, and that their best chances of survival would most likely result from following them. Things are different today. A Man is somewhat likely to live a successful life without ever being forced to use physical force to fend off predators. But you must get back to these roots to fully embrace the Alpha Male mentality. For this reason, Men who wish to develop themselves as Alphas are often recommended to take up some sort of physical combat sport. The best options are martial arts, boxing, MMA, fencing, or wrestling.

These allow you to develop the skills that come from fighting but to do it in a safe way, so you don't land in prison. Tapping into that primal urge is important. Men are natural warriors, but how can you say that you're a true Alpha Male warrior if you have never had to defeat an enemy in a physical altercation? You have to learn how to train, know what it feels like to be knocked down and learn how hard it can be to get back up again. The discipline you will learn will serve as a powerful metaphor for the rest of your life.

Step 12. Be Aware Of Your Wardrobe

If you're only buying baggy graphic T-shirts off the clearance rack at discount stores, you'll need to really up your game. They say "the clothes make the Man," and to some extent, this is true. Start doing some fashion research and put some time and effort into your wardrobe every week. Make this an important part of your weekly routine. Set aside the time to shop and go to a tailor. Plan your outfits and make sure you have the right outfit for every occasion.

A mighty Alpha Male will always arrive well-dressed and ready for whatever life might throw at him. He'll stand out enough to turn heads, and he'll be dressed fashionably enough to impress, too. You don't need to spend a ton of money to put together some awesome outfits, but investing time, effort, and energy into your wardrobe is important. If you start from the bottom, go shopping at thrift stores! There's no shame in purchasing clothes at a discount. What counts is that you put your time into it and that you do your best, in all circumstances, to look your best.

Step 13. Read More Books

Continuing their education is extremely important for every Alpha Male. Buy or borrow books from the library, and set aside the time to read every day. Even if you're just reading for 10 to 20 minutes each day, this time will enrich your life and teach you things you didn't even realize you didn't know. It can also be helpful to read blogs and articles, but there is no substitute for reading quality books. Plus, reading a real, paper-bound book in bed will calm your mind. In contrast, reading on an electronic device can actually keep you awake and disturb your routine. If you don't know where to start, try asking people you look up to for recommendations. Even fiction books can help you learn and become a better person, but self-help books are usually the number one choice.

Step 14. Learn How To Be Successful With Women

A lot of Men are infatuated by beautiful women, and rightly so! They are sexy and exciting, and spending time with an attractive woman can be intoxicating. At the same time, a powerful Alpha Male needs to learn how to control himself. He may be drawn to beautiful women but he must also realize that, in his life, women do not come first. His priorities will always be to himself and his goals. This is part of what makes such an attractive Alpha Male. He's going to treat a woman like a princess, but he's not going to sacrifice either his well-being or his sense of self to make her happy. That's partly why Alpha Males may seem "hard to get" when they're not even trying to play games. But pick-up artists can play hard to get, too. Alpha Males just do whatever they want. That is the biggest difference between the two. Unlike pick-up artists, Alpha Males just live their lives and pursue their goals.

In reality, some Alpha Males don't even date long term because they want to save their resources for their ventures and goals. Of course, this is entirely up to each individual, but the fact remains that you have to learn how to keep your head in the game by not allowing women to wrap you around their fingers. An Alpha Male always retains control over his feelings and emotions. For this reason, they learn how to attract and how to treat them well. But, once the fun is done, they also learn how to get back to business.

Step 15. Push Yourself Constantly

An Alpha Male needs to keep pushing himself. He needs to constantly broaden his horizons. The Alpha Male mentality will be killed by stagnation. It is necessary that you keep pushing yourself to do new things, reach new limits, and achieve new goals. Remain self-aware enough to know when you've started stagnating, and break out of the rut by setting a new target and pushing yourself towards that goal. If you begin to reach the peak of your social group, find new social groups full of people who are better than you. People who make more money than you, are busier than you, and have bigger goals than you are great people to spend time with, as they will motivate and encourage you to do even more.

Step 16. Be Aware Of Your Money

A wise Alpha Male knows how to track his money. If you want to consolidate your position as a true leader among Men in life, then you have to do the same.

Budget your money, get your finances under control, and take full responsibility for every dollar that flows in and out of your wallet. True Alpha Males always have enough money to do what's needed. They don't blow their money on unnecessary toys or trinkets. They work hard, they save, they invest, they diversify, and they find ways to hustle to earn even more money.

Proactiveness is at the center of all of this. You have to be diligent about taking on your finances, but you have to reconcile this with self-control as well. Too many Men purchase flashy watches or fancy cars and then end up going broke. Many Men blow their money buying drinks for girls, hoping to score a quick hook-up. But the true Alpha Male never spends a single dollar (or volunteers), unless he has it to spare, free and clear. A strong Alpha Male can prevent crippling levels of debt. If he goes into debt, it's going to be for a good reason.

Step 17. Learn How To Treat Women

Whether you're trying to find someone to marry, dating to play the field, or going steady, Alpha Males know how to treat a woman. They are always gentle, affectionate, and kind, but they also have a clear idea of what they want and what their priorities are. They don't play games or lie. They never promise something they can't deliver, and they are clear about their sexual interest in the women they date. They won't just be the nice guys like Betas and Omegas. They'll make it plain and clear that they want her. When dealing with a woman, true alpha ,ales do several other things too. They always ask for the check, even though the bill is always split with Betas and Omegas! (One exception is if the woman is very insistent. It's easier to let her pick up some or all of it rather than fighting over it.)

Alphas open her door. If she is cold, they give her their jacket. They schedule dates and take action. They choose where to eat, what to do for entertainment, and lead the conversation. They make it easy for the woman to have a good time and don't force her to make any decisions.

They think about her emotions and feelings. They're strong enough to handle anything that she might throw at them. They are not sucked into needless arguments. If the woman is worth spending time with, she's worth the patience it takes to cope with her feelings.

A true Alpha Male is a nobleman on the streets, in every sense of the word, but an animal in the sheets! He is going to respect her and keep her honor, but as soon as it is time to play, he'll be ready to flip the switch. That said, a true Alpha Male also knows how to please a lady in bed. So make sure you are conscious of what you do!

Practice makes perfect. Even if you don't get a lot of opportunities to practice, study up! Study what the ladies are searching for and be aware of how she responds when things get heated. It will make a big difference if you pay attention to the way she responds to you and just try to see what she enjoys when you're together. This will help you figure out what you are doing right!

Step 18. Constantly Look For Adventure

A true Alpha Male never allows life to weigh him down. He'll be exploring and looking for new adventures forever. Life doesn't happen while you're sitting at a desk, and the Alpha Male knows that. Therefore, he will always meet new people, try out new experiences, and create excitement in his life and in the lives of those around him.

This is not the type of guy who will sit around and play video games. This isn't the type of guy who'll be happy to sit at home and watch porn. While it's true that video games and porn can be fun, in reality, these things aren't fulfilling. They're items on a display.

Have adventures and go out. Have sex with real women. Challenge yourself. Play real sports instead of online sports. Instead of playing first person shooter video games, play paintball, or take a trip to the shooting range. Instead of playing fantasy games, learn how to swordfight and fence in real life. If you're married, take your wife out into town and have adventures together. Try rock climbing, then go to the bar. Go on the ocean. Run along on the beach. Try sailing. Do things that get you out of the house and into the real world. Meet cool people, have adventures.

Step 19. Watch Your Body Language

It's important to learn how to carry yourself. An Alpha Male doesn't slouch. He doesn't avoid eye contact. He holds himself upright, with dignity. He looks people in the eye. He doesn't keep his hands in his pockets. He doesn't fidget, or touch his beard, hair, or tie continuously. He makes an effort to look good, and he knows, when he finally gets around, people know he looks good.

Body language is incredibly important, as it signals to people what you believe about yourself. It subconsciously lets other Men know you don't feel threatened by them, and lets women know you're the real thing, not just a pretender.

Here are a few guidelines on how to gain Alpha Male body language. Make sure to walk confidently, not fast and nervously.

If you are sitting down, act if you were sitting on your throne. Don't act nervous and hunched over. Lean backward. Get comfortable. Stay relaxed. Stand open with your chest and shoulders back. Give people a proper handshake when they greet you. Look them in the eye. Extend your hand, and allow them to come to you. Learn how to communicate without speaking. Be expressive, and let the person you talk to know you are listening to them. Don't be a blank canvas. Show them what chemistry feels like. Show off when something looks funny. Show when you find something to ring true. You can do all those things without saying a word.

Keep eye contact. Learn how to feel comfortable looking another person in the eye at a. Look away only if you need to look at something else. Avoid looking away out of nervousness.

Step 20. Avoid Negativity

The number-one thing separating an Alpha Male from a beta male is a positive mentality. An Alpha Male is always positive. The only exception is that, when the need arises, the Alpha will not be afraid to take a stand and be confrontational. He doesn't fear calling things the way they are.

But Alpha Males, as a general rule, don't bash other people, talk trash behind their back, or exude negativity. Those are male Beta and Omega characteristics. Thus, in your life, practice positivity. Avoid speaking down to others. Stand up for yourself and don't shy away from confrontation. But also, express that you are mentally healthy and confident. These are true traits of the Alpha Man.

Step 21. Live Responsibly

An Alpha Male will only take calculated risks. He does not make stupid decisions.

Before blowing money on something needless, make sure that:

- Your bills are paid.
- Your wife and children are provided for.
- You have set aside money in savings.
- You have looked ahead to plan for unexpected expenses.

An Alpha Male has always saved money so that he is not caught unprepared for anything. It is true that we can't prepare for everything, but we can be accountable for what we have.

A true Alpha Male also knows when and when not to take risks. Walking up to that attractive woman and having a chat? That may well be a good risk. Have reckless, unprotected sex? No. Exercise responsibility and use common sense. Alpha Males are not all bravado and no brains. We combine wisdom with bravery. If you want to be a true Alpha, you have to be willing to do the same.

Step 22. Build Other People Up

A true Alpha Male is confident enough that he doesn't need approval from anyone else. He acknowledges when other people are not entirely confident, and then helps them feel better about themselves. He will compliment their clothes. When needed, he'll provide encouragement. He'll give them positive feedback. Instead of focusing on the negatives, he will brag about the good things people do.

A true Alpha propagates positivity and improves his world. True, he can give precedence to himself and his own purpose over everything else, but he also understands that there are ways to treat people well and build them up that will help everyone in the long run. If you catch somebody talking smack or gossiping behind his bros' back, that is not an Alpha. That's a Beta or Omega, always fighting to get the spotlight!

Step 23. Be Conscious of Your Own Mortality

One of the most prevailing things an Alpha Male can do is to remain conscious of the fact that he is one step closer to his death every day. Life is not forever, and the Alpha Male knows that every day is priceless at the core of his being. It is good to be at peace with that knowledge. It's good to be reminded of that every day, too. A true Alpha isn't going to waste time on small things that don't matter.

So make every day meaningful, and use your time as you wish. We often treat time as if we had an unlimited amount of it. We are wasting time just to be entertained. Some of us act as if all that matters is consuming entertainment and content, and it shows. But an Alpha knows that what matters isn't what we consume, but what we create. We need to leave our mark in the world and create a legacy for ourselves. The only way to do that is to get away from the TV screen. Take action, and remember that it could be our last day.

Step 24. Get Your Priorities Straight

What are your concerns? Who matters to you? When does your life come first? What are your values? Having your priorities in order is very important. If you don't have your priorities in order, you'll be wishy-washy and never know exactly what to do or what to do.

Men who don't know what their priorities are live life in chaos and confusion. Their thoughts and instincts drive them. People sometimes destroy their own lives, and their wishy-washy actions often hurt the people around them. This is how Betas and Omegas act. As an Alpha, you have to figure out your priorities and learn to make decisions about them. At any given moment, you have to know what is more important to you. Is it your job? Your family? Their bills? Are you healthy? Your goals? Feeling happy? Your friends? Think about this, and meditate on it a lot. It will help you become much more confident in your ability to make rational, short notice decisions.

Step 25. Be Good Without Expecting Anything In Return

This may be the biggest difference between an Alpha and a Beta. An Alpha is working hard to be a good person, because he wants to be a good person. On the other hand, Betas and Omegas try to be good people, so that other people are good to them. The difference is enormous.

An Alpha male has a life of his own. He does not need help from anybody else. He doesn't have to try to' hand out' good deeds. If he does something good, it is because he wants to do it, not because he expects a reward. He follows the idea: Do good things, but only if you really want to. If doing the good thing is not in itself a sufficient reward, then don't do it. Alpha Males do as they please. And when that includes good or charitable things, it's just because they wanted to be good and caring.

Doing something well and expecting something in return is a sign of weakness. If you are going to expect something in return, then don't even do the good thing (unless you make a business deal). Charity and business deals are two things that are completely different. One comes from your heart's goodness and the other is a transaction.

CHAPTER FIVE

SELF HYPNOSIS, SLEEP LEARNING, MEDITATION & AFFIRMATIONS

Important Techniques To Take Control Of Your Mind And Build Your Ideal Personality

NO MATTER how much valuable advice you receive, your self-improvement is ultimately up to you. You're the only one in charge of yourself. That means that the focal point of control in your life needs to be internal. Many people have an external locus of control, meaning that they consider powers outside of themselves to be responsible for their lives and their well-being. This is an appealing frame of mind because, when something goes wrong, it gives them someone or something else to blame.

The problem with this mindset, however, is that it commonly results in a lack of motivation and personal drive in life. People with external loci of control are overly influenced by the moods and mannerisms of those around them, to the point where they avoid making any special effort to succeed. Furthermore, by assigning responsibility to others, they refuse to learn from their own mistakes in life.

Psychologists refer to this concept of internal and external loci of control as "attribution theory." According to research, individuals with internal loci are the most successful in life. The reason for this is easy to understand. If you consider everything to be within your control, virtually nothing is outside the realm of possibility. You know that your destiny is entirely within your own hands. Think, for instance, of self-made millionaires. They're typically self-reliant and have succeeded in life because they took control of their situation.

With this in mind, remember that if you believe yourself to be an attractive guy, you'll naturally find yourself exhibiting attractive behaviors. But where can you find that faith in the first place? Does it come from performing well in previous sexual encounters? If so, you're relying on an external locus of control. This makes you vulnerable to a "rewards and punishment" mindset, in which your morale depends entirely on consistent success. If you begin to do poorly in your encounters with women, your confidence will plummet, leaving you with no motivation for self-improvement.

On the other hand, if you're comfortable with yourself and believe in your own desirability, you'll be able to keep your head high regardless of whether or not women have the good taste to pursue you. The permanent solution to unstable self-confidence is simply to stop thinking that women and their opinions are all-important. Yes, that's right: when it comes to the game of love, the belief that women are the most important thing will only get in your way. When you're first beginning a relationship, try to view the woman as a source of fun, excitement, and sex--no more, no less. If you start out by looking at her as a potential girlfriend, you're likely to put too much stock into her approval. Not every relationship has to be emotionally intimate or committed. Half the fun of dating and sex is just that: fun!

Easy Alpha Male Exercise

At one point or another, pretty much everyone will end up fixating on external influences. When you get stuck in this mindset, how can you escape? One easy technique is by making a list. Take a moment to write down all the negative aspects of your life that you feel to be outside of your control. Your list is likely to end up looking something like this:

- *My parents did a bad job of raising me.*
- *My boss is holding me back.*
- *Classmates hurt my ego by bullying me.*
- *I'm objectively bad looking.*
- *My economic circumstances are bad.*
- *I haven't been given the same opportunities as my peers.*

...And so on and so forth. Once you get started, you're likely to find that the negative influences in your life are practically endless. If you really start thinking about the sheer weight of them all, you're likely to feel immobilized, and therefore find yourself unable to enact change.

Now, let's try approaching the list from a different frame of mind. It's true that none of these things are within your control. But, since that's the case, why are you worrying about them in the first place? Stressing about things that can't be changed is ultimately a waste of time and energy. Why be cynical when you could choose not to be? Why give your parents, bullies, and bosses the power to ruin your life?

It's been scientifically proven time and time again that we can exert a huge impact on our behavior and well-being merely by believing ourselves to be in charge of our situation. The more we take charge of our circumstances, the less likely we are to give up. When you move towards developing an internal locus of control, you'll become more optimistic. You'll have the willpower to improve problems in your life--even those that you may have initially thought to be beyond your control. For example, if one of the items on your original list had to do with unattractiveness, you can choose to hit the gym, improve your diet, and focus on your grooming habits.

When you take responsibility for your own empowerment, you'll become more determined to improve yourself and this will enable you to achieve anything you want in life.

Your Thoughts

Most of our perceptions originate from our feelings, which may seem irrational and outside of our control. But the truth is that, as thought-oriented beings, we have the ability to regulate our emotions. It is indeed within our ability to choose either a positive or a negative mindset. The tricky part is that a negative frame of mind is usually far easier to maintain. Staying optimistic takes hard work. There's no way around that fact.

For instance, say you're attending a speed-dating event in which women will check "yes" or "no" to indicate whether they're interested in seeing you again. If the latter happens, it's easy to make assumptions. You might feel like a loser or like nobody will ever want to talk to you again. You could easily feel inferior to all the other guys at the event, and might wish that you had spent the evening at home playing video games instead.

Let's think about a better way to look at this. What aspects of your situation could you have controlled more effectively? Maybe your anxiety resulted in a hunched posture and a furrowed brow, making you less attractive to the woman who said that she would no longer like to see you. If you correct those major errors in body language, you're guaranteed to do better next time.

If your predominant attitude towards life is a concerned one, you're always going to find things to worry about. If you're hopeful, on the other hand, people will find you attractive and enjoy spending time with you. If you intend to be a successful Man, start by thinking positively. Reminiscing about the past will only produce negative thoughts. Sure, you've made mistakes--we all have. The trick is to let go of them.

It is absolutely critical to understand that the past only exists in your mind. Once you've learned from your mistakes, there's no further use holding onto them. Do away with negative thoughts--not only pertaining to yourself, but also to the world at large. Certain people have pessimistic approaches that inhibit their ability to grow and improve themselves; it's your responsibility to cut them out of your life. The news can also be a downer, especially when it's practically inescapable due to the prevalence of the internet. To the best of your ability, avoid being a news junkie. There's really nothing to be gained out of scouring doomsday headlines every day. If the world really is ending, someone is going to tell you so!

Developing a Positive Mindset

Why would any woman be attracted to me? I'm just too short, you find yourself thinking as you walk into your afternoon class. You sit in your usual place, behind an attractive girl who's never given you a second glance. Today, though, she turns towards you.

"Can I borrow a piece of paper?" she asks.

"Yeah," you say, and pass a blank sheet to her.

Neither of you speak for the duration of the lesson. Later that night, alone in your room, you can't help but think about her, and about how she must see you as a complete loser.

What you don't understand in this scenario is that the girl made an effort to talk to you. Chances are that she didn't really need a piece of paper--or, if she did, she could have asked a friend instead of a virtual stranger. But she chose to speak to you instead. The "paper" thing was just an excuse--in her mind, she's given you a clear sign that she's interested in you. But you made the mistake of putting your insecurities first and assuming that no girl like that could possibly find you attractive. Because of this, you've completely missed a solid opportunity. You need to believe in your own attractiveness in order to pick up on the signals that girls send in your direction.

When negative thoughts crop up, don't flee them. Instead, identify them, acknowledge them, and let them go, leaving more room for positive thoughts and feelings. Choose to be inwardly confident and happy, no matter what's happening to you on the outside. Be satisfied with yourself, and know that, no matter what happens, you'll find a way to be happy. Never forget that every day is another opportunity for self-improvement.

Here are a few easy ways to start building a more positive attitude:

1. Constantly envision yourself as the person that you want to be. Imagine how your idealized self would act and work to embody those behaviors. Visualize how much money you'd like to make, the house you'd like to

live in, and the body you'd like to have. Albert Einstein once said that "Your imagination is your preview of life's coming attractions." Don't forget it!

2. Cut out negative influences in your life, including people who dampen your mood with constant cynical remarks.

3. When you think about the past, focus on your achievements. Recognize that mistakes are temporary and often the result of bad luck.

4. Assume that you will be successful in your endeavors. Think of yourself as confident and work on believing that you're every woman's dream lover.

5. Make use of affirmations. If you inundate yourself with positive statements, repeating them over and over, you'll eventually find that you're feeling better about yourself. These statements, known as "affirmations," are the opposite of the self-deprecating thoughts that we often find ourselves having.

Let's talk a bit more about affirmations. They have three main purposes: changing your beliefs, strengthening trust in yourself, and encouraging yourself.

The more you tell yourself something, whether it be positive or negative, the more ingrained it becomes in your subconscious. Though something like, "I'm so ugly!" or "Women hate me!" may feel like a throwaway thought, it can actually be incredibly damaging. When you imagine something enough times, you start believing it.

How can you use this in the opposite manner? You can reprogram your mind by repeating new beliefs over and over again. For instance, take the sentence, "I'm becoming more extroverted." At first, your mind will reject the idea, labeling it as bullshit and trying to block it out solely because it feels so radical--after all, you've likely spent years convincing yourself that you're introverted and antisocial.

But the day *will* come when you find yourself doing something that you never would have expected of yourself. Maybe you're waiting to check out at the grocery store and decide to exchange light banter with other customers in line. You'll do this without even thinking about it because you've successfully convinced your subconscious that extroversion is one of your core characteristics. When you realize this, it's an absolutely incredible feeling.

Remember, though, that affirmations work very slowly. If you look at yourself from one day to the next, you won't be able to detect any change. This can be discouraging, but keep at it. Sooner or later, you'll find yourself adopting new and better behaviors.

One way to make affirmations work better and faster is by using all of your senses to visualize them coming true. If you're walking down the street and telling yourself, "I enjoy being a totally confident Alpha Male," take note of how your body responds to the words. Visualize your perfect self, and it will begin to become reality: your muscles will relax, your shoulders will straighten, and your strides will become longer and slower. When you're alone, it can also help to speak each affirmation out loud in order to fully engage your sense of hearing.

Think of affirmations as a sort of mental weightlifting. Hard, consistent work is the only way to build up muscle, and you need to maintain your exercise patterns in order to keep yourself from sliding back into an unhealthy state. This means that you'll need to repeat old statements from time to time, even if it feels unnecessary.

SUPREME ALPHA MALE BIBLE. THE 1NE.

While trying out affirmations, feel free to experiment with different techniques. Some people find that the most effective method is to write affirmations down with a pen or pencil, giving themselves both visual and tactile associations with each statement. Someone more auditorily inclined, on the other hand, may prefer to save recordings of themselves speaking affirmations out loud.

Go ahead and try it right now. Pick an affirmation and repeat it to yourself a few times, then do the same thing tomorrow, the day after that, and so on. Even though they work slowly, positive affirmations are truly miraculous. You'll be amazed at how effective they can be.

Self-Hypnosis

Self-hypnosis is a great method for training the mind. It works to make the brain highly sensitive to suggestions by relaxing and making your mind blank. In this state, ideas take root in your mind with ease and help you change your behavior. The brain is a very agile organ. It constantly thinks, rationalizes, and reasons. Still, you will sometimes avoid accepting new thoughts and beliefs that would help you build a better life. That's where self-hypnosis comes in. Self-hypnosis is a gradual process, just like affirmations. You'll need to program your mind to do what you want each time you practice it, but in time, the programming typically fades. So you need to continue your sessions of self-hypnosis regularly before your mind is fully convinced of the new ideas that you are teaching it. You don't need any fancy equipment or software for this, only a tape recorder. Follow these instructions to build your self-hypnosis practice.

Self Hypnosis - How-To

1. Make sure you are in a place free of distractions. Switch off your cell phone and unplug your landline. You don't want any interruptions.

2. Do not worry about stumbling over words while reading the script, just soldier through. When you listen to the tape later, any blunders you made while reading the script will seem so trivial that you will hardly notice them.

3. Check that there is no background noise, like air conditioners or road traffic.

4. Use your regular voice when you start reading the script. Speak at a moderate pace–not too fast and not too slow. As the recording moves into the "relaxing oxygen" talk, slow it down, using a more relaxed voice. You will move into a deeply peaceful state when you listen to the tape, so you need the tape to have a calm voice on it.

5. Turn off any phones and eliminate other possible interruptions while listening to the tape. You do not want sudden interruptions when you are in a deeply relaxed state.

6. Get comfortable when you listen to your tape, with your body spread out and relaxed. I like to lie on a sofa.

7. Listen with an open mind. Follow the directions that you give yourself.

Tape Script:

Close your eyes.

Take a deep breath.

Let your body feel relaxed.

I want you to feel all of today's stresses, all of your worries, clustered right on your forehead in a small little bundle. Feel the tension in your body when you think back about girls ' rejections.

Feel the stresses gathering up in your forehead from life, your job, your goals and everything else.

I want you to believe that all those stresses are slowly draining away from your body right now. Let them drain from your forehead, your nose, your chin and neck, your shoulders, your stomach, your hips, then your legs and your feet, until they leave your body.

All the stress is going out of your body. You feel completely relaxed.

I want you to believe, as you breathe in, that you breathe in the warm air and that you relax. Feel the soothing oxygen give you a tingly warm feeling inside your chest cavity. Feel the warmth radiating out of your chest and all over your body.

Allow your breathing to deepen, gradually taking in the calming oxygen. You sink deeper and deeper into calmness with every breath you take.

(Pause 15 for seconds.) I want you to repeat these affirmations to yourself internally. As I say the affirmations, notice how completely relaxed you feel and focus all your attention on my words.

I'm feeling good about myself (pause after each of these, to let the listener — that is, you— repeat them).

Being an optimist helps me achieve everything I want in life.

I'm feeling better about myself every day.

There's no limit to what I can do, so I'll program my mind to become successful beyond my wildest dreams.

I know this will work because I have the same mentality as Men who are productive already.

Now that you've said your affirmations, I'm going to count to ten, and you're going to become even more comfortable with each number I say aloud. One, I feel happy. Two. Three. Four. Five, relax deeper. Six. Seven. Eight. I am feeling quite relaxed. Nine. I'm feeling good. Ten. I'm feeling pretty good.

Now you are at the deepest possible level of relaxation. Now you're going to take this opportunity to reconfigure your mind to achieve the maximum benefits. You're a hot guy. You can make a woman as happy, just as any other guy can.

You want to have sex with hot women. You have control over your personal life. No one else does. Whatever you do, you can choose to become totally successful. You enjoy having this strength.

You radiate an aura of poise, elegance, and still, steady faith and you have such a solid, optimistic mindset. You have an amazing mind, and your willpower is growing stronger and stronger. You are determined to achieve the goals you set for yourself.

Take another deep breath. Enjoy the sense of deep relaxation. Repeat to yourself the following affirmations.

- I release the need to allow others to control my life. Again, pause to let your listener— you— repeat the affirmation. I need to accept myself.
- I couldn't care less about what other people think of me; I'm the one in charge of my life.

- I am a powerful Alpha Male. I walk like I'm a superhero and I think very highly of myself.
- I love women because they are a source of fun and pleasure in my life.
- When I have sex with a woman I do it enthusiastically. I am capable of thoroughly satisfying myself and my lovely partner.
- I fancy having sex with women. I just love making love.
- I love giving affection.

Now it's time to just listen. Don't say anything. Just continue to enjoy how good you look. Let your mind be completely at ease while you allow those thoughts to come in. Remain calm and relaxed when you are with a woman, no matter what happens, you're in control of your life. You're not putting all that much thought into what she thinks of you; you know you're a nice, interesting Man, and she's lucky to be with you. You're the world's number one male. You're amazing and any woman would be fortunate to have you.

You deserve all you get. You radiate love and joy.

You will never be subservient to anyone again -- not to anyone, male or female.

You are not a follower; you are a natural leader.

You are living an active life. Every day you have fun and you find new adventures, even in small things.

You're taking care of your health because you want to be healthy, desirable, and have a long life.

Life is interesting. You love to tell women stories about the fascinating things that are happening in your life.

You have an intense desire to be financially successful. You know you can do whatever you dream of, and you enjoy moving toward that dream.

You feel optimistic and want success with women, fitness, good friends, financial wealth, and the hobbies and interests you enjoy.

Now take a deep breath and relax.

Pause for an instant, and appreciate the feeling of being in complete control of your life. If you choose to, you can be totally successful and you will love every minute of that success. You love it when your dreams come true, just like they are now.

You will soon emerge from this relaxed state and become more alert. Become more and more alert as I count to five. Just. One. Two, become more alert. Three. Four.

You awaken feeling totally refreshed, full of energy and vigor, and incredibly optimistic. Five, have your eyes open. You are an Alpha Male. Four, fully alive. You feel completely refreshed and in a good mood!

Sleep Learning

There are just 24 hours in a day and about a third of it is normally spent sleeping. So, over-ambitious Men have always wondered: Can this time be used to learn a new talent, or even a language? To put it another way, is sleep learning possible?

The answer is yes and no, but depending solely on what we mean by "learning." It is almost definitely difficult to absorb complicated knowledge or pick up a new ability from scratch by, say, listening to an audio recording during a nap. However, research indicates that the sleeping brain is far from idle, and certain types of learning can occur. However, it has yet to be determined if that's worth losing sleep over.

The idea of learning while you sleep, or hypnopedia, has a long history. In 1914, the German psychologist Rosa Heine conducted the first study showing memory and learning gains from sleep. She found that learning new information before sleep in the evening leads to better memory compared to learning during the day.

Many studies have shown that sleep is key to creating long-term memories of our daily experiences. During sleep, the brain creates long-term memories in the Hippocampus. It then stabilizes the memories, and proceeds to store them in the neocortex. Since memory formation happens during sleep, it makes sense to wonder if memories can be altered, improved, or even reformed during sleep.

One popular sleep learning method during the 1930's was the Psycho-phone. It played motivational messages to sleepers, such as "I radiate love." The idea was to help people digest new ideas in their subconscious so they would feel confident and rejuvenated when they woke up.

At first, research seemed to support the concept behind devices like the Psycho-phone. Some early studies showed that people were absorbing the information they came across during sleep, but those results were debunked in the 1950s, when scientists began using EEG to track brain waves during sleep. Investigators found that, if any learning had occurred, it was only because the participants had been awakened by the stimuli. These faulty experiments discarded sleep learning as pseudoscience.

However, other studies have shown in recent years that, during sleep, the brain may not be a completely inert mass. These studies indicate that information can be processed by the sleeping brain, and new memories created. The catch is that the memories are either tacit or unconscious. This method of learning is, to put it another way, incredibly easy, far simpler than what your brain would do if you wanted to study German or quantum mechanics.

Now, these results have lifted sleep learning from the pipe dreams group and put it back on scientists' radars.

"Scientific literature has been suggesting that sleep learning has been difficult for decades. Therefore, only seeing the most simple form of learning is fascinating for a scientist," said Thomas Andrillon, a neuroscientist at Monash University in Melbourne. "But people aren't really interested in this simple method of learning." Andrillon told Live Science that the recent findings have boosted expectations for future applications for scientists. The implicit essence of sleep-learning, for example, makes the practice useful to those who want to shed a bad habit, such as smoking, or develop new positive ones.

Multiple studies have shown that there could be a fundamental process of learning, called conditioning, during sleep. For example, a 2012 study by Israeli researchers published in the journal *Nature Neuroscience* found that people could learn to associate sounds with odors during sleep. The scientists played a tone to the participants in the sleeping test, while they released the unpleasant scent of rotten fish. When awake, the people held their breath upon hearing the sound, expecting the bad smell.

"It was a simple finding that people can create new memories during sleep," said Andrillion, who was not involved in the research.

In a study published in the *Neuroscience Journal* in 2014, researchers found that, even though the memory was implicit, it could still influence the actions of the participants. For example, smokers smoked fewer cigarettes after spending a night exposed to the scent of smoke combined with rotten eggs or rotten food.

Andrillon and his colleagues found that sleep learning could go beyond pure conditioning. In a study published in the journal *Nature Communications* in 2017, Andrillon and his colleagues found that participants were able to pick out complex patterns of sound they had heard during sleep.

Sleep learning skills can lead to word learning, too. In a study published in January, 1991 in the journal *Current Biology*, researchers played pairs of composite words and their supposed meanings to participants. For example, the participants were told, while they slept, that the word "guga" means elephant. When awake, the participants performed better than chance when they took a multiple choice test and had to choose the meaning of made-up words used in the study.

What all these studies have in common is that they implicitly display memory. "It's not any knowledge that they will be able to use naturally, so they don't know that even there is this knowledge," Andrillion said. "The problem is,'Where do we go from there?'" There are several different layers involved with learning a foreign language: understanding the sounds, learning the vocabulary, and mastering grammar. To this date, evidence indicates that it might be possible to get acquainted with the sound and accent of a language, or even the pronunciation of words, while sleeping. The study also found that, although people can learn new words while asleep, they learn to a lesser degree than they would during the day.

So you have to weigh the cost then, said Andrillion. Stimulating the sleeping brain with new information is likely to interfere with sleep processes, negatively affect pruning and reinforce what we've learned over the previous day, he said.

Although losing quality sleep to theoretically learn a few words isn't a good trade-off, researchers continue to study sleep learning in specific cases. The compromise may be worth it. Sleep learning, for example, may be helpful in cases of phobias and post-traumatic stress disorder, where people decide to change a habit or modify stubborn upsetting memories.

And some types of implicit learning can occur more intensely during sleep, which can aid in that situation. For example, the conditioning that occurred in the study of smoking and rotten eggs does not work well when performed during wakefulness. When you smoke near a garbage bin every day, then you know that the two sources of the smells are different, so you don't associate one with the other. Once we are awake we are not easily fooled, but our sleeping brains aren't quite so clever. We can use it for our own benefit.

Meditation

Meditation is a fascinating subject, but it can be hard to describe because you're sure to offend someone, and you're sure to come across anyone who disagrees with you regardless of what you say (usually a self-proclaimed "expert"). Although I deny any expertise, I have been a practitioner of various types of meditation for nearly a decade, and I believe the modern Man can benefit from an easy, practical approach to meditation.

Meditation isn't difficult; it's usually the "gurus" that can make it sound needlessly arduous or dogmatic. All you need to do to obtain the benefits of meditation is dedicate a bit of time every day, and have discipline to stick to your practice. You can meditate anywhere, practically without any fancy supplies or gadgets. Although pillows, bells, incense, etc., can be useful tools for meditation (I own them), they are not required. In fact, some of my most intense meditation experiences were spur-of-the-moment meditations in the woods, on my back porch, or even in my office during lunch.

Throughout the different spiritual traditions, there are five key styles of meditation.

1. Mindfulness

The purpose of mindfulness meditation is to relax and calm your "monkey brain." What's the monkey brain? It's the continuous and restless shifting of thoughts that is going on all day in your head. Mindfulness meditation attempts to silence the thoughts clamoring for your attention and to focus your attention on one thought or sound that serves as your "anchor." Your anchor may be the sound of flowing water, the repetition of a phrase or even your own breath.

This type of meditation is usually performed in sets of 15-30 minutes. It's a great tool for relaxation, or as a primary tool for spiritual practice or other forms of meditation. When thoughts come into your mind (and I know they will), just try to ignore them. You may notice that one single, pressing thought continues to recur. If that's the case, take the time to contemplate why this thought, right now, and why that thought is so important. Ask questions like "Why does this matter? What effect does this have on me? How can I handle this effectively?" Of course, if your recurrent thought is a trivial thing like a funny YouTube video you saw earlier that morning, reject it and seek to get back to your anchor.

One effective technique for mindfulness meditation is the Buddhist breath meditation "vipassana." In vipassana, you simply observe your breath or use a "breathing package" to anchor your mind. Inhale and count (1, 2, 3, etc.) for a breath set, and then exhale and count (1, 2, 3, etc.) until you hit your set. Repeat.

Feel the air coming through your nose/mouth, reaching and filling your lungs, and then release it through your nose/mouth. Seek to ignore the thoughts as they come into your mind, and return to concentrating and watching your body.

2. Active Meditation

This form of meditation includes physical activity to enable the synchronization of your body --a practice or experience you do to feel peace, calm, and clarity. This is something that many people practice or experience without even understanding. Ever feel like you're "in the zone" playing a sport? You may have heard of people "losing themselves in the music" when they were dancing. Or maybe you've felt the "runner's high." These are all examples of people who, to one degree or another, are practicing active meditation.

This form of exercise can be as easy as going for a walk, doing yoga (which isn't just for girls – if done correctly, it's a hell of a workout), dancing, or just working out. Just like in mindfulness meditation , the aim is to clear your mind and to use the exercise or physical activity as an anchor to clear your mind of mental garbage. Concentrate only on your body's movement, and the task in front of you. If thoughts start to crop up, ignore them or investigate them, depending on their meaning. During this process, you can also repeat a mantra to add another focus or stimulus.

3. Mantra/Affirmation

This form of meditation involves repeating a sentence or a phrase over and over again. The sentence acts as a catalyst for clearing the mind. The movement Transcendental Meditation (TM) has transformed mantra/affirmation meditation into a common form of meditation. Adherents in TM repeat a mantra (word or saying) time and time again. That's what other people think about when they talk about "meditation:" A bunch of people lying on pillows singing "Aum! Boom! Aum! Boom!" Or something like that. Essentially, the words or phrases are meant to serve as an anchor, as well as a stimulant to clear your mind so that you can reach the next level of spiritual development.

Repeating the Lord's Prayer one word at a time is one of my favorite things to do. Start with "our" in your mind, and say "our." Try to imagine it in the eye of your mind and just concentrate on "our" for 10-15 seconds (don't think about being precise because that defeats the purpose). Then clear your mind and say, either mentally or aloud, "Aum!" three or four times profoundly and gradually, then move on to "Father." Keep going until you reach the end of the prayer.

You may also repeat a positive affirmation or sentence (Tony Robbins style) such as: "I'm fine," "I'm a nice person," "I'm a powerful person," etc. You can also meditate on a specially motivational quote that will help you concentrate on a positive situation and ignore a negative one.

What you use as your mantra or affirmation is your choice. Choose mantras and affirmations that work for you, and improve your mood.

4. Insight

Insight meditation is intended to analyze one thought or feeling and to concentrate on it. It's important to have a very calm mind before starting insight meditation. Start by doing breath (mindfulness) meditation to help quiet your monkey mind. When you feel relaxed and calm, you'll be able to step into your insight meditation.

Choose a subject. Any line. It could be "love," or "rage," or "justice," or even "death." When you've got your subject, let the mind go. Don't try to control your emotions. For example, if you choose "heart," you might think of your father, wife, child, lover, Mother Teresa, your grandpa, an old couple holding hands, etc. Let those thoughts move along. Do not judge them, or seek to interpret them. Discover what love is, and what it means for you.

Often, thinking about a negative subject, like "hate," is good. When you are using a word like "hate," let your mind race. Maybe you're shocked by what comes up, but don't judge it. Let your mind work. It is helpful to understand why you associate the word "hate" to the images that come to mind. Once you make these associations, you can start working through your anger.

If you're going to practice insight meditation on a negative topic n, it's important to finish your session concentrating on something positive. You don't want to leave your meditation on a bad note. Additionally, ending on a positive note can give you a better picture of how you really feel about a subject. You can find that a thought you associate with a negative subject ends up coming back as a positive experience.

Meditation on wisdom is incredibly helpful for clearing your mental garbage. It causes you to explore and make associations that you might have long forgotten about, but maintained a subconscious level that still affected you.

5. Guided

These meditations are directed by someone who takes you through a certain scenario (in person or in a recording), or even an archetypal dream-type world. By creating a "plan" for your meditation, you can build your own guided meditation. Where are you going? What kind of guys are you going to be your role models? How are you going to respond to the challenges along the way?

Guided meditations allow your imagination to run wild and to consciously explore mental associations. Think of guided meditation as watching an amazing film where you are the creator, producer, and star.

In your guided meditation you can imagine visiting your younger self to deal with problems, having a chat with a deceased loved one to work through some unfinished business, or even seeking advice from someone you admire.

The Power Of Affirmations

Our ideas create our reality. We eventually become the things we think about constantly. This means that, if you have insecurities, you probably have recurrent negative thoughts about your confidence. You might be the kind of person, for example, who dreads the idea of speaking to a group of people, even if you know them all. Some people don't even have the bravery to speak at family gatherings because they don't have the courage to speak. Simply put, they lack confidence. In such cases, you say to yourself that you can't speak to people for different reasons, and try to justify your point of view, even when you know you really want to talk to them.

Negative self-talk is likely to affect the way you think about your skills, your looks, your height, your health, and your thoughts, so you end up second guessing everything you do. If you feel this way, the odds are you won't want to take any risks because you are afraid of failing. The truth is, you will never achieve anything in life if you are not willing to take risks. If you always tell yourself that you are not good enough, you will never take risks. Negative self-talk can only be described as a kind of affirmation that reinforces negative notions in your life.

As I mentioned earlier, our thoughts make our reality; if you're constantly thinking about how inadequate you are or how you don't look good enough, you're going to lack the confidence to believe that you do deserve more. As a result, you will settle for less than what you deserve. The best antidote for the effects of negative self-talk is to start declaring positive thoughts about yourself to yourself. This will help you boost your confidence, and will help you grow. The reasoning behind repeating positive affirmations about yourself to yourself is that you have to get to a point where you believe what you are saying about yourself.

Human behavior is very complicated. Our actions don't always reflect our true intentions. For example, even if you don't want to think negatively, our culture is so riddled with negativity that it influences our lines of thought. Negative thinking comes more naturally than positive thinking, thanks to the negativity found in the media, advertising, parents, and everyone around us. For example, our past personal conflicts with others carry a lot of negativity within them and can cause us to think negatively about ourselves. These thoughts, in turn, make us attract more unwanted situations in our lives, which, in turn, make us even more unhappy and further damage our self-confidence.

When we think, we tell the universe what we want in our lives. It doesn't matter if you thoughts are positive or negative. When we think we're defeated, we tell the universe that we can't be good enough. As a result, the universe will respond by manifesting something that reinforces our idea that we are not good enough. The manifestation may be in the form of never getting promoted, never finding opportunities to make money, or never finding an avenue for us to explore what we really want out of our lives. So if you wake up to find only disasters in the morning news, you might find it hard to find something uplifting or positive to think about. Since your subconscious mind is often the biggest culprit of negative thinking, even when we want to see ourselves from a positive light, we need to change the way it perceives life, so that we can actually start thinking positively subconsciously. In this case, when you affirm yourself, you could describe it as tuning the positive thinking radio in your mind. That way, you can begin to think of yourself as a powerful and confidence-filled individual who has everything in his or her control.

New experiences will change the way you think about particular issues. As a result, the next time you are faced with a similar situation, your brain will activate the neural pathways it created after the original experience and refer back to them. As a result, you will respond in the same way you've responded in the past. This is where the subjective thinking problem comes in! We become trapped in our minds because we have the same old habits and reactions. Our mind wishes to confirm that the truth is what we perceive of that situation.

If you have problems with self-confidence, you'll find yourself searching for opportunities to justify why you can't approach your dream woman, why you can't pass exams, why you can't apply for a job in your dream company, why you can't start your own business, and why you have to continue working at a job that makes you dread getting up for work in the morning. You will also start looking for faults in your physical appearance, height, gender, race, academic credentials, and other aspects of life. As a result, you will find it very difficult to unleash the power of self-confidence within you; you have already convinced yourself that you don't have what it takes to reach your goals. You won't even be able to speak in public because your subconscious mind will always tell you to focus on how disinterested the audience seems in whatever you're talking about. To better understand the affirmations, let's talk a little further about our subjective thinking.

How Affirmations Work

In this case, the more you repeat positive affirmations, the more they become part of your reality because your subconscious mind will begin to "remember" them more frequently. Once this happens, you will realize that these results are all the proof you need that affirmations work and that you ought to continue believing in them! In this case, you will be transforming your negative subjective thinking into positive thinking. As Albert Einstein put it, "if we want to change our present subjective reality, we need to change the thoughts that occupy our subconscious mind."

Simply put, when you've achieved a goal, you stop being afraid of failure and your subconscious mind already believes you've overcome that obstacle. Think of your preschool days; you probably thought differently about things like life, friends, and happiness. Back then, life was simple: going to school, playing with your friends, being happy and carefree. Nowadays, your thoughts about life, friendship, and happiness have changed. You have grown up, and that means that the way you perceive the world has changed, too. The way your brain processes different experiences has changed, and as a result, the way you think about life has changed, too.

Our thinking patterns are largely influenced by our family upbringing, life experiences, social setting, education, and other experiences. Our thinking patterns describe our subjective reality. So, if you're poor, you probably think of yourself as a poor person because that's the subjective reality you've been taught to believe. This is different from somebody who is rich because he or she thinks like a rich person. So, if you want to change your economic situation and become wealthy, you need to start thinking like a rich person.

I know it may feel strange to start thinking like someone who's the complete opposite from the person you actually are. You can, however, start transforming your thought patterns with affirmations so that you can start thinking as someone who already has what they want. Going back to the subject of building confidence using affirmations, your goal is to transform your thought patterns, so that you can really start believing everything you say. It even gets to a point where you don't even need the affirmations anymore because you already have built up a confident personality.

By deliberately changing your thoughts over time, you start creating new neural pathways which, in turn, will help you create new thought processes. In this case, when presented with challenges, you will not be falling back into old, negative thinking patterns. Instead, you will be using your new, positive ways of thinking.

There is no way for your brain to filter between positive and negative thoughts, and your mind doesn't actually distinguish between imaginary and real situations, either. With affirmations (positive or negative, deliberate or subconscious), you feed your mind with things that depict the reality you desire. The more you use affirmations, the more that your mind will begin to believe them. The more you believe what the affirmations are telling you, the more your mind will attempt to match your inner beliefs with the outer reality. When we create our inner storyline by using affirmations, we begin to see opportunities we never saw before, when our minds were under the influence of negative thoughts. That's the role of affirmations!

So, how do you get to a point where you can change your negative self-talk, so you can generate positive self-talk about your confidence? First, let's understand how affirmations work, so you can start creating your custom affirmations to deal with your unique life situation.

How To Create Good Affirmations

If you don't know how to create new affirmations, you will not create the right affirmations. So, here's a list of do's and don'ts on how to make powerful affirmations that will transform your life forever:

1. Make sure your affirmations are in the present. You don't want to wait forever for the future to come! In this case, don't say things like "when I go to the interview, I'll be confident." Instead, say "I am

confident in every aspect of my life," or "I am prepared for the interview I have today."

2. Use the word "choose" in your affirmations. The word "choose" denotes that you make a conscious decision to be whatever you want. In this case, you can say something like "I choose to be confident in every aspect of my life."

3. Stay positive. Your subconscious mind will make no distinction between what you want and what you don't want. So rather than saying what you don't need, just say what you wish for. In this situation, the law of growth and development takes effect, since what you are manifesting is the things you are focusing on. In this case, don't say you don't want to freak out when you're standing before an audience. Instead, describe how high your level of confidence is so that you can't wait to present to the audience.

4. Repeat! Repeat! Repeat! Do not get tired of repeating your affirmations, as this is the only way they can stick to your subconscious mind in a way that makes you begin to believe what you are saying. You can begin by repeating your affirmations at least twenty times in the morning and twenty times in the evening; in fact, the more the better! You should write them down at least twenty times a day, too. Writing is an even more effective way of learning than recitation. As a rule of thumb, you should repeat the affirmations until you get results. Don't give up!

5. Use a mirror. Sometimes when we tell ourselves affirmations, we don't believe some of the things we say. Mirrors are a great way to boost self-confidence, as you can affirm whatever you want to happen in your life while looking at yourself in the mirror. Look

closely at your reflection in the mirror and repeat the statements as many times as possible. This helps to connect with the subconscious mind.

6. Memorize and recite affirmations using the card technique. If you want to remember the affirmations wherever you go, you can write all your affirmations in a pocket card,so you can affirm yourself wherever you are.

7. Keep your affirmations short. An affirmation in a single sentence is good enough. Don't write affirmations that are paragraphs long!

8. Make sure you understand every single word you say to yourself.

9. Recite the affirmations when you are calm, and make sure, in your subconscious mind, that you can hear them.

10. Have absolute confidence in whatever you say. Failing to believe that whatever you say is true, means you have negative self-talk, which will not help you manifest whatever you wish. The negative self-talk, in any case, will always push you to look for excuses to justify why you cannot believe what you say!

Now that you understand everything about affirmations and how to create them, let's look at a few assertions that you can start using today to transform your confidence into new heights.

30 Self-Confidence Affirmations That Will Transform Your Life:

#1. I emit beauty, attraction, and excellence.

#2 Now that I acknowledge my self-worth, my confidence level is at its highest.

#3 Many people want to emulate my rampant level of confidence.

#4 I'm very self-confident and I stand out.

#5 I have an infinite capacity to overcome my anxieties and challenges.

#6 I have all the qualities needed to achieve everything I set out to do.

#7 I am always overwhelmed with creative ideas that transform my life with every day that passes.

#8 I am extremely talented and will begin to use my talents today to make a difference in my and other people's lives.

#9 I am the architect/author of my life; all I build is courtesy of my creative mind and my extensive experience.

#10 People and companies are always looking to me to offer a solution to their needs.

#11 My future is a clear copy of what I now envision.

#12 I choose to inhale confidence whenever I breathe and exhale all timidity.

#13 I love to be around new people every day, as they challenge me to get better.

#14 Being around strangers unleashes my natural enthusiasm and boldness.

#15 I look forward to changing, since I can easily adapt to changing situations.

#16 I live in the present and exude unrivaled trust in the future.

#17 I am a problem solver; I always find the best solutions to the problems that people are having.

#18 I deserve the best in my life and release any need for misery and suffering.

#19 I love myself and accept myself without reservation.

#20 I'm totally content with my uniqueness.

#21 Every day I become more self-confident.

#22 Despite my fears, I will go ahead with the plan.

#23 I feel comfortable attracting friends because I am fun to be around.

#24 I choose to be open to trying new things because I don't fear change.

#25. I am now successful.

#26 I am very confident, intelligent, and capable.

#27 I always appeal to people who bring out the best in me.

#28 I love the person I have become.

#29 I allow all negative thoughts and feelings about myself to go away.

#30 I always exude my best qualities.

The daily repetition of the above affirmations and the creation of other affirmations aimed at boosting your self-confidence will certainly transform your life. By combining affirmations with meditation, sleep learning, and self-hypnosis, you'll boost your ability to focus on positive thoughts each day.

These are just some of the most powerful ways to deal with some of the challenges that come with failing to find a perfect way to focus on the affirmations. If you find that negative thoughts often crop up, then you should blend affirmations with meditation and self-hypnosis, as these two can help in building focus.

Confidence is one of the two traits that women find most desirable in a Man. It can show a lot of different things: a confident Man is comfortable in his environment, high in social status, able to take a leadership role, and capable of adapting on the fly. When you act in a confident manner, you're showing a woman that you can handle anything that comes your way and that the little things don't faze you. While a beta male may get nervous in a new situation, an Alpha Man will approach it in a relaxed, poised manner.

At this point, we've done a lot of work on your mindset and internal growth. In the next chapter, we'll turn our attention to your physical looks, and how they can be optimized in order to match your developing inner alpha.

CHAPTER SIX

LOOKING THE PART

HOW YOU LOOK IS a critical part of becoming an Alpha Male, but it's not as important as you might think. And not necessarily in the way you think, either. Your physical appearance can make up 20 to 30 percent of your attractiveness to feMales. Other factors that may make you more or less attractive to women, are your level of confidence and self-confidence, your social standing, and how you make women feel in your presence. Think about this: do you think that, if Johnny Depp – a guy whose looks get a 10 out of 10 (according to my current girlfriend)—was a miserable wimp who slouched all the time and trembled at the thought of talking to the girls he had just met, he would still be considered one of the sexiest Men alive? Probably not. So, it's not all about the looks. Your attitude, demeanor, and self-confidence also play a huge role in becoming an Alpha Male.

All things being said, it is obvious that looking good would add to your appeal. In this chapter, you will discover the secrets that will instantly double or triple your looks to transform your appearance as soon as tonight.

While it's true that the way you dress doesn't really determine who you are, the style of clothing you choose says a lot about you. For an Alpha Male, it's not all about how you dress, it's about principles, values, habits, and way of life. Being an Alpha Male is about who you are as a Man and not so much about what you're wearing, but that doesn't mean that Alpha Males don't care about how they look. Caring about your appearance is about being confident and proud of who you are. And that is something an Alpha Male definitely cares about.

One of the best ways to build confidence in yourself is by dressing well. While it's true that confidence comes from the inside, it is also true that the clothes we wear can enhance that confidence. And when your morale is up is when you know you are on your way to being top dawg or Alpha Male. Before teaching you the art of dressing well, let me convince you why dressing well is valuable for building your self-confidence and, ultimately, becoming an Alpha.

The very first – and obvious – benefit of dressing well is generating the best first impression you can muster. This is true when you meet people, in general, and crucial when you first meet that hot girl you want to hook up with. I don't want to sound like most Men, but it doesn't matter what anyone says: Women care about looks, and they want to be with a Man who looks as good, or better, as them. So, believe me when I tell you: If you take pride in your appearance, the girls will notice you more. In the end, no matter how hard we try to convince ourselves to "not judge a book by its cover," we always end up doing it, whether we realize it or not. If you can't beat them, join them!

The reason appearances matter to society is, perhaps, due to the way we evolved as a species. Back in the Stone Age (not the stoned age), humans did not have the privilege of giving menacing-looking species, like a Saber-tooth Tiger the benefit of the doubt. No one said "Oh, he must be an adorable cuddly creature deep inside, just give him a chance." Those who did became dinner that night!

While unpleasant, that way of thinking was an important mechanism of survival at the time, and as such, it was passed on from generation to generation. However, the danger these days lies not in being shredded to pieces by an apex predator, but in being swindled, or worse, committing to an exclusive relationship with an extremely unstable person.

You'll need some degree of social validation if you want to be confident. Or to put it another way, you won't become a confident person without other people's support. Let's face it: There's no chance you can become an Alpha male without other people willing to follow your leadership. It would be like saying that you're valedictorian of a one person class! And making a good first impression can go a long way to gaining self-confidence and becoming Alpha.

Control Your Ideal Self By Controlling How You're Seen

All of us experience life a little differently. Though we may share experiences, our minds process them in different ways based on our memories, personalities, perspectives, and beliefs. Because of this, pretty much everything is subjective--including our own image. People will treat you not as the person that you are, but rather as the person whom they believe you to be.

This means that people will project different qualities and characteristics onto you and then treat you accordingly. This can be a good or a bad thing, depending on the person. The key point is that, once you understand that people are projecting an identity onto you, you can take actions to shape that identity into your ideal self.

How to Compliment a Woman Effectively

Suppose a woman admires you, and looks up to you as something of a role model. Is that a sufficient foundation for a relationship? Surprisingly, the answer is usually no. If she considers you to be out of her league, the two of you aren't likely to have good chemistry--and even worse, spending time with you may give her feelings of inferiority. This is due to the fact that she sees you as better, smarter, and more attractive than herself.

Many intelligent people, including Alpha Males, frequently find themselves in this predicament. This can be frustrating; if women find you appealing, why aren't they willing to start or maintain a relationship with you? Both sexual relationships and platonic friendships can be inhibited by a perceived power imbalance. Luckily, there's an easy solution. All you need to do is encourage the people around you to feel good about themselves while in your presence.

The trick to doing this is to give a genuine compliment, then *immediately* follow it up with a personal question. For instance, you might say something like "I love your outfit! Do you study fashion or the arts at all?" When you ask a woman something straightforward like this, you're basically demanding an answer--meaning that she doesn't get the opportunity to turn down the compliment. You're also displaying genuine interest: you care about who she is and what she does and you're eager to learn more about her. Once she responds, you can use that information to start into a new angle of conversation. In this case, she might reply that she's actually a biochemistry major, which opens the door to a whole new array of questions: What made her want to study biochemistry? Has she always been interested in science? How does she plan to use her degree in the future?

This strategy will help to work around one of the most difficult obstacles in your love life, which is the fact that women often refuse praise. Since society has conditioned them to be modest and timid, they automatically tend to brush off compliments, assuming that they come from a place of dishonesty. Many Men don't know how to fix this, resulting in a frustrating scenario for both parties--the Man feels upset that his flattery is rejected, while the woman is convinced that he's only complimenting her for the sake of being kind. By avoiding this situation, you immediately stand out from the pack, and women will start actively seeking opportunities to spend time with you.

With this in mind, never offer an insincere compliment. Women are very perceptive, and their predisposition for self-deprecation will only make them more likely to tell when you're fibbing. Unless you're an accomplished actor, it's going to be very difficult for you to pull off a lie--and, if you aren't convincing, the consequences could be disastrous. As the saying goes: if you don't have something nice to say, don't say anything at all.

Your compliments should be frequent, but not overbearing. You don't want to overwhelm her, especially if she already finds your presence intimidating. Remember that a conversation is an equal exchange, and that she's interested in learning about you, not just in being endlessly flattered.

The Secret to Good Listening

Let me tell you a secret: just about everybody struggles with shyness and self-consciousness. If someone is attracted to you, they'll feel good if they think that they've won your attention, and they'll likely make attempts to impress you whenever possible. To detect whether or not someone is expressing interest, look for hidden meaning in everything that they say to you. Just like you, a woman will have her own motivations, and she may not be willing to put them out in the open. With a little critical thinking, however, anyone's intentions should become clear.

Here's an example. While conversing with you, a woman poses a seemingly random question: "What percentage of genes do you think humans share with chimpanzees?" Why in the world would she ask you something like that? Chimpanzees aren't exactly the most flirtatious topic of conversation. In a way, she's assessing your intelligence and depth of knowledge about a subject that she finds interesting. On a deeper level, though, her goal is to impress you by showing off her own expertise.

With this in mind, how should you respond? It's possible that you have a subscription to *National Geographic,* and you remember reading that humans and chimps have 98.5% shared genes. Do *not* give her this answer! Since she's looking for a chance to show off for you, it would be nothing short of crushing to learn that you're already ahead of her. Instead, play dumb with an answer like "Oh, I don't know--we can't be that close, right? Maybe fifty percent?" She'll be delighted to blow your mind with the actual statistic, and she'll feel as though she's earned your approval, making you more approachable during future interactions.

This isn't the only situation in which you should understate your own knowledge and abilities. Women will often be eager to share experiences or plans that they have and you won't always be very impressed by them. It can be tempting to try and one-up a woman in this situation, thinking that it will make them admire you more, but the truth is that bragging comes across as being desperate for validation. Suppose a woman tells you that she's going on a trip to Panama City Beach. If you've been to Hawaii, Panama City is small fry--but you definitely shouldn't say so. She's excited, and she wants to share her enthusiasm, not be shot down. Instead, use the opportunity to learn more about her and the things she enjoys. Say things like, "I've never been there! Is it your first time? What part are you looking forward to the most?" If the conversation plays out in your favor, you could even sneak in a suggestion that the two of you should go together some day. There are few things more romantic than a beach vacation!

Above all else, you should genuinely be interested in what a woman says to you. If you find yourself bored with the conversation, you can safely assume that the two of you aren't a good match--even if she's got the body of a supermodel. No amount of sexual attraction can make up for incompatible personalities. You should look at each girl as a new opportunity to learn, and getting to know her should be an enjoyable journey rather than a chore. Take your time and be a good listener. It will always pay off.

Two Magical Words That Make a Woman Understand Your Kind Behavior

The most successful people tend to be the most gracious and accommodating. When somebody offers you a gift or a service, they're doing so because they view you in a favorable light. It's your job to legitimize their favorable portrayal of you by expressing gratitude. And gratitude is best conveyed in two simple words: "Thank you."

These days, there's an odd tendency among many people to deny favors and presents. "You shouldn't have!" is a common approach to receiving an especially nice gift. While many people treat this as a polite response, the fact of the matter is that you're suggesting that you don't deserve what they've done for you--or, even worse, that you're ungrateful. You should believe that you deserve good treatment, and you should make it clear that you value her kindness and thoughtfulness. Expressions of kindness should always be met with earnest gratitude. No exceptions.

Nine Nonverbal Cues That Say, "I'm Likable"

When it comes to successful conversation, the things you *do* are just as important as the things you *say*. Body language is a huge indicator of personality and motivations, and if you aren't careful, you might come across as distant or unapproachable. There are several easy ways to avoid this. Take a look:

1. Lean forward when you're having a seated conversation. This expresses interest and the fact that you're mentally present, while also bringing you physically closer to the other person. If you draw back, you're playing "hard-to-get," rendering you cold and distant in her mind.

2. Smile. This one is simple. Don't grin constantly to the point where you look ridiculous, but do make sure to toss in a smile here and there, especially when agreeing with something or expressing excitement.

3. Sit comfortably, and let yourself spread out a little bit. By physically "opening up" your body, you're demonstrating the fact that you have nothing to hide and that you're confident enough to be fully relaxed.

4. Be mindful of your outfit, and try to dress just a *bit* better than those around you. If you wear a suit to a

casual cafe, you'll look like an idiot. But if you pick a patterned button-up shirt rather than a boring black tee, you'll come across as hip and sophisticated. In general, lighter-colored clothing signals friendliness and approachability.

5. Establish and maintain mutual eye contact. Don't stare, but definitely don't avoid the other person's gaze. Eye contact is one of the easiest nonverbal ways to build trust.

6. Make sure that your voice is friendly and confident and that you sound engaged in the topic of the conversation. Being too quiet, being too monotonous, and staying mostly silent are all red flags.

7. Steer clear of inappropriate facial expressions, stiff mannerisms, and uncomfortable postures. Trying too hard will always make you unattractive.

8. Remember to strike a balance between superiority and likeability. You want to maintain the appearance of someone with a high social status, but you don't want to seem like you're looking down on her.

9. Avoid coming across as pitiful. A lot of Men are overly clingy when they're starting a relationship and will make self-deprecating statements in an attempt to get women to feel bad for them. From a psychological standpoint, this is literally childish behavior; young boys will say similar things in order to spur the nurturing urge in their mothers, thereby getting what they want. For obvious reasons, you don't want to make your date feel like you're her child!

3 Big Mannerisms that Instantly Convey that You're Not Alpha

If you can avoid the three habits described below, you'll already be more appealing than about 95% of your competition. These mistakes are so common that women have come to expect them; by subverting their expectations, you stand out from the crowd and make a great, lasting impression.

1. Bragging

"You should see my beautiful house."

"I'm about to collect six figures a year!"

"You won't believe the size of my cock."

There's something very ironic about the act of bragging. By showing off, you're actually expressing a need for validation. If you're comfortable and confident in yourself, you shouldn't feel the need to say so out loud. Aim to stop explicitly verbalizing your good qualities. Instead, let your actions speak for themselves, so that the woman can draw her own conclusions. This will also make you more intriguing, and she'll want to get to know you better in order to learn what other impressive features you might possess.

2. Putting yourself down

However, you definitely don't want to swing too hard in the other direction. Self-deprecation is a huge indication of low social status--Men tend to be overly humble because they want to avoid offending others at all costs. Alpha Males shouldn't aim to be seen as modest. Women are attracted to high self-esteem. If you think highly of yourself, she's likely to do the same.

The only exception to this is when you're obviously joking. For example, if you're a fit guy with prominent muscles, a line like, "I'm so frail--I don't think I can lift that heavy thing!" comes across as charming rather than pathetic.

3. Putting others down

When you put others down, what you're really doing is disclosing your own insecurities. Say you're walking down the street and make a snide comment about a homeless Man's shabby outfit. This Man isn't a threat to you, so why would you behave as though he were? If anything, you're basically inviting your woman to defend whomever it is that you're insulting.

You also shouldn't criticize other guys who are competing for a woman's attention. Once again, this exposes your own vulnerability and insecurity. Instead, choose not to pay attention to them. They aren't worthy of your time or consideration.

Social Standing

No matter how many Men tell you that being confident and Alpha is all about being yourself, both things require a certain degree of high social standing. Again, if you're the only dog you can't be the top dog, right? Being on top of the social food chain can make you more confident than ever before. And nothing can uplift you faster to the eyes of other people than to be well dressed.

Sense Of Control

When you dress well, you can exercise control over an area of your life that can impact your success significantly. This will, in turn, increase your self-confidence even more! Every time the people around you admire your style, you get a confidence boost. And as you get more compliments, you're motivated to dress even better. In the end, your self-confidence will snowball to become an epic avalanche of never-before-seen proportions!

Branding

Truthfully, the way you dress will become the foundation for how people brand you, which can be beneficial or detrimental for your self-confidence. Even if you feel confident about yourself, if people keep throwing jabs at you over how lousy you look, your confidence will eventually erode. But if you dress well, people will admire you, and their admiration will strengthen your self-confidence even more. Who knows, in the end, you may grow to become as confident as Shaquille O'Neal or Yao Ming!

Suits project a very particular image to people. They tell others that you are a successful businessman, a CEO, or top-notch lawyer. That's a good example of how you can use your clothes to help you brand yourself in a positive way. Dressing well brands you as a Man of confidence and success – an Alpha Male! Dressing poorly, on the other hand, brands you as your social circle's man-bitch.

Authority And Influence

Ever wondered why, most of the time, the best speakers in the world are sharply dressed? It's because dressing well can give you authority over people – to some extent. Imagine you are attending a conference about personal finances and how to build wealth. You have attended two presentations by two very different speakers on the topic of how to build a stock portfolio that will make you wealthy. One of the speakers is wearing a nice, crisp dress shirt tucked in a great pair of jeans, Cole Haan shoes, and a nice blazer. The other is wearing a round neck T-shirt and baggy jeans with a pair of worn Chuck Taylors. Who do you think inspired more respect and authority to the audience? Whose advice would you follow? Exactly.

Assume You Know Nothing

Let's get real here, dude – you're probably not confident or happy about your personal style, that's why you're reading this section. Recognizing this insecurity puts you in the best possible position to actually do something about it. I salute you!

Now that we have established this, I would like to suggest that you think about what you now know about fashion and style. Your ideas of "fashion" are probably the opposite of how you want to look. As such, you probably know very little or – I'm going to be bold here – nothing about how to dress well and with elegance.

The best place to start is to assume that you don't know anything about dressing elegantly. Learning how to dress well is easier if you accept that you don't know anything, compared to thinking that you know something that you believed was legit. It's like creating a piece of art: You need a blank canvas if you want to create a masterpiece.

Now that you realize you really don't know anything about fashion and how to dress well, you are in a better position to ask for help from other people. And there are three ways to do this: hire a fashion consultant, ask a fashion-savvy male friend to help you rebuild your wardrobe, or simply research your own.

The first option is the best, but it's probably the most expensive one, as with all the best things in the world. Unless you're married to a fashion consultant or are best friends with one, you probably won't be receiving these services for free. The reason hiring a fashion consultant is the best option is because professional fashion consultants do this for a living. Their job is to stay on top of the latest fashion styles as well as the classic ones. It is like asking a professional mutual fund manager to manage your investments versus asking a friend who is a part-time stock market trader.

The second option is a good compromise between hiring a professional consultant and doing your own research. It offers the advantage of having a second opinion about what's going to look good on you and the cost-effectiveness of doing it for free. When it comes to how you look, it is always best to have the opinion of someone who knows fashion. We all have blind spots and we can't really trust our own opinions of how fashionable and stylish we are until we've learned to dress well (what works for us and what doesn't).

If you don't have the budget, and if you're mostly hanging out with people whose sense of fashion is straight out of *The Big Bang Theory*, you really don't have any option but to do things yourself. The good news is there's a whole world of online and print media sources (books, magazines) out there. Keep in mind, though, this should be your last resort; this option doesn't give you the benefit of an objective outside opinion.

Stick To The Basics

The best way to look really good is to stick to the basics, especially if you're not used to dressing to impress. If you get the basics right and add your new personal style to the equation, you will be 75 percent of the way to success in most of the social situations without a hitch and full of confidence.

What are the basics, then? These are items of clothing that will make you look good in just about any social situation. These include white crew neck T-shirts, dark blue jeans, a dark blue navy blazer and a good pair of sneakers and loafers. These clothing items are not only adaptable to most social situations, but they can also serve as your training ground for personal style as you work on mastering the basics and eventually developing your own trademark style. Just be careful to resist the temptation of accessorizing – do this only after you have the basics right.

Be Suave And Simple

Many Men think they can learn a lot from women when it comes to their own personal style, for example, how to accessorize to achieve an elegant and striking look. Well, this is a thang for ladies, dawg! For us confident, alpha people, it's a lot different – it's all about being simple and suave. Simplicity is actually the ultimate in sophistication.

So keep it simple, yet smooth. Confidence isn't all about trying hard. Trying too hard only projects insecurity and a great need for people to accept you, which is the confident Alpha Male's antithesis.

You Can't Look Good If Your Clothes Don't Fit Well

If there are ten commandments to dressing well, the equivalent of "you won't have other gods before me," is this: stop forcing yourself to fit in clothes that are either too tight or too loose! It doesn't matter if you've got the face and body of the world's two hottest Ryans, Ryan Reynolds and Ryan Gosling; if you're wearing shirts and pants that are at least 2 sizes too small, you'd only be able to look as Alpha Male as Richard Simmons. I smell something burning... it's got to be your fat! If you wear clothing that's at least two sizes two big, you won't look like an Alpha, you'll look like Alvin and the Chipmunks. Only a few select men (mostly hip-hoppers), like Snoop Dogg and Jay-Z can pull it off.

So what exactly fits you well? The primary indicator for shirts is the line to the shoulder. Both lines should rest on the edges of your shoulders – not before or after. If it's before the edges of your shoulders, you'll notice the shirt is feeling a bit tight, and if it falls below the edge, it will feel too loose. Another way to tell if your shirt's too long is by checking how it looks on you untucked. If your shirt's bottom edge falls past your crotch area, then it's too long. If it's above your crotch area then it is too short.

As for trousers, you also want them to fit. The last thing you want is to look like you're attending a Hip-Hop convention using the suit and tie version of M.C Hammer's pants (if you look like this, your pants are too big). On the other hand, if your crown jewels feel like they're too snug, to the point where you sound like Mike Tyson, your pants are just too tight. Go for a middle-of-the-road approach.

Just Enough

Having too many clothes is as inconvenient as having too few. Being aware of this will help you keep your wardrobe within a reasonable budget. Clothes are like drinking alcohol: the right amount of drinks make you merry and help you loosen up and have a good time. Too many drinks, and it can get very bad. It's the same with clothes, except that the next day, instead of puking and having a really bad hangover, having too much in your closet can burn holes in your pockets and cause you to suffer from paralysis when deciding what to wear. One way to make sure you don't have too many clothes is to check your wardrobe periodically for clothes that either no longer fit you well (loose or tight, whatever) or clothes that are already a little faded in color. Throw them away (or donate them) so that your closet can have more breathing space. Later you will have more space to add newer clothes that will make you look better and feel great!

Diversity Is Friendly

Last but not least, looking good can make you confident, but don't fall into the trap of thinking that you can achieve looking good by always wearing the same clothes. Looking stylish is not the same as never changing your style. Can you imagine Jake Gyllenhaal wearing that same shirt and pants for a month every day? His male alpha status would dip, even if he did this two days in a row. Since you are not Jake Gyllenhaal, wearing the same rag day-in and day-out will ultimately cause significant damage to your image and, as a result, to your confidence. That's why it's important to wear different types of clothes that look stylish and match the occasion.

It's important to clarify that quantity does not mean variety. All that means is different colors, different styles. It means having a few white t-shirts but solid color T-shirts and print T-shirts, too.. Just remember to have enough variety to fit into an ideal-sized wardrobe (just enough, no excess!). For example, when it comes to shoes, you can't go wrong with 3 pairs: casual, formal and athletic.

How To Dress Like an Alpha Male - Quick Tips:

1. Buy Some Jeans - When you don't know what to wear, start with jeans. This is solely because the public has been conditioned to believe that individuals who wear jeans to look more manly. Regardless of whether it's due to the rough jean finishes or advertising effect, an Alpha Male needs a nice pair of jeans. Choose a darker jeans color preferably. When buying a pair of jeans, you need to make sure they are the right length. You want them to be a little long, especially if you like to wear boots. If possible, buy fitted jeans, but not "skinny" jeans. This type of fit can make you look less manly.

If you hate wearing jeans, does that still mean you need to wear jeans? No. Jeans are a great starting point, but if you don't like wearing jeans, you can opt for other choices, such as a pair of khaki pants. Light brown, beige, or khaki navy-blue pants can make you look cool and interesting.

2. Get Some Plain T-Shirts - Once you got the perfect pair of jeans, it's time to hunt for the right shirt. Your best bet is to choose a nice, but dull t-shirt. Go for shirts you can throw on at the gym, beach, work, and match the jeans you've chosen.

You don't have to spend a lot to get brand T-shirts here, but some solid color T-shirts will do the job well. First, buy slimming and plain colors. If you want, you can opt for brighter T-shirts, especially if your jeans are dark. An Alpha Male looks good when it comes to tees, so you can always buy more T-shirts and keep them in your wardrobe.

As for the size, that all depends on how you're built. The general rule is that you want your shirt to fit snugly around your arms and a little loose around your torso.

3. **Get A Few Button-ups -** What if you don't like wearing T-shirts? Well, you can go for a button-up shirt at all times, but go for an unusual design. Do not go for a simple white dress shirt with black shoes; go with a shirt that has some red in it, for example. A shirt with multicolored color prints is also a great place to start.

An Alpha Male doesn't wear really colorful or flowery shirts. So go for full patterns and muted colors. When you're wearing clothing that is too colorful, people will think you're neither serious nor easy-going. This kind of attire will make you look funny because it is too flamboyant. If you wear a button-up shirt, don't forget to tug the bottom into your jeans, otherwise you will look less mature and not reliable. Choose shirts that are not too long, of course they will make you look shorter than you are.

4. Groom Like An Alpha Male - Grooming is a very broad topic, and an important one. However, it is not as important for an Alpha Male as you think it is. Just remember that you shouldn't over-groom; an Alpha Male radiates with confidence. While grooming gives you more confidence, over-grooming does the opposite, making you look like you are trying too hard, which is a sign of insecurity.

Never shave your arms or legs. And if possible, opt not to pluck your eyebrows. If it really gets out of hand, you can choose to trim your chest hair and keep your hairstyle personal. It's OK to grow a beard, but never let your beard grow too long and make your face look messy. Make sure you trim and cut your beard from time to time.

What type of hairstyle suits you best? Everyone is different, and being an Alpha creature, your hairstyle will reflect your identity. You don't have to spend too much time or effort getting a flawless hairdo, just go with what God gave you (but make sure that you take care of it).

5. Get Some Jackets - You will need at least one winter and one spring jacket. Make sure that the jackets you choose match the rest of your wardrobe. To ensure that your jacket matches most of your clothes, make sure you choose a neutral design and color. Do not go for a complicated design, it will be a nightmare to match and you'll never want to wear it. Choose something neutral which you can wear regularly.

Bright colored jackets aren't really recommended because they get dirty easily and, unlike shirts, you'll have to wear the jackets often – almost daily. So go for a darker or more neutral color and pair it with a bright colored shirt. You should buy a good quality winter jacket. These are a little more expensive, but you will be wearing this throughout the winter season, so you will want a warm jacket, made with the best materials you can afford. There's no point in being cold just for the sake of fashion. You may think it's worth it now, but after you've had to withstand freezing temperatures a few days in a row, you'll surely change your mind.

6. Time For Boots - There are plenty of masculine boots out there. The key is to find quality boots that will not break the bank. Two or three pairs of boots should suffice. If you're just going for two pairs, choose one pair of a lighter color and another pair of a darker color. That way, you'll get the best of both worlds. Your boot choices depend on your occupation and your location. For example, if you live in the US, you may choose a pair of cowboy boots. If you live in another part of the world, you may choose to buy a pair of black steel-toe boots. Those may look very nice on you too. If you work in the corporate world, you will need a nice pair of leather shoes.

7. The Right Watch - Is it really necessary to have one? Not at all, but every Man, especially the Alpha Male, should have a watch. A watch will make you look sleek and mature. Wearing a watch in the business world can make people feel that you value your time and that you are a reliable person. The brand of the watch doesn't really matter, just make sure you choose one that matches the nature of your work. For example, if you work outdoors, choose a watch with a leather strap, if you work in an office, you may choose to go with a metal strap watch.

Many Men have a dream watch they would love to own. Spend some time doing some research on the internet and spend more effort selecting the right watch. Watches can be expensive, so make sure you are getting the highest quality for a price you can afford. Keep in mind that you only need one or two watches.

8. Get A Suit - Now, you don't have to spend all of the money to buy an expensive designer suit. It all depends on the nature of your work. If your job requires you to fit in, then by all means get one or two. The key to choosing the right suit is to find the right size for your body, and then consider quality. You don't have to buy expensive suits, but try to find a suit that will give you the best value for your money. Tailor-made suits are an excellent choice, if you can afford them. Choose a suit that fits comfortably because you'll be wearing it often. If you only wear a suit for special occasions, then just go for the quality. And make sure you pick a suit that matches your shirts and pants.

9. Quality, Not Quantity - Buy a ton of outfits. Don't just go for quality. You may need to spend more money at the beginning, to buy quality clothes, but buying quality clothes you can afford will save you a lot of time and money in the future. Remember, cheap clothes are made with poor quality materials that wear out quickly. While not all quality clothes need to be of brand names and super expensive, if your clothes are good quality, they will make you look good and that can make you feel more confident. Lots of studies have confirmed this, so make sure you are choosing quality over quantity. Being an Alpha Male also means keeping up with your image. You may struggle to find your personality as an Alpha if you wear all kinds of different designs and colors every day. Choose quality over quantity and go for consistency.

10. It's All About You - Remember that being an Alpha Male means being authentic. There's no point in imitating and copying how others dress or behave. You need to be comfortable in your own skin, not someone else's. You have to be yourself. For example, if you like the athletic look, wear more sneakers, shorts, and dry-fit gear. If you like boots and jeans, just go for them. It's about bringing out what's inside of you. Your clothes should be a reflection of who you are, and they should bring out your confidence for others to see. Your attire counts, but your character as an Alpha is more important. Just dress up like a guy. An Alpha Male does not dawn on accessories. They are not so worried about what they wear that they spend more time grooming themselves than a lady. Men, particularly Alpha Males, wear simple clothes that last through their own lifestyles. Remember, what you wear doesn't define who you are, but you're the one that should be confident about how you wear it. Always dress up to fit your image as an Alpha.

The 5 Right Mindsets For Dressing Like an Alpha Male

There are many websites and magazines dedicated to telling Men how to dress in order to appear powerful and influential, but they end up creating followers, victims, and people who overspend on clothing without any real power. While how you dress is important, your character is what really counts. In addition, if you want to be an Alpha and a leader, your mentality and character matter more than how you dress. Below are the five mindsets you should adopt before dressing like an Alpha Male.

1. Have Self-Confidence Without Being Egotistical

Never be too concerned about what you wear, settle for being pleased with how you look. The prouder you feel about what you are doing, the more valuable you are going to be. When you value yourself and are proud of what you're wearing and what you're doing, people will notice. This type of pride and confidence shine from within, and they have nothing to do with what you're wearing.

Most people focus too much on their looks and their image. While it's true that how you dress can make a statement, you'll never feel confident and comfortable if you don't have pride, no matter what you wear. Never let your clothes determine who you are; rather, make your clothes a part of your aura and feel pride.

2. Understand Your True Value

Expensive suits, luxury cars, designer watches, and jewelry don't really hold true value. The memories you have of your first vacation with your lady is likely to hold more value for you than your watch. With this said, your experiences are what create your values. Why do you think you want people to wear branded goods and drive a luxury car? It's because they want to portray themselves as a wealthy and influential person, but if they've never experienced hardship, the rewards are just not worth it.

To bring out the best in you, you must understand what you really value. This understanding will make you a true leader and an inspiration to others. For example, a simple watch given to you by your business partner when you fought through the hardships may be more valuable to you than a designer's watch. So don't fall into the trap of thinking that expensive things are inherently valuable. An Alpha understands the real value of things.

3. Never Be Disappointed By Society

A lot of people like to compare their lives to others', especially on social media. There is such a thing as a condition called "social media depression." It happens when people become depressed after comparing their lives to other people's on social media.This is not surprising. If you spend your days constantly comparing yourself to other people's highlight reels, you will become depressed. You need to work on your self-awareness, discipline, and honesty about who you are. Although these days most people are buying into the idea that a brand name makes items make items more valuable, do not fall into that trap. People who think this way need to be their own Man. This is much easier said than done, of course. You need to know what you want, and not be swayed by what other people say. You must have the discipline to pursue your goals and never be influenced by seasons or trends, or by what someone else telling you.

4. Never Do It To Impress

People wanted brand items and expensive things because they want to impress others. Never let that happen to you. Your freedom is more important than your image. You shouldn't trade your freedom just to impress others with expensive things like clothes, cars, and watches.

Plus, you don't want to envy other people. A true Alpha is one who never compares himself with others. If other people are looking at you and want to be like you, you don't mind. You are happy and proud of who you are, what you do, and what you enjoy. It doesn't matter if you wear jeans and old boots and the person next to you is decked out in the most beautiful suit that he probably can't afford. Being an Alpha means you won't wear something nice to impress others. You dress up like who you are and what makes you feel at ease.

5. Live Simply & Frugally

Last but not least, you have to know that what you wear is not as important as what you do. Society and the world have deceived people into thinking that image is everything, but it really isn't. The Alpha dresses with pride because he wants more power or is more influential. His clothes are a reflection of his state of mind, not the other way around. A real Alpha dresses with simplicity and frugality because he spends his money on other, more important things. You must understand that power is not found in the clothes that you wear or the finest timepiece that you own. True power is about understanding what you want, taking action to achieve your goals, and standing by your decisions without being swayed by other people's influence.

CHAPTER SEVEN

PHYSICAL EXCELLENCE LEADS TO MASTERY IN LIFE

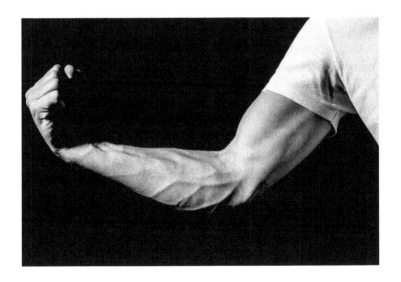

Rock Your Body

BODY LANGUAGE IS AN EXTREMELY useful tool. Even before the development of spoken and written languages, humans used their bodies to communicate with one another. As a matter of fact, according to experts, between 80% and 90% of effective communication can be attributed to body language rather than spoken words. This is both exciting and frightening: while it can be empowering to understand the impact of our body language, the fact that so much communication is done subconsciously may feel daunting.

Think about it this way: even if you say you're a Man worth following and admiring, your body language can easily prove otherwise. If your posture is slouched, your gestures are hurried, and your hand movements are fidgety, you will come across as weak regardless of how confidently you speak.

The body language of the Alpha Male should be confident and sexy, catching the attention of every woman in the room without the slightest effort. This can make him stand out within any group, compelling people to take a closer look at him. It demonstrates utmost confidence, high intelligence, and complete control of any situation.

In order to become an Alpha Male, therefore, you'll need to master the appropriate body language. This means learning how to calculate each and every movement you make with the goal of increasing your attractiveness. Without further ado, let's take a look at the kind of mindset that you'll need to adopt in order to demonstrate Alpha Male body language.

The first and foremost thing to keep in mind is *confidence*. The principle of this is simple enough: if you can't be confident in yourself, then you can't expect anyone else to be confident in their interactions with you--least of all an attractive woman. Women love to see confidence in a Man; it makes them feel safe and secure in his presence. Three good ways to manifest confidence in your body language are by holding your head high, making eye contact while you speak, and speaking in a deliberate manner.

Alpha Males also naturally exude *power*. No matter how much the feminist movement insists that Men and women are equal, women will always see Men as their protectors because this perspective is wired into their subconscious. Does this mean that you need to go looking for conflict in order to demonstrate your ability to protect your woman? Absolutely not. Instead, it means that your body language should communicate a sense of power. Just by looking at you, a woman should be assured that you can and will protect her in the event of trouble.

Acting the Part

While the idea of adapting your body language may feel over-whelming, the truth is that you only need to prioritize a few key gestures, postures, and movements. Body language, although impactful, is relatively straightforward and its subtle power should not be underestimated.

Eye Contact

Nothing expresses more trust, manliness, and raw power than making and maintaining eye contact. Why is that? To find our answer, let's consider the following questions:

- Think about a time that you misbehaved as a kid--for instance, let's say you spilled spaghetti sauce all over your mother's expensive couch while she was out shopping. Chances are that you were terrified of what was going to happen when she found the stain. When the time came for you to admit what you had done, were you able to look her in the eye?

- Imagine that you accidentally revealed a friend's secret crush, and that the whole school knew about it within a day. When your friend confronted you, did you meet his gaze, or did you make a point of avoiding it?

Your answer to both of these was almost certainly a resounding "no." These serve as examples of how eye contact expresses self-confidence. When you look in someone's eyes, you are establishing a sense of trust between you and the other person and they will immediately feel more comfortable around you.

Next time that you're speaking to someone else, especially an attractive woman, remember to maintain eye contact. Keep your gaze evenly aimed between her eyes rather than jumping from one eye to the other. Don't overdo it, though--while *looking* someone in the eye expresses confidence, *staring* at them can come across as aggressive or creepy. To avoid this, make sure to occasionally point your gaze towards something else, such as your surroundings. This helps you come across as relaxed and naturally confident, rather than stiff and forced.

Posture

When you hear the word "posture," your mind probably jumps to the phrase "stand up straight." This is for a good reason--standing upright is hugely beneficial to both your appearance and your physical health. When it comes to the posture of the Alpha Male, however, standing up straight isn't enough. In addition to that, you need to stand up *tall*.

What, you may ask, is the difference between "straight" and "tall" in this context? In order to adopt a "tall" stance, you'll need to take the following steps.

- Start with your legs. Your height is primarily determined by the length of your legs, and if you want to come across as tall, you need to make sure that you're using them to their fullest capacity. Keep them straight and extended at all times--don't bend your knees or let your waist sag.

- Focus on your spine. If you're hunched over or leaning forward, you aren't standing tall. Your spine should be curving slightly inward, as if to form a reverse letter "C." This will push out your chest and pull back your shoulders. Both of these communicate strength and confidence.

- As in the case of eye contact, remember that moderation is key. Don't push your chest out to the point where you look like you're being pulled by an invisible chain; that quickly changes your appearance from confident to ridiculous.

Facial Expression

Facial expression may be the single most important facet of body language. Numerous studies regarding the impact of facial expressions have been carried out, and several books have been published on the subject. When it comes to the particular area of self-confidence, however, your facial expression should serve to *enhance* your self-confidence; it should be a supplement, not a basis. Here are some tips to help you master the look of a confident, charismatic, and attractive Alpha Male:

- Smile. This is absolutely crucial, especially when you're first meeting someone. Smiling doesn't just communicate openness, but also gives the sense that everything in your world is okay and that you're comfortable and happy with who you are. Make sure to keep it genuine: a smile should extend to your eyes, not just your lips. Smile often, but not constantly--a perpetual grin makes you look overeager and naive, both of which are traits that any true Alpha Male would not possess.

- Do not stare. As mentioned during our discussion of eye contact, staring is intrusive and unlikable. Similarly, if your eyes are opened too widely, you'll seem surprised, anxious, and unsure of yourself. This makes it look as though you have no control over your situation when the opposite should be true.

- Lastly, mind your setting. While these general guidelines will work for most casual interactions, they certainly don't apply in all cases--there's nothing alpha, for example, about frequently smiling during a funeral. Stay attuned to the mood of the people around you and make sure to adjust your facial expression accordingly.

Holding Your Head High

As subtle as it may seem, how you hold your head plays a huge role in communicating your level of confidence. If you keep your head tilted down, you seem insecure and antisocial. Looking up too often, on the other hand, makes you look like a kid in a candy factory: innocent, unassuming, and overly eager to please.

Instead, you should aim to keep your head levelled straight forward, neither high nor low. This conveys trust, security, and dominance.

Hands

How you hold your hands is key to enhancing your overall body language. If you keep your hands at your sides, you come across as relaxed, confident, and open. In keeping your hands folded in front of your chest, on the other hand--pardon the pun--you communicate insecurity, close-mindedness, or even aggression. Putting your hands in your pockets is a fairly neutral gesture, but you should be aware of how it may serve to supplement other aspects of your body language--for instance, if you're slouching and looking at your feet, pocketed hands may serve to further emphasize your lack of self-confidence.

Walking

Last but not least, the way you walk is also indicative of your alpha status--or lack thereof. Confident Alpha Males take long, slow steps, while omega Males are more likely to take short, quick ones, giving the impression that they're always in a hurry. These shorter, faster steps communicate agitation and anxiety, both of which suggest an inability to control oneself and one's situation.

As you can see, there are many body language secrets that can help you to come across as a true Alpha Male. By changing your mindset to incorporate them, you can make a massive difference in your image. We'll take a closer look at body language and its significance later on, but for now, remember to keep these basic tips in mind.

From The Inside Out or the Outside In?

You might wonder why the focus on body language starts with your mind, as mentioned in earlier chapters. Yes, it starts with having the right mindset. But it's worth noting as well that repeating a behavior can also affect your mindset. That's why Alpha athletes train so hard; it's the way they stay sharp and even get sharper at their game, which further reinforces their confidence in themselves. Using the right body language before each practice session is as important as taking a thousand shots. When you have the right mindset, you become confident enough to work on your body language continuously, which makes you even more confident, and the cycle continues. Without acting on your mindset, you either stagnate, or worse, slide back into the deep, dark world of insecurity and lack of self-confidence. I don't know about you, Sherlock, but that's as frightening as the dark pits of hell to me!

Few people exemplify self-discipline and dedication better than professional athletes. What an average person sees when looking at an elite performer – say, a world-class tennis player – is that his abilities seem normal, basic. They conclude, "he must have been born with this," but they could not be any further from the facts. They only see the result – the act of winning. What people don't see is the thousands of hours spent prac-ticing that were required to win the event. His sore body, count-less hours of drills, missing matches, and all the rest that made him the tennis player he is today. With talent alone, he'd never achieved to win, never would've beat anyone else.

Success is the result of a long process that takes years – some-times decades, not just days or weeks. Some of his success could have something to do with his innate talent – physical qualities, such as great hand-eye coordination. If it wasn't for the relentless self-discipline to put those qualities to work, though, he would never have become a world class tennis player. Working on your physique to increase speed, strength, or flexibility is a perfect introduction to the world of building self-discipline. Without commitment, long-term preparation, and determination, you won't achieve any of your goals.

Physical fitness is an important part of building a healthy life. And no, this is not about becoming a world-class athlete or a perfectly sculpted human being. Working diligently on your health and fitness – according to your ability and biology, not comparing yourself to others – is what will help you achieve discipline in life. You cannot build a strong body in a couple of months, which is why strengthening your body is a great way to challenge yourself in order to build self-discipline and create healthy habits. If you stick to training towards a goal for years on end, until you see results, you will learn to value the process, which in turn, will help you develop self-discipline. The transformation to Alpha Male happens when you move on from being results-oriented to process-oriented.

It's Time For A Workout Plan

Going to the gym (or any other form of regular fitness activity) is a useful indicator of how disciplined you are. There are two pieces to the puzzle of reaching the ideal physique. The first is physical activity. The second and perhaps the more important thing is to maintain the right diet. A dose of daily discipline is required for maintaining both regular physical activity and a healthy diet. By following these two daily habits, you will build a powerful source of discipline that you can use to achieve other goals in your life.

Let's begin with physical activity. Just as there is no ideal diet plan, there is no perfect workout plan either. The only prerequisite is to introduce some sort of monitoring system to your weekly schedule and adhere to it. For example, you'll work out an average of an hour a day, and do it no matter what. You won't be dissuaded from exercising either by nature, laziness, or your friends coming over for the weekend. Weightlifting and other anaerobic types of exercise can build muscle and help you achieve a tougher, better-looking body (and that's true for both Men and women–dear ladies, don't be afraid you are not going to get huge). Anaerobic workout is characterized by small periods (up to 2 minutes) of high-intensity activity leading to increased strength, velocity, power, and muscle mass. Good choices include:

· Weightlifting: As already described, it is probably the best choice for most people because of its ability to develop the entire body in perfect harmony (contrary to popular belief, proper weightlifting is not about building huge biceps, but about building a strong body with healthy proportions)

· Sprinting: Especially hill sprints, which are healthier for joints and more effective overall.

· Swimming: High-intensity bursts of activity instead of an hour-long marathon when done in short. Yoga can also be a healthy way for both genders to build a well-rounded lean body.

Maintaining awkward positions is, in itself, a great exercise to build up discipline. Calisthenics (workouts on body weight) can be a perfect replacement for weightlifting if you are actively working towards more demanding exercises. All of these sports encourage athletic, muscular and effective bodybuilding. Getting those results is crucial to developing self-discipline.

Progress and reward will fuel your efforts to keep going despite losses, but ideally, most of your inspiration will come from within – regardless of the outcomes. In addition to anaerobic activity, introducing some variety to your workouts and doing some aerobic activities is also good. It's all related to discipline as well – a relaxed person has a much easier time resisting the temptations and sticking to his plan than an over-pressed person. Here are a few suggestions for aerobic exercises that are a lot of fun and provide amazing health benefits:

- Cycling: Long rides can be exhausting, not only physically but also mentally, making them a perfect activity for self-discipline building.
- Walking or jogging: Simple, easy, low-cost and gives you a feel-good runner's high.
- Tennis: Probably one of the most difficult sports to learn, requiring a lot of self-discipline.
- Inline skating: A fun exercise that almost doesn't feel like exercise.
- Swimming: Unless done in short high-intensity exercise bursts. One of the best types of physical activity for obese people (unlike jogging, swimming puts no pressure on your joints).
- Martial arts: Mental development is a huge aspect of martial arts, making it a perfect holistic workout.

How To Stick With A Fitness Program

The five most common reasons people quit their fitness programs (and lose their self-discipline) are:

1. False Encouragement

There are two types of encouragement: Internal and external. Internal motivation (also known as intrinsic motivation) occurs when we act without any apparent external rewards. We just enjoy an activity, or see it as an opportunity to explore, learn, and realize our potential. Extrinsic motivation, on the other hand, includes while we are engaging in a sport (or any kind of activity) in the hopes of receiving some sort of external reward aside from the satisfaction of participation in the activity. Intrinsic motivation is the kind of encouragement you need to stick to your fitness program and develop your self-discipline.

You're not supposed to develop your self-discipline just because you want to impress someone, so you shouldn't go to the gym because you think someone is going to praise you or respect you for that. If you work mainly because you expect an external reward, and by doing so draw little to no personal enjoyment or fulfillment, reconsider your motivation. If you keep doing something, you develop your self-discipline precisely because it makes you understand your full potential, and not because it can make you look good in other people's eyes or offer you bonuses. If you do not seem to be able to find intrinsic motivation, try another, more enjoyable sport, which will encourage you to explore, learn or realize your potential. If you hate it, you're not going to do it anyway in the long run.

2. Lack Of Pleasure

It's nice to have a lot of discipline but it doesn't mean you always have to do things you don't like (do not equate it with doing something that's difficult for growth purposes).

3. Lack Of Support

While it's nice to have ample self-discipline to achieve your goals without others helping, it doesn't mean that it's always the best way to do things. In reality, other people's support can often make or break resolutions. Working out with a partner is a good way to keep motivated and make progress in aerobic workouts. Furthermore, working out with a slightly better partner makes you more persistent. It is because of the Kohler effect, a phenomenon in which an individual works better as part of a group than when he works alone. If when working with a group you can work harder and develop better discipline, why not take advantage of it and get support?

4. Wrong Expectations

Regular physical activity strengthens your self-discipline by teaching you two things: How to stick to a specific plan, and how to be patient while waiting for the results. However, if you start your workout plan with the wrong expectations, you're likely to quit before your mental toughness improves. Because of the phenomenon known as False Hope Syndrome (Making frequent attempts at change attempts while maintaining unrealistic expectations about the probable size, quantity, ease, and consequences), you're likely to set unrealistic goals and expect things that can't happen within a specified time frame. Study what kind of outcomes you should expect realistically to prevent discouragement, and set them as your targets. When developing self-discipline, small victories are more important than holding on to the hope of achieving something grandiose or amazing.

Lack of Time

Normally, lack of time is the least valid reason to quit a fitness program because it hides a different kind of problem. If you can't find time to look after your body, then the problem isn't your lack of time, but your lack of priorities. Few people would disagree that the most important thing in life is health, yet that is not necessarily how they live their lives. In this situation, you need to define your values, you need discipline, and most importantly, you need to live your life in such a way that it represents those values. If wellness is one of your main values in life (and it should be; if you don't feel good, everything else matters very little),you should be willing to compromise one of your lower values (say, ascending the corporate ladder) for it. Probably the time has come to figure out how to balance family and work. It would be easier to ignore them, in order to stick to your workout routine and develop lasting self-discipline as a result. Nonetheless, your family and your job are also important parts of living a balanced life, so even though it may feel challenging, you need to include the appropriate amount of time to spend with them in your new lifestyle. Don't forget that all of these challenges are there to help you get better – it's your job to figure them out, not to use them as reasons for giving up.

Win Against Yourself

Mostly, when you don't have the motivation to do something, you use your determination and do it anyway. In the case of fitness, that involves going to the gym and lifting weights (or doing the high-intensity sprinting or swimming workout, despite a lack of motivation or encouragement). If you can perform a workout during a light rain, you're already ahead of the pack. These little wins build up like a muscle and improve your determination. If you can be consistent for years, you will likely be sufficiently disciplined to achieve anything you want in life. Do not misunderstand your body now and act against it. Do not be irresponsible; if you don't feel well or if you injure yourself, stop working out, find out what's wrong (not enough rest, too much stress, a chronic illness, etc.) and get back when you're ready.

To avoid burnout, take a week's break every 3 months or so. Strategic breaks will not hurt your performance and will provide a welcome break which can bring both physical and psychological benefits. A break (and eventual return to your daily regimen) will be an additional benefit to testing your self-discipline. It's harder for people with low motivation to get back to the fitness center after taking a break. So, it's nice to see how solid your workout habits are. If you feel anxious during your week off and are looking forward to getting back to the gym, it's safe to say you've developed a strong regular workout discipline.

Maintain A Healthy Diet

In today's world, most people find few things in life more difficult than maintaining a healthy weight. Temptation is everywhere – billboards promoting fast food, your favorite bargain treats at the supermarket, friends asking you to grab a bite in a burger joint, or unhealthy food just a phone call away, delivered in 30 minutes or less. Luckily, obesity is not a condition people are born with. Many people are obese becuse of a lack of self-discipline, aside from a few cases of legitimate medical problems. Controlling your weight is not optional – if you want to become a self-disciplined person, you must maintain a healthy weight. This is especially important if you want to become an Alpha Male. At the risk of sounding politically incorrect, if you can't deal with your extra pounds, you're not likely to attain success in other parts of your life.

Surprisingly, there is no perfect diet. Different diets have been associated with promoting health and preventing disease as long as it is made up of "close to natural, primarily plant-based, minimally processed foods." When you concentrate on and adhere to unprocessed foods, your body will change. And when all the fresh habits become a way of living for you (not a diet, but a lifestyle), you will also notice changes in other parts of your life. You will have more energy – which you will want to use to spend more time doing activities that improve your well-being. As a result, you will have more clarity of mind, which will allow you to learn new things and grow as a person. Plus, you will develop a better work ethic that will help you stick to your new resolutions and more easily achieve your goals.

Sticking To Your Diet

The biggest challenge when modifying your eating habits is to switch from your old, unhealthy ways to the new, more beneficial ones. There's no doubt that most people just can't handle the overpowering feeling of hunger (even if it's only a few hours since their last meal) or the feeling of longing to consume an unhealthy meal. Although removing entire classes of foods completely from your life isn't the best approach (after all, eating is a major part of life's enjoyment and you shouldn't deprive yourself of it by never consuming anything less than 100 percent healthy foods), it's important to know how to deal with food cravings, so you can take charge over what goes in your body. An individual who can say "no" to a powerful temptation is the one who is more likely to say "no" when he feels tempted to give up or choose laziness over to working towards his goals. Meanwhile, here are three quick tips to help you properly handle cravings:

1. Distract yourself

The easiest and most effective method is to remove the temptations from view. If you have no tempting foods at home, avoiding the urge to cheat will be easier. There's a difference between being 15 minutes away from a store with a chocolate bar on its shelf versus having the candy bar on your shelf. The same applies to any other things that might make you feel tempted, like TV ads, driving to your favorite fast-food restaurants nearby, etc. Waiting for fifteen minutes for the craving to go away is normally enough. If it is still there after fifteen minutes, keep distracting yourself until it passes (instead of trying not to think about the temptation, try to concentrate on something else altogether). Developing a default habit to do this, instead of eating unhealthy food is good for you. Any time you feel the urge to drive to the nearest pizza joint, for example, take your shoes and racket and move out to the local tennis court.

Eventually, the brain's less-than-helpful portion will forget about the lure, and concentrate on other tasks. As the hot-cold empathy divide suggests, we normally find it hard to understand how it feels to be in the opposite state. It's hard to understand how hunger will take over our power when we're satiated. If we're angry or sad, then it's hard to understand how good it feels to be happy. If we're not sexually aroused, we don't foresee what kind of risky sexual choices we might make while in the "hot" state.

It's hard to imagine that eating unhealthy food won't be delicious. When you feel the emotion you'd never anticipated during your "cold" state, it's only then you give in (then you find it hard to believe you couldn't resist the temptation because the experience turns out to be dissatisfying).

There are other negative effects of giving in to a craving, such as getting an upset stomach or the food tasting awful instead of amazing. When you're in the "hot" state, it's hard to think about these negative effects, so it's important to be realistic about the urge by considering all the potential outcomes.

Instead of (again) being puzzled about why you envisioned your banned food as something delicious (and finding out it's not really that incredible, and you're only getting guilt as a reward), think about it before making the wrong decision. Logic doesn't always work to stop the wrong choices (it's an emotional addiction after all), but it can help.

2. Don't Make It Too Difficult

It's good to be a self-disciplined person, but this doesn't mean you need to make everything as hard as possible just to boost your willpower. The better your diet is, the less likely you are to give up on a challenge. Science agrees that easy meals are worthwhile too. Overeating (while on a low-calorie diet) helps to increase leptin production levels for up to 24 hours by about 30 percent. This rise in leptin post-cheating, which controls body weight, improves metabolism and may also lead to improved motivation. Unfortunately, leptin levels only affect high-protein, high-carb, and low-fat cheat days. Furthermore, you have to say no to pizza, ice cream, chocolate, and other fatty foods if your sole purpose of cheating is to raise your leptin levels.

This doesn't mean you have to strictly control your cheat days, though. This deception has both physiological and psychological consequences. Even if you cannot get the full physiological benefits because you choose not to have a low-fat day, you can still enjoy the psychological effects. Giving yourself a break once in a while will save you shame. Instead of following the inevitable post-guilt loop ("I've already screwed up, it doesn't make sense to get back on track") – which will surely happen because few people can stick to a strict diet with 100 percent consistency– introduce cheating into your food. It is about long-term commitment, not depriving yourself of everything and hoping to fight off every single temptation. So, as long as 80-90 percent of the time you are upholding healthy eating habits, you'll be perfect. The more you adhere to a healthy diet, both your health and self-discipline will improve, even with occasional returns to unhealthy foods.

3. Shift The Cravings

People don't just succumb to cravings because they don't eat pizza, hot dogs, ice cream or French fries on a regular basis, they cave in because they never establish permanent alternatives. If you don't create a fun alternative to the unhealthy foods you love, you'll always miss them and it will be very difficult to resist cravings. Can you imagine how easy it would be to sustain a diet that allows you to eat whatever you want? The key is finding healthy alternatives that will give you what you want but aren't unhealthy. And let's be honest here --you can't replace the fine, sweet taste of melting chocolate on your tongue with a bland piece of broccoli. Nevertheless, you can definitely do it to some degree with:

- All sorts of berries (strawberries, raspberries, blueberries – is there anyone who doesn't like them?)
- Dark chocolate (it's much healthier, and because of its rich flavor–here we're talking about 70 percent cacao content – you need much less to satisfy your sweet tooth)
- Smoothies
- High quality honey (there's a world of difference between cheap store honey and organic varieties – play with different flavors)
- Carob (although not necessarily something you can consume on a daily basis as a healthy alternative, it's better than regular chocolate)

Many forms of unhealthy foods can be rendered healthier by using healthier ingredients. For example, pizza with homemade tomato sauce and a high quality cheese can be made with whole-wheat flour. Instead of eating store-bought ice cream, you should eat natural frozen yogurt and add in some berries. Instead of buying oil-coated frozen French fries, you can make your own.

Spices and herbs have a great deal to do with taste, too. Many vegetables do not taste that amazing on their own. If the right spice or herb is added to them, they become a lot more flavorful, and you can begin to cultivate a craving for these foods. To give you only a few examples, here are spices and/or herbs that alter the taste of certain healthy foods dramatically:

1. **Eggs:** Chives, black pepper and/or salt. Scrambled eggs can be a bit bland on their own. Adding any of these makes the taste significantly better.

2. **Zucchini:** Cayenne pepper, basil, cumin, powdered garlic, oregano or thyme. Zucchini goes well with a lot of herbs and spices. Few people enjoy this vegetable alone, but just adding a pinch or two of these flavor-intensifiers can make a world of difference – especially if you grill it.

3. **Brown rice:** Cumin, turmeric, or soy sauce. Many people who are used to consuming white rice aren't as pleased with the flavor of brown rice. Try to combine it with a cumin or turmeric, or add soy sauce. You can also test for rice in the Asian spice mixes.

4. **Vegetable soups:** salt, black pepper, spice, bay leaf and/or garden lavage. Add a lot of onions to boost flavor. Quick, regular vegetable soups are perfect for anyone who doesn't like to cook

every single day. Every Monday, you can make a big soup pot, and eat it until Thursday. You will certainly develop a craving for soup with the right mix of spices (like I have).

5. **Potatoes:** Butter, rosemary, paprika, oregano, basil, parsley, cayenne pepper and/or dill. The potatoes are not as unhealthy as people think, when eaten in moderation and not in the form of French fries. The trick is not to fry them, but rather steam, bake, or boil them. With the perfect mix of herbs and spices, steamed potatoes can become more attractive than oil-coated French fries.

Experimentation can go a long way toward preventing, or at least greatly decreasing, cravings for specific foods. Sustaining your healthy eating habits will be simpler if you set up permanent alternatives as delicious (or tastier) as you would have liked. It'll also be a great lesson in innovative self-discipline – working around or avoiding an obstacle entirely rather than caving in.

The Importance Of Sleep

If you go to sleep after waking up at about the same time every single day, and feel well-rested, you may be able to skip this section. When you find that your sleep schedule needs a certain amount of work, focusing on this part of your life will increase your health and help you build more self-discipline. There is a major caveat about waking up early. Although waking up early is generally perceived to be a virtue, a habit everybody who wants to succeed should cultivate, science doesn't necessarily agree. If you don't feel well despite your normal sleep schedule, don't use that as an excuse to wake up late, though. I used to go to bed at 3 or 4 every morning and wake up at 2 p.m. I could have claimed that I was a night owl, but I never felt well-rested.

I eventually found that waking up early was the best option for both my time and overall productivity, as I went from one extreme to another and started waking up at 6 a.m.

There are two strategies you can use if you want to start waking up earlier. If your target is to wake up at 6 a.m. you can either set your alarm for 6 a.m. and take it from there, or wake up one or two minutes earlier each day until you reach your goal, usually after at least a few weeks. Few things are more challenging to your self-discipline than the alarm clock forcing you to leave your cozy, warm bed and start a new day – especially if you start it with something you don't particularly enjoy. It is therefore a great exercise to develop mental toughness and learn how to conquer your weaknesses. If waking up early is a particularly challenging task for you, consider staking up.

It takes a lot of determination not to learn the habit of staying up late and repeatedly hitting the snooze button before getting up. When you change your sleep schedule permanently and start waking up early on a regular basis, you will undergo a powerful self-disciplinary shift. You must build your own strategies to stick to your goals, even if you are already half asleep and likely to choose the easy way out. If you're not an early riser, you might develop a habit of sleeping and waking up at regular hours (but please test your theory and spend at least one month after a routine in the morning). You also need to develop the self-discipline to go to bed at the same time every night to make sure you get enough sleep. Your body needs a routine, and waking up and going to bed at the same time every day helps you plan your day better.

Fashion

Want to make a statement with your appearance? The way you dress matters. Men are often led to believe that they shouldn't be interested in being particularly fashionable or well-dressed, but this couldn't be farther from the truth especially when it comes to attracting women. Your personal image and the manner in which you express yourself will determine whether or not people take you seriously. From picking up women to interviewing for a new job, every single social interaction will be impacted by your choice of clothing.

What to Wear

There is no universal standard for what looks good on guys. Your height, weight, build, and mannerisms will all play a part in determining your unique style.

Skinny Guys

If you're very skinny, the last thing you want is something that makes you look even thinner. Stay away from vertical stripes, which tend to be slimming. Patterns, in general, aren't the best idea; try instead to wear solid colors.

One easy way to mask extreme thinness is by wearing your clothes in layers. Thermal jackets and long-sleeved hoodies-- bulky, but not baggy--are your best friends. Put these on top of vintage style T-shirts or button-up shirts. If you do choose to wear a button-up shirt, however, be mindful of your sleeves because long, closely fitting sleeves will also emphasize your thinness. Long sleeves should therefore be rolled up to the elbow, exposing your forearms. Additionally, don't be afraid of clothing that fits your body type--although you certainly don't want anything to be skin-tight, a snug fit can actually make your body appear bigger and stronger.

When it comes to pants, the most important thing to ensure is that they fit well with your shoes. Jeans are usually a safe bet and slacks work for more fancy or formal occasions. Stay away from skinny jeans, and never tuck in your shirt; both of these have a slimming effect.

Big Guys

If you know that you're tall, it's a safe bet that other people notice your height, too. This might make you feel self-conscious, but don't worry: if you're at peace with yourself, then everybody else will be. With that in mind, *what* you're wearing is less important than *how* you wear it.

Nevertheless, there are still some key points that you can keep in mind while choosing what to wear. Vertical stripes have a slimming effect that can be hugely beneficial to more heavyset guys and button-up shirts also look good. A matching jacket or sports coat completes the look.

When it comes to your lower half, avoid baggy pants. Jeans or slacks are your best bet. Additionally, you should always make sure to wear fitting shoes; if your shoes are undersized, they emphasize the size of your stomach, which is probably the last thing you want.

Average or Athletic Guys

If your build is on the athletic side, you're in luck: most clothes are going to look nice on you. With this in mind, it's important to make sure that you're wearing the right size to properly accentuate your body. Don't be afraid to ask for help while shopping--the workers in clothing stores know their stuff, and their goal is to help you find your optimal fit!

Style

You can and should use your clothes to express your unique personality. Horizontal lines, contrasting colors, patch pockets, different fabrics, and layers are all things that you can use to make yourself stand out from the crowd. Keep in mind that balance and moderation are important. Don't wear loud colors or patterns solely with the intent of being unique. This can actually have the opposite effect of making you look like you're trying too hard--a situation known as "peacocking," after the vibrant feathers that male peacocks possess and use to attract a mate.

The extent to which you accessorize is entirely up to you, but the more you "peacock," the more attention--both positive and negative--you're going to receive. Be prepared for this, and dress accordingly.

Shirts

There are all sorts of combinations of shirts and jackets that you can wear. You can try a button-up shirt over a T-shirt or individual shirts under a jacket. Or maybe a long-sleeved shirt beneath a T-shirt is more your style. Lots of guys tend to throw on a T-shirt and call it a day, but there's tons of room for experimentation and a number of combos that work well.

Pants

Your pants usually aren't going to be the main focus of your outfit. Because of this, it's best to choose them based on your top, rather than the other way around. Make sure to keep plenty of jeans and dress pants in your dresser; with those two on hand, you're prepared for just about any situation. Jeans with a more rugged look, such as distressed jeans, can put a fun spin on your style. Only wear those in casual situations, however. If you're headed to a high-end club or a nice restaurant, you'll want to go for something more formal and less flashy.

Belts

They may seem like a relatively insignificant accessory, but belts can actually be very useful in showing the world your style. Large, flashy belt buckles attract attention, while thinner, more stylish belts lend you a sophisticated look. The utility of belts also can't be overstated--keeping your pants on is extremely important!

Another lesser-known tip is that your belt should match your shoes. Both of these are small details of your outfit that may be easy to overlook, but if you coordinate them appropriately, you'll exude style--a trait which women find extremely attractive.

Shoes

Speaking of shoes: they're much more important than you may think. As strange as it seems, shoes are actually one of the first things that women notice, making them key to establishing a good first impression.

There are many, many types of shoes to choose from, ranging from sneakers to boots to sandals to loafers. Each type of shoe is appropriate in a different situation. As long as you're aware of that, you won't have much to worry about. Though shoes are essential, they should serve to accentuate your look, not define it.

Lastly, remember that women tend to love shoes and shoe shopping. This means that you can actually use your shoe choice to initiate conversation--or even as a setup for a first date! When you ask a woman to help you pick out new shoes, you're establishing yourself as non-threatening, while also demonstrating how much you value her insights and opinions.

Accessories

Accessories are another in which you can ask for help from a woman. In addition to utilizing shopping as a bonding activity, you can also increase her interest in you by making a point to consistently wear an accessory that she picked out. It's an easy way to demonstrate that you care about her and that you believe she has good taste.

Grooming

Grooming is a universal habit across the entire animal kingdom--that alone should be enough to show you just how important it is. Over thousands and thousands of years, humans have developed very specific grooming rituals, and with good reason. Some guys may be averse to maintaining good, clean looks, likely due to the concern that they'll come across as effeminate. The truth, however, is that women love a Man who knows how to keep himself neat. Good grooming patterns convey maturity, responsibility, and a confident self-image.

Hair

Most Men don't get their hair cut nearly as often as they should. If you really want to stay on top of your hairdo, you should be cleaning up your haircut at least once a month. This helps you avoid a shaggy, careless look. It also lets women maintain a consistent image of your looks, which improves patterns of trust.

As long as your haircut is consistent, you can do pretty much whatever you want with it. Messy, spiky, short, long--anything can work, depending on your looks and on your woman's particular taste. Keep in mind, though, that while models and celebrities may make messy hair look effortless, there's a good deal of work involved in maintaining it. This is where gel and other hair care products come in. If you choose to use a specialized hair product, make sure that you're *completely* sure of how it works *before* you begin slathering it all over your head. Watching a YouTube tutorial or two is never a bad idea. And, last but not least, always remember to wash your forehead after application of the product, as most products often leave a greasy-looking film on your forehead.

If you've begun to lose your hair, the best thing to do is shave it off. Some Men worry that this will make them look older, but that isn't the case at all. Hair regrowth products are unreliable at best and it's pretty much a guarantee that women will be able to tell when you're trying--and failing--to cover up your bald spots. Shaving your whole head, meanwhile, puts you in control of the situation. It makes your baldness look deliberate, thereby conveying that crucial sense of self-confidence.

Eyebrows

You probably don't want to shape your eyebrows like a woman would, but you still shouldn't neglect them entirely. If you have bushy, uneven, or conjoined brows, you can make a huge improvement by tweezing them regularly. Getting rid of a unibrow, for instance, can easily bump you up from a four to an eight on the attractiveness scale. It's always worth it to put in that extra mile!

Nails

This one is simple: keep your nails trimmed at all times. This applies to toenails as well as fingernails. Overlong nails don't just look unappealing; they also make physical contact uncomfortable. Everything from sex to handholding can be ruined if you're sporting raptor claws.

Facial Hair

When it comes to facial hair, the choice is entirely up to you. Preferences regarding shaving vary between women and what looks good on one guy may be awful on another. As in the case of your other hair, the most important thing is consistency. Once you find a look that appeals to women and makes you feel good, stick to it. Daily maintenance is essential here.

Colors

Just like how our body language conveys our thoughts and attitude, the colors that we wear send a subconscious message to onlookers about our personalities. For example, pink is considered to have a soothing effect. Because of this, it's been used everywhere from prison cells to visiting sports teams' locker rooms. Red, on the other hand, is a color that increases your appetite, hence its frequent use in restaurant advertising. Think about it: How many fast-food restaurants have red logos? This isn't a coincidence!

The right color to wear depends on the impression that you want to make. Because of this, you should own clothing in a variety of colors, so that you're ready for any situation. Here are a few of the most commonly worn colors, along with the subconscious feelings that they inspire.

Black

Black conveys authority and sophistication, which is why it's so often considered to be a staple of formal wear. It's also a slimming color, meaning that wearing black can make you look thinner. Lastly, black can be seductive--for instance, if a woman wears black panties, that suggests that she wants a Man to see her in her underwear.

White

White is typically associated with innocence and purity. It can also represent cleanliness and sterility. The latter is the reason that doctors wear white lab coats. You probably will want to stay away from this color for the most part. Innocence usually isn't the vibe that you want to emanate--plus, it's a huge pain to keep your white clothes clean.

Red

Red is an extremely powerful hue that shows superiority, passion, and sexual energy. Use it well!

Blue

Blue is one of the most common colors used for clothes, in large part due to its versatility. Generally, it indicates intelligence, authority, loyalty, and commitment, all of which are valuable attributes to show off to women. It also causes the human brain to release calming chemicals, which can make you seem more approachable without being a pushover.

Green

Green is another calming color, suggesting love, sustainability, wealth, and vitality. But beware of the fact that it can also be loud when it is a hue that is particularly bright. Like red, green should be used in moderation; this will make it all the more impactful when you do choose to wear it.

Yellow

Yellow is a tricky color to work with. Though it symbolizes optimism, excitement, and playfulness, it can also feel childish or indecisive. Furthermore, yellow is one of the most difficult colors for the human eye to process. Your best bet is probably to steer away from any vivid yellow items of clothing.

Purple

Historically, purple has been the color of royalty. It stands for luxury, wealth, and sophistication. It also has a feminine romance to it, which isn't necessarily a bad thing--if a guy can wear purple proudly, it shows that he's truly confident in his masculinity. Purple can also feel mystical or "special" due to the fact that it's rarely found in nature. Because of this, it's a reliable attention grabber, to use as you see fit.

Brown

It's hard to go wrong with brown. While purple is unusual and exotic due to its rarity, brown--being the color of the earth--represents consistency, reliability, and comfort. This is many Men's preferred color of clothing, and with good reason. If you want to stand out from the crowd, though, you might want to get a bit more adventurous with your choices.

CHAPTER EIGHT

UNDERSTANDING WHAT WOMEN WANT

"WOMEN ARE TOO HARD." "Women are too vulnerable." "I don't understand women." You still hear all sorts of nonsense. And, honestly, these are all cop-outs. Some Men say that because it's easier to treat women like mysteries that can't be understood, than trying to wrap their minds around how to understand women. Here's what you need to learn about women, and don't worry, it's good news: on a basic, biological level, they are very sexual creatures. Indeed, they likely enjoy sex even more than we do.

Ever noticed how much more women moan during sex than Men do? Sadly, in the rational part of their brains, society forces women to believe (not the emotional component) that enjoying sex is "wrong." Since women tend to be social creatures (more so than Men, for evolutionary psychological reasons), labels such as "slut" or "whore" have a heavy, negative effect on them. Neither penalty applies to Men who have a lot of sex.

The overarching irony of the misogynistic system created by religion and society to repress the individuality of women is that Men everywhere have more of a gender problem than they would if they were to live back in times of pre-civilization when women were wild and uninhibited. In modern society, your role as a Man is to get around the societal conditioning of a woman to draw the natural woman inside her.

Sounds tough? Believe me, it's not! In a way, women are like padlocks. They seem difficult if you use the wrong keys, but they open easily once you find the right one. To bring out the natural woman that lies deep inside each girl, you always have to bear in mind that women love sex and they want it just as much as (and possibly more than) we do. And as if the social conditioning to which women are subjected is not bad enough, a much more powerful force lies within them: biology. Babies are a perfectly natural consequence of having sex and every woman knows that.

She knows that if she gets pregnant when she is not supposed to be pregnant, people are going to talk. Therein lies women's ultimate tragedy; despite loving sex they cannot be comfortable with their sexuality without being branded as a whore. So when you – as a sexual Man – make a move towards sex with your partner, you need to prevent her from feeling like a slut. (By the way, it's for your own good to be discreet around women. The last thing you should always do is to be like the attention-seeking Beta Males who brag about the women they've bedded to their buddies).

Your buddies' approval is not necessary, so skip the locker room talk! Real men don't have to do that. Have you ever spoken to guys who tell you, "We Men will never understand women?" Women aren't really as mysterious or hard to understand as guys think. We are not as isolated from each other as some of us would imagine. As we know, women want sex, and when you connect with them it's OK for you to have sex in your agenda. Basically, it's a really good idea.

What you should stop, however, is verbalizing your thoughts at all costs. You don't want to tell the woman anything about sex or your desire to have it. Whenever you tell a woman about your sexual intentions by saying something about it, you activate the logical part of her mind that allows her conditioning to kick in. "Oh, yeah," she says. "This guy is tacky, disgusting, grumpy. And I might end up being treated like a slut here." So avoid being overt about sex, and keep in mind how much women love it, and focus on projecting your own sexuality without saying anything about it at all. Useg body language, not verbal language.

What Women Like

Don't listen to what women say when they talk about the kind of Men they want; rather, watch their actions and look at the kinds of Men they are pursuing. If a woman were truthful, she would say that the type of Man she wants is "a romantic Man who will build an opportunity for sex and persist until he gets over my defense mechanism." But she doesn't dare say this because she's frightened people will call her a "slut." Women like relationships, but they don't need a Man for that. Women have very close relationships with their female friends, after all. And here's another biological bummer: when it comes to sex, women usually take on the passive role. That means that you, the guy, have to take responsibility for the sex by steadily moving the encounter towards the layman. Don't expect her to take the lead. I mean, think about it: She is living in fear of the slut label and you expect her to start sex? It's no wonder so many guys are having difficulty getting laid. That's way too much to expect – a woman simply won't go out that far on a limb.

You'll have to create a situation for you to get laid, where the woman feels like she can have sex with you without any repercussions for her. For example, I picked up a woman at a happy hour last month. We talked about a few topics (which I will reveal later which make women super chatty) for a couple of hours. We hit it off, and then she tells me (two hours into our conversation) that she has a boyfriend. There were two ways I could have answered at this stage. Most of the guys would either have:

- Left in disappointment, feeling bitter about how the woman "led me on."
- Tried to talk up and persuade the girl to leave the other guy for me.

Most guys will vote for either A or B. Believe me, I used to do this, too. Therefore, I've found that what I consider "Choice C" is the best thing to do: respond nonchalantly, retain my Alpha

Male calm, and prove that what she's saying doesn't bother me. (Meanwhile, if a woman connects with you but doesn't have sex with you, mark my words, she will find another guy to hook up with and fulfill her carnal desires). That is what women are afraid of. You've also heard of women looking for out -of-town flings on holiday. Ever wonder why they are doing so? It's because they cannot be held accountable; they won't be called a whore. Sex happens naturally because the circumstances are right. A woman can satisfy her carnal desires thousands of miles from home, and no one from her hometown ever needs to know.

Don't Reveal Too Much

There is a certain mating ritual humans engage in. It's like a dance that lasts several hours. The ritual of mating has to follow the proper steps for sex to take place. We guys have an unfortunate tendency to always want to clear the air and find out straight up from the woman what's going on, where everything is between you two, and how she feels about having sex. That is an enormous mistake. Never verbalize anything about where you stand with a woman in the mating ritual. Don't tell her what your thoughts are, specifically. That is a logical thing to do, Man. Logical things kill emotions, and it is important for her to feel emotions to be sexually responsive to you.

By not thinking about sex, you'll make it look like the two of you were randomly having sex. You are going to keep her emotional part engaged, while her mind's rational component remains disengaged. And that's a good thing – it's the logical part of her mind saying, "No!" When you come across her as a genuine gentleman with whom she really hit it off, then she'll rationalize having sex with you on the first date as an exception. Only remember: a good time for a woman is with a Man having good sex... And she wants you to take the lead.

Non-Verbal Cues That Scream "I'm Dominant"

What do you think is the one thing that attracts a Man most to women? It's the illusion that you're a dominant Man. And no, you don't have to scream, kick, and jump around like a caveman to demonstrate superiority. You express your dominant male status simply by acting the way dominant Men do, deliberately manipulating the nonverbal signals you send out, creating the impression that you are Alpha.

This methodology is called the theory of connection. A woman sees you as a Man with attractive masculine traits while dissociating yourself from unnecessary "nice guy" traits. This is the way magicians perform. The magician carefully manages the way the audience sees him while on the stage. By diverting the attention of the audience to items they relate with magic – like his spinning wand – he prevents the audience from seeing the thing that would make him look unmagical: the fact that he uses his hand to do the trick!

Similarly, you may use perception management to influence what a woman thinks of you. And here's some really good news: you'll eventually grow to become an Alpha Male by adopting the right mindsets discussed in this guide. Today you can start moving in that direction by adopting an Alpha Male's behavior. What is superiority, then? It's the social power which comes from being assertive. As you go through your self-improvement process, you'll finally internalize this book's ideas and become an Alpha Male. Right now, by using your voice, your eyes, your actions and your attitude, you'll learn how to perform like an Alpha Male, giving the impression of superiority.

The number one nonverbal signal that lets people know you are an Alpha Male is your eyes. A powerful Man doesn't hate looking at people directly. You express submissiveness by averting your attention. You express self-consciousness, guilt and a sense of low status when you look down. There's no limit to how much eye contact you can make when you're the one who is talking. Research has shown that the more eye contact created by the person speaking, the more the listener perceives the person as being dominant.

The opposite is true when you're the one who is listening: the less you gaze at other people while they talk, the more dominant you are. (You're always curious why adults say to kids, "Look at me when I'm talking to you"? It's a way to reinforce the superiority of the adult over the kid.) Of course, you don't want to exaggerate and make the woman think you're staring at her. If you are seen to be too dominant, then your likeability begins to suffer. So, every now and then, give your eyes a break.

Your voice is another sign of your superiority. Interactions are controlled by dominant people. We always talk in a cutting voice and do not fear interrupting the other person. Research has shown that if you use a calm, quiet voice, you will give the impression that you are not assertive.

Try letting your words flow as you speak and don't be afraid to speak your mind. Individuals who hesitate when they speak are seen as weaker than those who don't. Note the attitudes and mannerisms. Try to avoid nonverbal beta status indicators:

1. Using filler words like "oh" and "um" in conversation. Studies have shown that people see others who speak like this as lacking in confidence and not being strong. It is a form of nervousness. We say "um" because we are afraid the other individual will dislike what we're going to say. Do not be afraid to pause for

impact instead. When you pause between important points, you will feel more confident and people will remember what you are saying.

2. Talking too fast. It gives the impression that you feel anxious and have little faith in yourself. A natural, comfortable speaking speed will vary from 125 to 150 words per minute within a moderate range. So, slow down!

3. Speaking in a soft and unintelligible voice, also known also as mumbling. Individuals who speak in this way may cause discomfort to their audience and are seen as uninteresting and untrustworthy. So, change your tone and you'll be viewed as an alpha, outgoing man.

4. Making a long pause before answering a question. This suggests that you think too hard about your answer, which makes you seem indecisive. It also seems as if you are trying too hard to gain the respect of the other person.

5. Bad posture. An Alpha Male stretches out his arms and legs freely. By hooking your thumbs in your back pockets, you can improve your posture.

6. Hold your hands up before you. This is a sign of insecurity. Instead, remain open and vulnerable. (You're not weak; you're not afraid.) Relax your arms. No one will punch you, so why do you have to cover yourself?

7. Twitching hands or toes. Some people have the habit of playing with sugar packets or straw wrappers when they are across the table from someone else. Don't tap your fingers on the table either. Some women hate that.

8. Pressing your face when you're thinking. It means you're concentrating too hard, you're indecisive, or you're feeling nervous. Hold your hands together in a steeple formation in front of your chest or neck to show trust. (Many instructors do this when they lecture.) Another pose that will support you when you need to show that you are trustworthy and confident is to keep your hands on your hips. Cops do this when they are talking to a suspect.

9. Folding your arms. It's possible to fold your arms in an alpha way on rare occasions (see Brad Pitt in the movie *Fight Club* for a successful example of that), but avoid it as a general rule.

10. Rigid stance or a hunched posture. An Alpha Male has a confident stance, whether it is sitting or standing. Avoid being hunched over.

11. Looking down. The Man holding his head high is the omega. It's showing zest. Looking down makes you the loser. Keep your head up. Expose your neck— do not worry, you won't be attacked by anyone! Look at the person you are talking with and remember what I said about using your eyes.

12. Nervous movements on the face, such as lip licking, pursing your mouth, twitching your nose and chewing your tongue. An Alpha Male has a good mouth and calm face.

13. Smiling excessively. Primate experiments have shown that beta Males can smile at stronger Males as a way to signal their harmlessness. Beta people are smiling to demonstrate that they are not a threat. However, an Alpha Male just smiles when there's something to smile about. And yes – he could be a threat.

14. Walking too fast. Instead, walk a little slower than normal, almost as though you were swaggering. You are alpha – no one chases you and you don't try to satisfy anyone else's desires. If you aren't in a hurry to get to a place, then walk as relaxed and confident as you are. Think: "I'm the one. I can make any woman happy." Walk as if you just had a huge success and felt on top of the world. Look at what you're doing to your body. You will notice you are moving your arms and bouncing slightly when you walk. Do it all the time.

15. Slouching. You don't have to stand so straight that you're uncomfortable, but you should have your shoulders drawn back. See Brad Pitt in any of his films for details of how you can comfortably keep your back straight.

16. Some blinking. Instead, you slowly open your eyes. Do not close your eyes in frustration. Just relax your eyelids and let them drop a little bit. But don't be blinking excessively.

17. When you are talking, your eyes shift back and forth. This is a beta behavior. Gazing at the face of the other person when you are in a conversation shows that you are paying attention. It expresses nonverbally that what you say is important and worth listening to.

18. Making too much eye contact when someone else is talking. Ignore the books of dating advice that advise you to keep eye contact all the time. Non-stop eye contact makes you look like a weirdo, insecure, socially inept, and dishonest. Let your eyes blur instead, and then look and make eye contact again. From personal experience, gazing at the woman for around two-thirds of the time that you are engaged with her is optimal. By the way, hold her eyes only when she tells you something truly interesting. Otherwise, focus on other things like her shoulders, her hair, things happening around you, and so on. Be comfortable with your eyes. The ultimate goal is to make your eyes happy, confident, assertive, and sexual.

19. Looking down or to the left before answering a question. If you need to look away to think before you reply, then look up and to the left. Studies have shown that people who do this are seen as more confident.

20. Fearing and avoiding touch. Be relaxed when you approach women—any nervousness can be detrimental to any kind of future relationship. Be alpha and touch her physically if you need to. Hold her hand to guide her around. Be gentle – if you use excessive pressure, you show insecurity. (Because you're an Alpha Man, she's going to follow you, so there's no need to be

anything but friendly and tender.) It's normal to touch someone as if you're making a point. Show some affection.

21. Turning your head up quickly when someone needs your attention. Use the movements you would make when you are at home – slow and comfortable. You're always an Alpha Man, remember?

22. Using long, complicated words. Alpha Men use short words that are specific and to the point. If you are tempted to use long sentences, stop.

Do not feel bad if you eventually slip up and sometimes use some of those nonverbal signals. No one is perfect, so don't beat yourself up, especially when you're talking to a woman. Let it go and keep the conversation going. If you think too much about these things, you begin to doubt yourself and when that happens, you feel insecure and anxious and it shows in your behavior. Instead simply work at all times on staying nonchalant and sincere. It's enough to just be aware of how you interact non-verbally. Being aware of that means you're going to start avoiding these behaviors a lot more.

How to Effectively Compliment A Woman

Suppose that someone looks right at you. Is that enough by itself to make them like you? Probably not. If you are more interesting than them, they'll worry that you don't have any chemistry and when they're around you, they won't feel good about themselves. This is because they see you as better than themselves.

Many people who are considered "smart" face this problem. Even though they are seen as really cool people, they give others performance anxiety. As a result, many cool people have trouble maintaining relationships (both sexual relationships and friendships). You should control how you appear to others so that they don't feel insecure about it.

You are probably wondering, "How do you do that?" You do it by acknowledging them in positive ways. The only way you can do this is to make a positive comment and then ask a follow-up question immediately, as if you are making sure the woman is willing to be with you. Remember, you're a good catch, so when she impresses you, she'll feel good.

Examples:

You: "You have incredible energy. What do you like to do for fun?

Her: "Blah blah."

You (thinking for a second about it): "Yeah, it sounds like fun. I would be willing to know more about it."

Another example:

You: "You really look cool. What is it you are learning at school?"

Her: "Blah blah."

You: "Blah blah."

You: "That is interesting, you know? I have a friend who's been researching blah blah."

As you can see, when you offer a genuine compliment, you should follow it up quickly with a question. This stops the woman from refusing the compliment and helps her prove her worth to you, too.

In fact, as long as you make her feel qualified to be with you, she will be basically eating from your hand and believing anything that you say. As an Alpha Male, you get approval without having to give your approval back. So, don't wait and thank her for the compliment.

Women often refuse praise because they see themselves in a lesser light. So, when you do pay them a compliment, they think that you've given them fake praise, which is the last thing you want. So don't give them the opportunity to reject your admiration

I like to follow up on my compliments with a question. Then that sets up our conversation in the context that, even though I found something I liked about her, if I don't like her response, my interest in her can still disappear. That puts me at a high value target, and makes her feel like she has to work in order to win my affection. This kind of attitude makes women much more interested in you than if they see that you are interested in them. Now, there's something you need to look out for: it's important you don't offer false praise because she'll notice you're trying too hard to get her to like you. Besides, offering a false compliment and making it sound sincere is hard and you certainly don't want to come off as insincere.

Beta Men sell themselves, Alpha Males don't have to. Another strategy which I like, especially when talking to someone I just met, is to change the topic quickly after complimenting them. "You really do seem cool. You know what I saw on my drive here?" This keeps me in charge of the conversation, plus it prevents the person from having the opportunity to refuse my compliment.

I like using compliments in my interactions with people because it keeps me focused on the outside. I'm not burdened with stressing and over-analyzing my every step because I'm worried about it.

The Secret To Good Listening

Here's a dirty little secret: almost everybody is a little bit shy and somewhat self-conscious. When they speak to you, it's because they think you're an interesting person (for example, a woman who is attracted to you will try to start a conversation with you) and they'll feel good if they think they've got your attention. To make sure other people feel like you're interested in the conversation, make sure to always follow-up what they tell you with a question or a comment. This will show them that you are interested in what they have to say. Once you've figured out how to do this, think about where the conversation can go.

Let's say someone asks you, "Which percentage of our DNA do you think we share with chimpanzees?" Ask yourself, why would someone ask you that? It's because they are checking your general knowledge on a superficial level. But the real meaning here is that they are trying to show off their own knowledge and, in all probability, they are teasing you. Suppose you're a well-read Man and recall seeing something about 98.5% in National Geographic about this topic. Are you going to offer this as your answer? No. Alphas don't play games with other Men. A much better answer would be, "I don't know, but we can't be that close. Is it about 50%?" This makes the other person feel like they got your attention. If they know the right answer, they'll tell you. At that moment you can compliment them by saying how cool it is that it is 98.5%.

If you believe you need to show your intellect, you're seeking approval from the other person and that's a sign that you're on a lower status. Suppose someone tells you they're going to Panama City Beach. They're doing that because they're excited about the trip they're going to take and want you to share their enthusiasm. So the worst thing you can do is to one-up them by saying, "Oh, that's nothing. You should see Hawaiian beaches!" The statement shows that you are oblivious to the other person's enthusiasm and it will make them feel that they are not all that special.

Instead, get them to think about things in Panama City Beach that they will enjoy. Say "Honey! I want to go there. I'm curious! Have you been there before? What was your favorite part of the trip?" And while Alpha Men interrupt when they need to, try not to interrupt people while they speak about something that is of interest to them. And don't worry if people interrupt you too much. Others interrupt you because they are interested in the conversation, which is just what you want.

When you are speaking to someone, be more focused on them than on yourself. Ask follow-up questions and explanations, show interest in people's opinions, and then follow up to make sure that you understood their explanations. This shows that you are satisfied with who you are and don't need to put anyone down. This, in turn, will make you more desirable and likable. Genuinely think and be interested in what a woman is saying. Each girl is a new discovery and you've got a lot to learn about her. So take your time and be a good listener.

8 Nonverbal Cues That Say, "I'm Likable"

I have already identified non-verbal signs of dominance. There's some overlap in body language—like persistently looking someone in the eye while talking, which expresses superiority and makes you more likable as well. Yet signs of dominance, such as leaning back, can sometimes make you seem more distant. You may need to align your dominance with likeability where necessary. Too much superiority makes you unlikable. Be mindful of the following quiet tactics that are sure to attract women:

1. Lean forward when you're sitting across from someone who asks you something. This conveys curiosity in what they are saying. Make sure that the woman is highly interested in you before doing this; drawing back is a means for you to play "hard to get" non-verbally. If she's interested in you, leaning forward will give her the impression that you're easy to talk to.

2. Align your body and face directly with hers. Before doing this, you should have control since you lose dominance when you are blunter with your body language.

3. Smile.

4. Stand comfortably and spread out.

5. Dress well. You'll be better off if you dress as well as, or better than, the people you're interacting with. You may choose to wear more casual and lighter-colored clothes and that is fine; just remember that this kind of clothes often detracts from your perceived dominance.

6. Establish mutual eye contact—go on and look into her eyes. But, as I mentioned earlier, don't do it more than 70% of the time.

7. Make sure your voice is friendly, engaging, confident, and that you sound excited and engaged in the conversation.

8. Avoid inappropriate facial expressions, lack of

movement, looking elsewhere, closed body language, and awkward posture.

Make sure that you strike a balance between superiority and likeability. If you never smile, then you will come across as if you don't like the woman. But if you smile constantly, it gives you the impression that you have low social status— you are trying too hard. Some things, like a relaxed, spread-out stance help you with superiority and likeability, so you should always be spreading out and relaxing.

3 Bad Habits That Instantly Turn Women Off

Avoid the three habits below and you'll have an advantage over about 95% of the guys out there. That in itself, when women feel it, makes them feel more comfortable around you instantly.

1. Bragging

"You should see my beautiful house."

"I'm about to collect six figures a year!"

"I've got a great sports car."

The irony about bragging is that it usually conveys the opposite of what you're saying. For example, if you brag about being wealthy, other people will automatically think that you're a poor guy who's looking for validation. Why else would you need to talk yourself up like that? Stop verbalizing your good qualities explicitly, and let the woman figure them out by herself. This demonstrates your self-confidence and also makes you a little mysterious in her eyes. Strive to be a never ending source of interesting discoveries for her, not a blowhard.

2. Putting yourself down

Lower status Men tend to be humble because they avoid offending others and want to be seen as respectful. Except for when it's an obvious joke, Alpha Men should lack self-deprecating modesty. Women are attracted to high self-esteem. Think of yourself highly and a woman will think of you highly. Let's look at the following examples (imagine a Man saying these in a playful tone of voice):

"I'm so frail, I'm not sure if I can lift that heavy thing."

"I'm unemployed, and live in my parents' basement!"

3. Putting down other people

"Ha ha, look at the rags on that bum!"

When you put others down, you reveal your own insecurities. The homeless guy on the sidewalk is not a personal offense to you, so why do you behave as though he were? And since women are emotional beings who feel sorry for the less fortunate, you're going to trigger her instincts to defend whomever you put down. Similarly, don't put down your sexual rivals; that, too, exposes your vulnerability. Just don't mind them because they're not worthy of your attention.

primal level. I realized this later. The unwavering conviction that he was a good catch represented everything about him and how he handled himself. It was the mentality of power from which all of his prosperity flowed. He would only have sex with women who had won this right because of his assumption was that he was a good catch and would only be affectionate towards women who did find him a good catch. He would also only show interest in what women said if they said something important.

Once you've fully embraced this mentality of being the catch (not her), you'll become more desirable. The fact that we prefer to attach a higher value to things that are not readily available is a basic part of human nature.

This is basic supply and demand: whatever is in short supply comes at a higher price than average. For example, as I write this book, there's a market shortage of artificial Splenda sweetener. The company that makes it tried to build a new factory because its existing factory is incapable of meeting demand. So now, thanks to news stories that mention this situation, people who would have never used Splenda in the first place, buy enough of the stuff to last them months or even years.

You should take advantage of this as an Alpha Male, and increase your "catchiness" by using these three techniques:

1. Don't be accessible to a woman if she's not worth your time. If you do this, you'll avoid being friend-zoned or putting up with women who are not really interested in you sexually or in a rela- tionship.

2. Don't immediately return phone calls. You are a busy Man as an Alpha Male and women need to accept that. If possible,

always hang up first as well, not because you're trying to be rude or are interrupted by another call, but because you're genuinely busy.

3. Don't go on dates when you have better things to do. Dating doesn't enrich your life or make you a catch for women. When you're unavailable at times, they will see you as more worthwhile than if you're always at their beck and call. Also, guide your dating decisions based on how your date acts when you turn her down. Don't compromise for someone who acts childishly when things don't go her way.

You live the life you want, as an Alpha Male, free from needing someone else's approval. Unfortunately, most people don't live the life they want for precisely that reason, i.e. they're afraid of getting disapproval. So, move away from things you don't need and only do what you want. You are a Man of great importance who deserves to be treated right.

Creating Your Own Reality

Life is what it is. You can read about other people's lives and experiences online and in books. Many religious sites, for instance, speak about God as if it is clear that He exists, whereas atheists would say that it is nonsense. Read on and you will find compelling arguments for both opinions! How can that be, considering that both sides cannot be correct? This happens because each person experiences life differently.

Is it bad to hurt someone? Like say, break their leg? You are probably thinking, "Damn right, it's terrible." But imagine you were a British soldier in 1914 and breaking your enemy's leg prevented you from becoming cannon fodder on the Western

Front. That would be the least you can do to defend yourself. So, here's the thing: you need to find your own version of the truth. Truth is objective, but personal truth is not. It is open to interpretation. Say it's a rainy day outside. If you want to go to a picnic, you'll probably be annoyed. However, if you're a farmer and it hasn't rained in months, you'd be ecstatic. Even natural disasters aren't catastrophic for everyone.

You thus have the ability to see the world as you wish. You can get your own perspective on things and frame them as it suits you better. An individual with a poor grasp on reality is drawn into the expectations of the world by other people. A person with a clear grasp on reality is unaffected by the opinions of other people and attracts others into their world instead.

Let's say you're going to a nightclub and can't find a parking space. That will annoy a beta male who lets external factors affect him. But you can phrase it in such a way as not to get annoyed. Since parking is so hard to find, it means that lots of people are out and about. This means that you'll be able to meet more people. Getting stuck in a traffic jam? That's all right if you have a chance to take a rest, relax, meditate, and perhaps listen to some soothing music. Don't let anger take over when things don't go your way. Take advantage of the situation any way you can.

Now, let's look at how you frame yourself. This frame will be the basis of your success as an Alpha Male.

Change Your Beliefs About How You Are With Women

You need to internalize the fact that women are fortunate to have you. Ponder the questions below and write down your answers. This exercise can be simple, but it is necessary because if you have not yet fully internalized the Alpha Male mindset, redirecting your thinking patterns is key. Plus, it's always helpful to find some stuff that you can re-read later when you need to relive your journey.

1. If you bring a woman into your life, how can you make her happy?

2. Imagine you've got little time as a busy Man for others' attempts to grab your attention. What rules do you have to decide who gets your attention?

3. What are some fun things you like to do that are usually pursuits for women as well? (Women need feelings to become sexually responsive, and they love emotionally relevant things like talking to friends on the phone. The best way to kill a woman's mood for sex is to talk about boring things like corporate balance sheets.)

4. What are the things that a woman would find attractive in you? What about some things you're going to be working on that would make you attractive?

5. What are the things you would expect from a woman to consider dating her?

Come up with your own responses, but note that there are certain things women need, such as great sex, fun, positive emotions, and common hobbies. While you're thinking about what makes you attractive to women, you also need to think about what you're getting out of the deal. For me, a lack of interest in sex, dishonesty, childish drama, and being obese and unhealthy are deal breakers.

Only you know what you're put off by and what attracts you in a woman. I encourage you to answer the questions above before moving on.

Now that you've completed the exercise above, you know more about yourself and your needs. You're on your way to knowing how amazing you are, to put it differently. You've discovered your value and what you bring to the table. If your interests aren't understood by a woman, then it is her loss not yours.

I like bringing an example of a luxury car at this point, like a Lamborghini. This illustrates your importance in the relationship. Depending on who you ask, a Lamborghini has no inherent value or it is the most important part of someone's life. For example, Lamborghini dealers are strongly of the opinion that their vehicles are of great value. As a consequence, they're not letting you test drive one of their cars right off the street, unlike Ford or Dodge dealers.

Sever Your Attachment to Outcomes

You must relax when you are talking to a woman. To do that, focus on what's going on outside of you at that moment, instead of criticizing and second guessing yourself. When you think too hard, it interferes with the aura of social dominance that you radiate. So don't rate or judge yourself while you are talking to a woman. Be more dynamic than formal.

Concentrate on the here and now. Don't think about the results; they'll be looking after themselves. And don't hesitate to make fun of yourself, too. Relax and don't pay much attention to any of your interactions or behavior.

Remember: you are not bound to the performance. You don't have expectations. What you'll do is build the right conditions for a casual encounter to take place, and then see where it goes. If a connection happens, then fine. If not, then simply shrug it off. Other possibilities will come up.

There are some things about life that you can't control, and certain things you can. The trick to happiness is to focus on the things you can control, while not giving too much importance to the things you cannot. So just relax and enjoy yourself. An example of something that you have no control over the outcome would be window shopping. You do it because it's exciting, not because it's something you need to do to stress about. You don't expect anything in particular.

You shouldn't be expecting any specific results with women, either. When you feel like you have to get laid, you will end up draining your strength and feeling insecure towards a woman.

Women can sense when a guy has an agenda. If you have a specific goal to get married, you'll end up sending the wrong vibes, and instead of an Alpha Man, you'll come off as needy. That would make you look bad. Forget what could happen at the end of the day. What you two are doing right now will be fun and enjoyable for you both. If she senses you're going to suggest that you two have sex, she'll think you're pushy.

You'll be far more laid back when you have no expectations. If you have any goal, it must be "the probability of getting laid." You can make yourself relaxed by setting up the conditions under which a woman will feel comfortable having sex with you and then moving on slowly towards a relationship.

Talking to a woman, even when she is a total stranger, is perfectly normal. Be romantic yet non-threatening, and be as polite as you can be. You don't want her to form any expectations of you either.

Make and hold eye contact and let the conversation run naturally.

"I have acne."

"I am too fat."

"I can't play sports."

"I live with my parents."

"I don't have a car."

I want you to think about any inner beliefs you have that have kept you from thinking you are desirable to women. Because your truth is whatever you build, if you have negative inner values that erode your confidence and make you seem unattractive to women, these need to be demolished.

I won't pretend it's easy; it's not. I used to be incredibly nervous. While my real issue was my fear of talking to people (especially girls), I rationalized it by telling myself things like, "I am an introvert and want everyone to stay away from me." It wasn't until I let go of my ego and re-evaluated my life that I noticed that shyness was a problem for me. I found I was too worried about what other people thought about me. I was frightened at the prospect of being rejected.

I was unable to humble myself and tackle that conviction head on, until I recognized the real core conviction that held me off. It was an incredible achievement for me. Once I dropped my ego, I finally got over my shyness around women. It happened, literally, overnight.

From that point on, if I spoke to people, I tried to concentrate externally — that is, on them and what the interaction was about — not on inner issues like, "I want this person to like me." You might have other inner values that serve you well. Identify and strengthen these. For example, when it comes to bodybuilding, I happen to be genetically gifted. And it increases my morale because I think of myself as a muscular Man.

Easy Alpha Male Exercises

1) Identify the positive, core values that you hold about yourself.

2) Strengthen them by improving what's good for you.

3) Identify the bad faith in your heart and get rid of it.

Again, this cannot happen overnight. It will take a while to be able to get through these three steps, so be patient. Take it slowly. Take baby steps to evaluate your habits and feelings and separate the patterns of thinking that are healthy from those that you want to eliminate. Do yourself a favor and save all your overthinking for later, when you're alone at home, not when you're talking to a woman.

Hold yourself focused outwardly when you are with a woman and just think about the conversation at hand. This will cause you to feel confident and thus more desirable to her as you express confidence, which enhances your chances of having sex.

Handling Your Fears of Rejection

Picture this: you're trying to talk to a hot lady. You see her standing in the supermarket magazine aisle, busy reading an issue of *Cosmopolitan*. Her hair is sleek, silky blonde, her skin is soft and pale, and--that's right--she's rocking some super impressive breasts.

You'll probably start to feel stressed right away. Excuses not to talk to her will pop in your mind: "I'm still in a tired mood," "I didn't dress well today," "I don't even know what to say to her," and so on. This pessimistic self-talk will ruin a potential interaction before it begins, reducing your chances of a sexual opportunity to absolute zero. You finish your shopping, go home, and sleep alone. When this happens, you're the only person to blame--you didn't give the girl a chance to do anything.

The truth is that you didn't hesitate because you were tired or poorly dressed, and you could have always found some conversation opener to break the ice. The real problem was *fear*. You weren't making an approach because you were terrified of rejection. "I wish I could just force myself to get over this ridiculous fear," you might think. But the reality is that, when we enter an unknown environment, we feel frightened. That's just basic human psychology, and there's no way around it.

Since this fear won't go away on its own, the only way to overcome it is to face it head-on. This means that, if you ever want things to change, you need to make the decision to start approaching people.

I used to be so afraid of talking to girls that my vision would start to blur if I so much as offered them a greeting. In every situation, I found another excuse to keep to myself. I kept waiting, and waiting, and waiting--yet my anxiety never ceased. I was immobilized, unable to find out why I was so afraid to speak to women, and spent day after day refusing to even just *try*.

Here's the truth: when it comes to talking to women, almost all guys are nervous because rejection sucks. It hits like a blow to your ego and it can be hard to recover from it. Everyone wants to keep their self-esteem at a high level. For emotionally healthy people, though, that self-worth comes from inside. They don't need to rely on anyone else to supply it.

If you adopt this mindset, rejection stops mattering so much. If a woman likes you, great; if not, you don't need to stress about it. You can't dictate how she feels, and there's not a single Man on earth who's capable of winning over every single woman. Sometimes things work, and sometimes they don't. It's really that simple.

The only way to be less afraid is by exposing yourself. Everyone feels anxiety when they're in an unfamiliar situation and in order to overcome it, you need to make that situation more familiar. At first, you're going to be extremely vulnerable and paranoid, but that's the case for everyone. It's up to you to decide that you're going to overcome it.

Here's the bottom line: everyone is haunted by an invisible specter that will never leave their side. Its name is Fear. If you let it control your life, it'll put you in a straitjacket--but it can also be your faithful friend. As long as you keep trying new things in life, fear will always be with you--but it will only get in your way if you allow it to do so. Fear will be there every time that you try something new and exciting, and that's okay. Even if it may not feel that way, you're the one in control of yourself. Nobody else is.

How To Eliminate Fear

You need to do three things to overcome your fear of talking with women:

1. Don't have expectations. Be social if you want to be social. Nothing more.

2. Chat with ladies. Know that doing the thing you fear is the only way to get over your fear. The sooner you commit to chatting for the sake of it, the better the results. When the inevitable rejection happens, you can think, "Been there, done that, it's not a big deal."

3. Identify what exactly scares you. This way, you can eliminate it.

Since fear is common when it comes to chatting with women, it is normal to feel anxiety about approaching a woman. Don't assume that your anxieties are uncommon. However, you need to do what you're scared of anyway. This is what distinguishes a Man like you from all the beta Males out there.

Some people let their fear and anxiety overcome them, not only about women, but other things in life, too, like their career. That's why, unfortunately, some guys never find the success they want. The reason most people never discuss their anxieties is that they don't know where they come from. Anxiety comes from inside. It is your brain that's causing it, not the likelihood that you'll be rejected. If you don't have expectations and open a conversation casually, you're less likely to experience anxiety and fear of rejection.

Since you have no expectations, don't just approach women you find attractive. Since you're looking for easy conversations, try approaching people who usually react best when talking to strangers. These are elderly people, generally, regardless of their sex. This may be because people in certain age groups experience more loneliness than others.

If it helps, set a time limit for interactions, such as speaking to one person for 30 seconds and then bailing out of the conversation. You can say things like, "Well, I'm on my way to meeting a friend. It was a pleasure talking with you" and then you can walk away without making a huge deal out of it. Once you establish a routine and are feeling comfortable approaching people to chat, you can start focusing on women you find attractive.

For instance, if a woman passes you by in a lobby, try saying "Hey--I need a fast female opinion on something," as though the thought had only just occurred to you. Once you have her attention, ask her something that you're genuinely curious about. Another trick from a friend of mine is to think of something hilarious right before you approach a stranger. A little bit of laughter will put you in a much more positive mood, which will heighten the chances of a successful interaction.

Sometimes things will go wrong, and that's okay. Instead of thinking, "Oh my God, this woman must hate me because I'm fumbling my vocabulary," try thinking something like "It's cool that I'm talking to this girl--even if she rejects me, then she's out of the way, and I'm one step closer to finding my dream girl."

If you're nervous, try to identify the parts of your body that are physically reacting to your anxiety. On a physiological level, nervousness is accompanied by muscle tension. In my personal experience, I find that I feel the most tension in my face and jaw. When I make a conscious effort to relax those muscles, it tells my brain that it's time to feel comfortable rather than anxious.

Another way to relieve anxiety requires an exercise in imagination. Before you open your mouth to speak to an unfamiliar woman, envision the scene as though it already happened and she has rejected you. This helps you feel comfortable for a number of reasons. For one, you can be invigorated by the knowledge that you're at least going to give it your best shot--

you're an Alpha Male who goes through life without excusing his needs or apologizing for his desires. Secondly, each rejection is a step closer to success. Every time you're turned down, you'll learn and improve from your mistakes, and your conversational skills will reflect that in the future. Third and lastly, you've made even more progress towards desensitizing yourself, meaning that your next interaction will be that much less intimidating.

CHAPTER TEN

WHAT IS BODY LANGUAGE? AND WHAT IS ALPHA MALE BODY LANGUAGE?

BEFORE WE DEVELOPED SPOKEN LANGUAGE, we were able to understand other people's signals through the way they used body language. Body language is still the primary means of communication nowadays. It is incredibly instinctive.

It's the easiest way of communicating with women's primal instinctive mind without interference. There's no denying we go through a lot of trouble to make ourselves presentable to the world. But why do we do this and what does body language have to do with our looks?

Body language refers to various forms of non-verbal communication in which a person, through their physical behavior, can reveal clues about unspoken intentions or feelings. Such behaviors may include posture, gestures, facial expressions, and pupil dilation. Often, it's as plain as "I got an erection" means "I'm sexually excited." It is so simple that animals also use body language as their key mechanism of communication. Body language is usually a subconscious reflex, difficult to control, just as you can control the flow of blood into your penis with difficulty. Therefore, body language can provide accurate information about a person's attitude or state of mind. For example, it can mean arousal, aggression, attentiveness, boredom, comfort, enjoyment, fun, etc.

Body language is essential for communication and interpersonal relationships. It is, of course, important to business management and leadership and other situations where people witness it. Although body language is non-verbal or non-spoken, it can reveal a lot about your feelings and thoughts, and understanding it can help you understand the feelings of others towards you. Understanding body language can help you both in your professional and your personal life. Body language can be used to express conscious or unconscious messages, which is generally helpful when looking for a mate.

Whenever I walk somewhere, I walk purposefully. I have an air of confidence and a touch of cockiness. I walk like I'm someone else. Some would say that I am walking around like I think that I am tougher than anybody else. I walk the same way whether I'm heading into a club or my work. I'm walking straight with my head up, my chest out. I smile at people, sometimes I laugh. I have more fun than anyone else. I am walking with a purpose, just like I own the place. When I am in a group, I do the same thing. With a steady gait, I walk tall. All the things I'm doing are sending off signals that I'm comfortable and I'm interesting, I have something to give, I'm having fun, and I'm fun to be around. I walk in, and everyone in the bar wants to make my acquaintance. This is the power of body language!

Let's break some of this down. It is nice to go places with women and to be seen with women. You get other women interested in you. In other words, other women will think, "All those girls are hanging out with that guy, he has to be really cool." When you walk into a bar with an attractive woman, other women will notice you. I like to take it one step further by smiling and linking my arms with my date. On top of that, we joke around and seem to have a great time. So, any girls I may later meet at the bar will likely think, "This guy must be really interesting, he's got girls all over him, they're laughing, he's fun, he's got something to give. I want to see him!"

Some Men who are on their journey to becoming an Alpha Male may be still scared by the competition. They're afraid that if they tell their friends about body language, the competition will be too much. Although that's true to some extent, by being in a cohesive group you'll get better outcomes than if you're on your own. People hang out in communities. Each group has a leader. Whenever we're socializing, there are not only Alpha Males, but also members of each leader's pack. These members of the pack will look to the strongest, most dominating Alpha Male. When hanging out with friends, I make it clear that I am the leader of our group, while they make up my "pack." I use subtle signs of dominance to show outsiders that I am the leader. This makes patrons become aware of my Alpha Male status within the group. I stand when my friends sit. When I talk to them, I might put my hand on their shoulder, or if I tell them a joke, I give them a pat on the back. These are subtle signs of dominance over others.

When I hang out with my friends, I stand approximately one shoulder-length away from them. You want to take space in your party to show you're the Alpha Male. Stand in a relaxed way with your head back and your chest out. Don't place your hands in your pockets. That is a sign of nervousness. Don't hold your drink in front of your face. This makes you look inaccessible to conversation; you just put a barrier up. Take up a reasonable amount of space and send out messages that say, "I'm available and accommodating." Instead of standing pigeon toed, point your toes out slightly. This may seem like a small thing, but it is not. Women notice stuff like this. I like putting out an air of confidence, so I move my hips forward. Depending on what I wear, I lock my thumbs in my belt or pants pockets, and let my hands hang down my legs. This is a relaxed pose that appeals to the erotic subconscious of a woman.

To be an Alpha Male involves a certain look. You don't have to be the best-looking guy, the tallest guy, the fittest guy, or the funniest guy. Your body language needs to send out the right message, however. This message is quite sexual and it helps you become the center of attention without even trying too hard. People around you all want to know what you're about and why you're successful.

You need to learn how to look, think, and act as an Alpha Male. You have to move and make sure your body language is screaming, "I'm huge, I'm ruthless, you don't want to mess with me!"

CHAPTER ELEVEN

MASTERING THE ART OF EYE CONTACT

EYE CONTACT IS the single most important part of being attractive to women and picking up girls, so it deserves its very own chapter. In this book, the concepts you will learn are all centered around eye contact and the signals women give. Why does eye contact matter so much? Because it's how we know a woman is interested in us. In interacting with women, anything and everything you do is directly related to body language and eye contact. Eye contact will tell you everything you need to know about any woman.

All body language is significant, but eye contact and a little smile will tell you what you really want to know. "I'm interested in you and I'm free," for example. That's everything you need to know about the pickup game. Now, of course, you're going to use body language to do a lot of things: make her interested in you, develop and continue to create sexual chemistry, and cultivate a friendship in your attempt to get the things you need. All of this is done with body language, but her eyes are what tell you, "I'm interested and I'm available." If you're willing to be proactive when it comes to women, eye contact is the foundation on which you will build your game.

Let's think of a situation. You're standing around a bar table with a few friends when you've spotted a hot girl across the room. She comes up to you and says, "I'm not sure what it is about you, but I would like to get to know you. I'm not dating anyone right now. Would you like to go somewhere quiet and get to know each other?" You walk off to a quiet corner with your future girlfriend or potential friend with benefits, while your friends wonder how the hell you just pulled that off. She seems to be a little out of your league, but somehow you, this guy who knows nothing about women, just picked up the hottest girl in the bar.

Wouldn't that be perfect if it worked like that with women? They come up to you and tell you how they feel. Well, that's exactly how it works. A woman tells you those things with her eyes, her legs, her arms, and her movements. She and her body language send out signals. When you take a look across the room and she makes eye contact she says, "I'm drawn to you, I'm at your mercy, I want you to talk to me!" You should respond by dropping a little smile her way. If she smiles back, she just told you, "I'm interested in you, come over here and talk to me so that we can get to know each other." In face-to-face conversation, the words you're saying make up just 10% of the message. How you say them makes up 30%. The balance is nonverbal, which means that 60% of what you say is achieved through non-verbal communication or body language. Your body language will always betray you and tell the world how you really feel, no matter how hard you try to hide your feelings.

Sure, it would be great if that beautiful blonde from across the room approached you. However, that's not how it works. It's not socially acceptable for a woman to come up to a Man. Ultimately, making the first move is up to the guy, but in reality, a woman will have given over a dozen signals before most guys make their first move. Women send out these signals to attract the guys they are interested in but save face by not doing it directly. If a guy turns down this advance signal, no harm has been done because the woman didn't do anything outright. Despite receiving the cold shoulder, she doesn't have to take the walk of shame back to her place. She leaves it up to the Man. If a Man is interested in a woman, he picks up her signals and comes to talk to her, taking all the risk of humiliation onto himself. The problem is that most guys have no idea what to look for. Most guys don't get the signals she's sending.

There could be another question at this stage, when fear of rejection sinks in. You are reading the signs, but you are being held back by your lack of confidence. You start asking yourself, "Is she really interested, what if I go over there and she dismisses me, what if I misread the signals, what if I can't think of anything to say?" But what if, instead of asking yourself all these questions, you didn't waste your time worrying about them and just talked to her? Well, then at the end of the night you might find yourself in bed with her. The guy who fears rejection will never make the move to speak to that girl. He will stay away from her and will never find the one he wants. What if there was a way of being sure this didn't happen? We can increase our chances by studying the signs that women give us. At that point, a rejection becomes a non-issue. Eye contact is the single most important component of being able to pick up signals. It's how we know a woman is interested in us. Eye contact will tell you everything you need to know about any woman. Here are some things to look for:

The Extended Gaze

Each time you lock eyes with a woman, it shows you're interested. If she's interested in you, she'll lock eyes with you and keep her attention focused on you for a second or two longer than a typical look would last. When you catch her eyes, keep eye contact. Holding eye contact is different from staring. You don't want to stare at a lady. You can get lost looking at a woman for the rest of the night if you wait too long to approach her. What happens is that you are always trying to reinforce the fact that she's interested in you, and you keep making eye contact again and again. She begins to lose interest after three or four times, until she is no longer interested. So, to avoid that, once you have established initial eye contact, approach her.

The Checkout

A woman will check out a guy just as much as a guy checks a woman out. The difference between the two is that the woman's approach is more subtle and it can be very difficult to pick up. When you find out what's going on with a girl, you see her face and quickly turn your attention over to her chest. You look back at her eyes hoping she didn't just catch you checking out her boobs and then run your eyes over the rest of her body. Women do the same, but in a more subtle way. They start by looking at your face, and then move down and check out the rest of the kit. If she smiles, then you know that she likes what she sees. Now, when she checks you out, she can't see a whole lot. She is however searching for a few things. She'll look at your hands and at your feet. She likes to see you're well-groomed and that your hands and fingernails are in good shape. This is a good way to judge your appearance. She'll also look at your shoe choice. Bottom line, it's time to approach her as she looks you up and down and smiles.

Dilated Pupils

Your pupils dilate when you see something you want. This holds true for Men and women alike. This is an intense physiological reaction and we don't have any control over it. You can tell if a woman is interested in you by watching her pupils. Photographic studies have shown that people with dilated pupils are considered more attractive. Magazines improve the look of their models' pupils in their ads. Did you always wonder why the most romantic meal is seen as a candlelit dinner with wine? The dim light dilates the participants' pupils and makes them appear more attractive. As we drink alcohol, our eyes dilate, and the effect becomes even greater. Are you familiar with the word "bedroom eyes?" This is the thing; with a woman you love, when you're in a dimly lit atmosphere, like in a bedroom, your pupils become dilated. When trying to gage if your new friend is drawn to you, one thing to think about is that the lighting will affect her pupils' size. If it is too dark, the pupils will expand and the opposite will happen if it is bright. Use this trick only in a regularly illuminated environment, not at the bar.

The Flicker

The flicker can be seen after you've spent some time talking to the target and building up sexual chemistry. This refers to making eye contact and focusing on one eye at the time repeatedly. Kiss her when you see this because she just gave you the approval.

As you're looking for goals, look around the room. Keep your eyes in the direction of a girl you like. When she looks back at you, maintain eye contact for four to five seconds. If she's interested, she'll respond; if not, forget about her and move on to the next target. Do not hesitate to approach her once you get the right look and start a conversation. If you're uncertain about the signal, keep catching her eye for about every five minutes without staring. She reaffirms her interest in you each time she keeps making eye contact with you. Make your move after a second or third instance, otherwise she will start losing interest in you.

This is the most important part of body language. It tells her, "I'm attracted to you and I'm accessible." Of course, you'll use body language to do a lot of other stuff, such as making her interested in you, establishing and developing sexual chemistry, and skewing the interaction to your advantage. If you wish to be successful with women, you've got to know it all starts with your eyes, however.

242

CHAPTER TWELVE

WHY YOU SHOULD ASSUME ATTRACTION

THERE IS lots of advice about picking up girls on the internet. All of it tells you to do different things to make a girl like you: tell them certain types of stories, bring them flowers or presents, or do things for them. The problem with all these techniques is that these are all born from a beta male mentality. They suggest you should work hard to make a woman like you. If you always try to say and do the right thing with a woman, then you are trying too hard to win her approval.

The truth is, if you have good body language, high confidence, a great personality, and have a lot going on in your life, you would naturally be more attractive to a woman than 95% of the guys out there. And make no mistake about it, if you're in the top 5% of male attractiveness, in theory, nearly all women will find you attractive.

For instance, when a woman acts spoiled and asks you some question like, "What made you decide to talk to me?" or, "Do you tell all the girls that kind of stuff?" The best thing to do is not to answer. Instead, the best way to react is by acting indifferent. This way you stay in control of the situation. Whenever you care about what a girl feels, that gives her control. There's never a need to feel like you've got to entertain a woman. Doing so actually makes you a beta man.

When you speak to a woman, communicate with her. Screen her to make sure she can carry on a conversation with you. You're the Alpha Male. Since you always believe the woman is attracted to you, the most important rule is to always be willing to walk away. This is how you keep control of the situation.

Even though I speak of patience until you are either rejected or in a relationship, sometimes it's nice to be the first to walk away (if it's a girl you don't like), just to know you can. Whenever possible, always be willing to walk away. This makes you seem like a challenge for the girl. If a woman sees a Man as a challenge, she will see him as someone interesting. It means she has to work for him, and that he is her reward if she wins his affections.

If you are ever a woman's "sure thing," that gives her confidence and causes her to stop feeling attraction towards you. So, if you just presume attraction, this will mean the woman still feels she's more drawn to you than you are to her.

Your Behavior

You should sit as close to her as possible. The idea here is that you feel horny and want her to feel horny as well. Friends tend to interact from a distance greater than 18 inches apart, according to anthropologist Edward Hall. People who are familiar with each other stay within 18 inches of each other.

You should keep a close distance between the two of you; this way you build an intimate relationship with the woman you are dating. Aim to stay within that 18 inch space at all times. You also want the two of you to be comfortable touching each other as you develop the dynamic of being within each other's personal space. Even though you will touch her for potentially innocent reasons, research into human communication has shown that a person is more likely to tolerate contact from another person if they feel attracted to them. When you touch the woman, you are:

1. Triggering the parts of her mind that say, "I like this guy!"
2. Checking her to see if she is worth pursuing.

If she has a negative reaction, then you know that you are wasting your time hanging out with her. It's also a trademark of Alpha Males to feel able to establish physical contact with others. So by being open to physical contact, you're expressing non-verbally that you're an Alpha Male and a guy who trusts women. After all, only a very self-confident Man can relax when he touches a woman. Treat the woman as if she were one of your friends. Don't make a big deal out of it. If she thinks it's a big deal for you (for example, if you're staring at your hand while touching her), then the dynamic becomes one of you actively trying to get laid, which causes her protective defenses to go up. When you're in public with her, make sure you do the following:

1) Touch her hand. You can make this fun by holding a thumb-wrestling game, for example. If you don't know how to do this, watch Arnold Schwarzenegger's movie, *True Lies,* specifically the scene where he and Jamie Lee Curtis say, "One, two, three, four, I declare a thumb war." Once you've got the idea that contact can be fun like this, then you can touch her hand during other moments, like when you want to find out about the cool ring she's wearing.

2) Touch her arm. Do this by noticing and admiring her watch or bracelet when you touch her hand.

3) Touch her forearm.

4) Touch her upper arm. Do this when you're asking her something important you just thought of.

5) Pull her head back. Do this when whispering a secret in her ear. At this stage, you two can touch each other comfortably enough to hold hands.

6) Touch her lower back. When you stand up, touch her lower back as you start walking out with her.

The number one thing to do during the course of the entire cycle is to relax (in case I haven't stressed this enough).

To remain calm, view the woman's engagement as not all that significant. All you're doing is talking to her and hanging out to get to know her and build a bond before you become more involved with her. Look into her eyes as you speak. Caress her skin in a way that is erotic. Speak in a soft, natural voice, as if you've been around her for a year and feel completely relaxed with her. Speak with her in a gentle, sensual voice.

Six Beta Behaviors to Avoid

A little-known fact about humans is that we are wired to respond more drastically to negative triggers than we do to positive ones. To get a better sense of this, imagine that you're having a conversation with a casual acquaintance. They seem witty, smart, and charming... right up until they tell you in complete seriousness that they identify as a "flat earther." Just like that, your perspective about them will change; your mental file on that person will be permanently stamped with the word "WEIRDO" in bold red lettering.

Since a single wrong move can be enough to sabotage one hundred good ones, it's extremely important to make sure that you avoid messing up even for a second. There are six particular mistakes that Men often make in conversations with women, all of which cause them to come across as desperate beta Males. If you keep these in mind and steer your own behavior in the opposite direction, you're much more likely to earn the respect and admiration of the women around you.

1. Seeking approval. This most often manifests in uncertain patterns of speech, such as finishing your sentences with "right?" or "isn't it?" These questioning additions can make you sound weak-willed, especially if they're paired with a rise in your vocal pitch.

2. Trying to win. For the most part, *trying* is antithetical to *doing*. If your priority is rising to the top of the herd, you're internalizing the assumption that you aren't already there. Assume instead that you are the best of the crowd and then project that superiority into your attitude. This doesn't mean you should be bossy; on the contrary, you should be polite when you ask people to do things for you. If you're a respected person of authority, you won't need to employ force in order to get others to do what you want.

3. Acting belligerent. The Alpha Male must be able to remain calm under pressure, and should always know when to walk away from a situation. Starting up conflict for its own sake is an automatic sign of low status. Naturally, battling to gain a woman's affection is the ultimate form of seeking approval--and if you come across as someone who needs approval, your attractiveness is reduced. That being said, if another guy starts something, don't be afraid to stand up for yourself.

4. Being too passive. Of course, you should always respect other people, but you should never end up bending over backwards to accommodate them. Oftentimes, Men will fail to impress women because they go along with anything a woman suggests to them. This can lead to one-sided conversations, which are almost always mutually unenjoyable. An Alpha Male is concerned with what he wants, not just what his woman wants. If he gets bored, he makes his disinterest known. Don't be rude, but don't give people attention that they don't deserve, either.

5. Bragging or showing off. If you're constantly trying to one-up people in order to demonstrate that you're smarter than them, everyone--especially women--will think that you're trying too hard. Smart people don't need to prove their intelligence, and Alpha Males don't need to prove their authority. You should be secure enough in your own abilities to recognize when someone is more knowledgeable than you are. Willingness to learn is never a sign of weakness.

6. Getting distracted by looks. If you try to make a move on every hot girl that you see, you'll inevitably end up getting involved in some unpleasant relationships. When you aren't used to picking up women, it's all too easy to jump on anyone who expresses interest--but you should have standards, just like they do. When you're putting effort into an interaction, expect the woman to do the same--and, if she doesn't, seriously consider directing your attention elsewhere.

Above all else, Alpha Males claim the mantle of leadership as their birthright and behave accordingly. We don't care a great deal about what others think; we're doing our own thing, not seeking approval. Confidence in ourselves is what makes us interesting, and what compels people to admire us. Being a follower of an Alpha Male is a sure path to increased social status, invigorating experiences, and stimulating conversation. To put it in simpler terms, Alpha Males are interesting. People want to pay attention to us.

How does the Alpha Male maintain that alluring quality? The answer is simple: he speaks about things that fascinate him. This draws other people into his reality, leading them to find interest in the same topics as him.

In order to generate topics of interest in the first place, you need to have a well-balanced, exciting life. Keep busy with family, social life, education, and self-improvement. Don't just sit around; go skydiving, take lessons in music, hang out with your long-time friends. When your life is exciting, you'll have plenty of intriguing topics to discuss with women.

And when the time comes to talk about your experiences, make sure to lead the conversation. You should be comfortable, confident, and captivating, but not aggressive in your approach; Alpha Males don't need to be bossy, they already have assurance that people will follow and listen to what they have to say. One of the best ways to achieve many goals is to "fake it 'til you make it," and manifesting alpha masculinity is no exception. If you believe in yourself, everyone around you will eventually learn to do the same. You're the only one in charge of your own world, and you should be secure in commanding it.

Another aspect of this is that you shouldn't be overthinking every bit of the conversation. If you're constantly looking for signs of approval or disapproval from a woman, you're projecting your insecurity without even realizing it. Alpha Males have no need for validation; they already know their own capability. Constant worry about what a woman is thinking will get you absolutely nowhere. Instead, just remember that somewhere beneath the surface is a horny, primitive woman who's seeking wild, passionate sex. Sit back and relax, present yourself as an attractive guy, and give her the opportunity to be attractive in return. If she doesn't want to be with you, that's her problem. Don't let it discourage you.

Always remember that success comes from faith. Assume that women find you irresistible. Be solid and determined, funny but not zany, a bit of a "bad guy" but never a jerk. You are an interesting Man, and women ought to want you.

From a broader perspective, do what you want in life. Stay true to your feelings. If you don't want to do something, then don't. Your actions should come from what *you* want, not out of a sense of obligation or societal expectations. In the end, you'll be happier than ever when you learn how to embrace your identity as an Alpha Male. Great sex will just be an aftereffect.

Alpha Males claim the leadership mantle as their birthright, and behave as natural leaders. We don't really care about what others think. We are doing what we want and are not seeking approval. At the same time, we are often of use to those who follow us— whether it's social status, anticipation, or stimulating conversation. Individuals naturally follow Alpha Males because they want to because Alpha Males talk about interesting subjects or because everyone else is paying attention to them.

And people— especially women— want to be part of the Alpha Male conversation because it is fascinating. Why? Easy— because an Alpha Man speaks about things that fascinate him. Therefore, other people are drawn into his reality, so they find it interesting as a consequence. So, how do you get to think about the interesting stuff? It is simply because you have a well-balanced, exciting life. If you do that, you will of course exude confidence in your favorite topics. Keep busy with family, social life, education, and self-improvement. Play video games but don't just sit on your couch. Go skydiving, take lessons in music, call long-time friends and talk to them. When your life is exciting and fascinating, you'll have plenty to talk to women about.

When speaking to a woman, lead the conversation. Look her in the eye. This is a habit that comes naturally when you display leadership. You don't need to tell others what to do. They'll follow your lead naturally.

Most people don't like following orders. Because of that, displaying leadership and being a role model will have people following you in no time. You simply have to display the confidence you learned as an Alpha Male. This brings up a significant issue. Do not adapt to what you think is expected of you. You create your own world. That means that you should be acting as if things are exactly the way you want them to be.

Don't act like any woman is a catch. Quite the opposite, think like she's nothing special and you can take her or leave her. This is the right mindset for approaching a conversation that may or may not lead to sex. Speak as if all your manly impulses are perfectly natural. You have no reason to apologize for your sex drive or cover it up!

Don't act like she's right all the time or what she chooses to talk about is more important than your own thoughts. Believe it or not, she'll pay much more attention to you if you do that. Most guys find themselves trapped by constant worry about what a woman is thinking. "Gee, she's rubbing her glass in response to the joke I made, does this mean she likes me?" Now it's time to stop thoughts like that.

Instead, you should remember that at the end of the day, she's as interested in sex as you are. Sit back and relax. This will make her attracted to you. Stay positive and keep your faith. You're eventually going to win. The right woman will find you irresistible.

Be solid, and be determined but don't let that detract you from also being funny. You can also be risqué if you so wish. Whatever you do, bear in mind that you can get whatever you set your mind to.

Also, whatever you decide to do, make sure that you stay true to your feelings. If you don't want something, simply walk away. Be honest with yourself and stand up for yourself. However, don't do things because others want or expect them.

Touching

We try to crack the barrier of touching. As you start the conversation with this goal, you start about two to three feet away from each other. You want to step closer to her as you continue to talk. It's important to remember that she is the one who needs to initiate this proximity. When you act too aggressive, she's going to back up and bring her defenses up. Remember, she needs to feel comfortable around you before she lets you in. The first time she leans in to say something to you, take this as an opportunity to move closer to her and close the gap. Let's say that as you talk back and forth and she touches your shoulder or arm. You are now free to do it again. Keep getting closer and closer until you're standing or sitting next to each other. This builds sexual tension and the slow build up and anticipation will drive her crazy.

Touch isn't necessarily sexual in nature. In reality, it is the innocent contact that we use to break the ice. She may or may not seek to shake your hand when someone introduces you to her. If she does, shake her hand with both hands, holding it for two or three seconds before introducing yourself. This shows trust on your part and that you have no fear of touching her. If a good friend of mine introduces me to a girl that I consider attractive, I extend my arms as if to embrace her. This might get you an introductory hug.

When a woman introduces you to another woman, you've already passed the "female test" and are considered to be a decent guy. While this embrace may seem innocent and polite to whomever is doing the introduction, it may be setting her up for later. If she turns you down for the embrace, tell her, "Don't let me hanging here, give me at least a high five." Whenever you're about to walk with the target, give her your arm and say, "Shall we?" You can take her hand as if to guide her through the crowd. This helps you approach her in a commanding way and take control.

Once you reach the point where you're comfortable with physical contact, there is no going back. The gentle touch will soon lead to something more sensual, like a back rub. If the woman starts touching you, you need to be able to respond. Touch her back without hesitation.

Repeating her name does two things. It helps you remember it, of course, but women also like hearing Men repeat their name. This could get her immediate attention, paving the way for a smooth relationship.

Dancing is a wonderful way to feel comfortable with a woman and become physically closer. You've welcomed her into your personal space by telling her that you fit together. By definition, this isn't dangerous, but what you're really doing is making your way through her defenses and pulling down her walls. If she says something flirtatious, you're in. It doesn't really matter what she is saying because you're flirting and you are suggesting it is okay for her to touch you. It is going to work every time.

There is no hidden code about how to approach a woman or a magic pickup line that works all the time. What worked for one girl might fail with the next twenty. Everyone has their personal style, what works for them, and what they're comfortable with. Fortunately for us, each goal is a unique challenge on its own. We learn from every pickup. It can be hard to get rejected, but you can get through it. You learn to differentiate between the signals she sent. From the instant she starts to become your objective, you need to be able to read her body language, so that you can turn the dynamic back in your favor. The more we understand, the easier it will be to manage any situation, to the point where no woman turns you down and you know how to overcome any obstacle.

CHAPTER THIRTEEN

NAVIGATING THE ZONES, APPROACHING WOMEN, & PICKING UP ON A WOMAN'S SIGNALS

TRUST IS about feeling comfortable within our own personal space. If you feel comfortable, you will give off signs that you are open to change, but if you feel threatened, you will put up a wall. Everyone reacts differently and has their own comfort level. Just as we need to understand the signals people are sending us, knowing your personal comfort zones will help you to know if you are moving too fast towards your goal.

The invasion of their room is a simple experiment you can do to test a person's personal space. Everywhere we go, any room we enter, we subconsciously decide what our space is and what the other person's space is. Usually, everyone divides up space equally depending on the number of people in the room. Take for example two people sitting at a table in a restaurant across from each other. They each have subconsciously decided they have half the table. When you enter someone's personal space, start taking up room gradually. Place your keys on the table and slowly slide them towards them. Move the menus or the salt shaker into the other person's personal space. Take your drink, and divide it in half. They're going to do one of two things, either they're going to react to your dominant behavior and begin moving those artifacts out of their own space and back into yours, or they're going to retreat. They'll move their chairs back, or push their plate to make more room. They don't even know they're doing any of this until you point it out to them. They are doing it subconsciously. People react to social situations in the same way. If someone moves too quickly into someone else's personal space, the person will either retreat, or take a step back to regain their space.

Even something as easy as sitting on a couch reveals how open you are to business, and how relaxed you are. If you're sitting on the very end of a couch, pressed against the floor, you're projecting the image of "I don't want anyone sitting next to me; I'm scared of my surroundings and trying to hide." If you're sitting in the middle of the couch, you're saying, "I don't want any company. I sit in the middle. I want you to feel uncomfortable sitting close to me. This is my sofa. If you want it, you'll have to come and take it from me." The alternative is to sit on one side, not pressed against the armrest or in the middle of the sofa. You are inviting a client, which is a female, to sit next to you. You say, "I welcome business, I give you enough room to sit here and be comfortable."

Personal space is split up into four different areas. For the sake of this discussion, we will call them zones.

Navigating the Four Zones

1. The Public Zone

An area located seven feet away and beyond is considered the public zone. This is reserved for large groups, a speaker, or an entertainer. Think of a speaker in a lecture hall. He is close enough to a large audience to see and hear them, yet everyone is far enough away from them so as not to present an immediate threat. The public zone is where you're looking for your targets, making eye contact with the girls you like and watching for subtle signals, like them pointing their body in your direction or changing their body posture to more flattering and appealing positions.

2. The Social Zone

The social area is found between four to seven feet. The most common examples are small groups shaped like a circle. Members in the community are able to communicate effectively with each other, but the small group also adds a dimension of privacy and exclusivity. People who "fit in" the group make their way into the circle, while those who don't "fit in" are slowly squeezed out of the group by their peers. In this situation, most of the body language you'll see is very conspicuous, so be careful. Women will point their bodies in the way of the Men that they find most interesting, trying to get their attention, or they will break up into smaller groups.

The most critical aspect of the social zone is that it helps a pair to break into their own personal conversation. Place yourself next to your chosen target and start your own conversation. This will make you shift to your own conversation and break away from the larger community. This way you can get to know the target better.

3. The Personal Zone

The personal zone is between one and two feet. You can reach out and grab the target's hand, or touch them in a non-sexual way but you still have enough room between the two of you to be relaxed. In this zone, most body language signals will either be provided through eye contact. The other person will also begin to touch you, as all other signals have failed. At this point, it's easy to look into her eyes and see if her pupils dilated or flicker back and forth. She could lean in to hear you better or press her body against yours. Every time she touches you is a clear indication that she wants you to do the same.

4. The Intimate Zone

The intimate zone will bring you in very close proximity. Touching, kissing, hugging, and any other touch in a sexual way are all part of the intimate zone. This is the personal space we share during intercourse. There's very little guesswork on your part at this point. She is yours to have and if you haven't made a move by now, she's going to make one on you easily.

You have to understand how to move from each zone to the next to be a true master of the game. You can't move from one zone to another without passing through each first, nor is this a linear process. A target may allow you to reach her personal space and then realize you're moving things faster than she's comfortable with. She's going to compensate by pulling back a zone or two to reclaim her distance before she knows you better. This can go to and fro all night long until she is, at last, relaxed enough to encourage you to steal a kiss in her personal space. It's the whole one step forward, two steps back attitude. You can gauge her reactions by reading her body language signals, and get feedback on how sensitive she is to you coming into her space.

Approaching Women

Approaching a woman is the most challenging and intimidating thing you will do when you first learn to pick up feMales. We may be familiar with all the signs and know great openers and how to shift the conversation to our advantage. But we struggle when it comes to the game's most important element: going from point A to point B and introducing ourselves. The only explanation we can give ourselves if we fail to complete this step is self-doubt. Before we even try, we speak to ourselves about the possibility of failing. In the rare cases when we do try, our unconfident body language and poor approach tell the target, "I'm nothing special, I'm not a worthy Man, turn me down please!" If a woman sees this, she's going to reject us, not because she didn't like us, but because she subconsciously reacted to our body language, which begged her to reject us. So, to further justify our behavior, we convince ourselves that we should have never made the attempt.

The Different Approach Angles

The position from which you approach a woman is important when you receive the signal from the target, and are prepared to try to approach her. There are three ways from which we approach the target, two that we will use constantly and one that we will use only in extreme circumstances

1. The Frontal Approach

The most straightforward and threatening way to tackle a target is to meet her head on. This method is really straightforward. You tell the target, "I see you, I'm coming to get you." While I like to be as straightforward as possible, approaching a woman from this angle will do more harm than good. It's a direct personal assault. You invade her personal space, which immediately alerts the target to put up her guard and be prepared for a confrontation. She's on the defensive now, and you'll need to smooth-talk her to get her to drop her defenses.

The only time I suggest the head on approach is when the goal is making direct eye contact. Only use this angle if throughout your approach you make and maintain eye contact. Your eyes are locked from the initial contact to when you introduce yourself. In this case, you want to take the shortest possible line straight toward her. The reason for this is that any hesitation or step away from the goal shows a lack of confidence on your part. The moment of hesitation is going to cause the target to see you as an unconfident male and you'll be shut down before you can even start.

2. Approaching From the Side

The most effective and non-threatening way to approach the target is from the side. She can see you coming in her peripheral vision or when she turns her head, but as it's not a direct assault, so you're not seen as a threat. If she doesn't want you to approach her, she may turn her back immediately, avoiding the confrontation, but without embarrassing you in public. It's her friendly way to say, "Don't talk to me!" If she accepts your advance, she will either turn her side towards you or invitingly turn her body towards you. The signal may be discreet and difficult to notice and follow, but any move in your direction is a positive signal.

3. The Approach from the Rear

Nobody likes to be caught with their guard down. You should never be approaching a target from behind at any time. This not only shows a lack of trustworthiness on your side, but is actually a sneak attack and has the same impact as stabbing the target in the back. Approaching from the rear exploits the weakness of the target and, as a result, she will respond by putting her defenses up immediately. Every effort on your part to engage in conversation would lead to disaster.

The only time you'll ever approach someone from behind is when you've got your back to the target, too. This scenario doesn't happen so frequently, but when it does, take advantage of it. Imagine that you're in a party with your mates and it happens that the target is behind you, she is a part of another group. In order to work, she has to be within earshot. You both have your backs to each other. If you were to step around her party to better approach her, you would look like a fool and you should not turn around and touch her on the shoulder, either.

What you do is turn your head while you hold your feet in place, so you can engage in conversation. And if you approach her from behind, your back is always exposed, rendering you just as vulnerable. She won't see you as a threat, and will be open to your advances. You should turn around once you have begun the initial conversation.

If you can, try to approach her from the right hand side. You may not be able to always do that. If there's a chance, then take it but don't push it. Always approach from the right, unless approaching from that direction reveals your intentions to the target and makes you look like a fool. In this case, a direct approach is better. Remember: approaching her and being shut down is better than not trying.

Leveling

You want to start building attraction immediately after making your approach, but for that to happen you need to be on her level. By this I mean that you are standing while she is standing, too. That way you are both at the same height. If she sits, then you're alone. If she's sitting and you're standing, you're going to look intimidating and she's going to try to retreat from your presence because it feels like a threat. The opposite is also true; if she's standing and you're seated, she'll feel superior over you, taking away the Alpha Male image you've created since you came into the room.

Proper leveling means being able to move, and moving in a comfortable way. If you approach an all-girls' table and they're all sitting down, then make your move. Introduce yourself and sit down in a chair that's open. If there is no chair, squat down, or tell a person, preferably the target, to scoot over and make room for you. Sharing a chair shows trust on your part and it helps you to crack the contact barrier in a matter of seconds. Leveling is about not hesitating. Never ask if you can take a seat or join the party. That gives them an opportunity to refuse your company and it makes you look vulnerable when you try to get their approval. You are the Alpha Male, and they're lucky to be there with you. Take your proper seat and join the party. Now that you're at the right point, the games will start. We are already conscious at this point that the target is drawn to us. We saw that in the initial touch, eye contact, and body language. Now we have to keep on developing this attraction. We have to let the target know that we are interested in her from the start. We do this by positioning ourselves and our body appropriately to demonstrate that interest. Open your body to hers, keep your legs open, keep your arms by your side, and show transparency. This is not the time to be closed off.

She will also send out signals during your interaction. We've talked about some of these signals before. She sends out signals with her eyes to tell you she's interested. She sends out signals to express interest with a smile. Some of those signals are going to be good and some are going to be bad. Let's call them "yes signals," and "no signals." "Yes signals" will be signals that you send or receive from a woman who says, "I want you, come get me, I'm interested in you, let me move forward, take me home." "No signals" are the ones you don't want to see. These signals mean that you need to correct the situation or change the situation in your favor. "No signals" can be stuff that means, "I'm not interested, you just turned me off, you said the wrong thing." Don't worry about a "no signal," however. We are going to discuss that in the next chapter.

We have already addressed some of the signs to watch out for when it comes to eye contact. Now let's take a look at some of the other ways a woman uses body language to send out signals.

Positive Body Language Women Use

Lips

The second most visible signal is coming from the lips. Lips can say many things without words. Lipstick is used by women to call attention to their mouths and to exaggerate the messages they send. Looking at your mouth continuously is a sign she wants to kiss you.

Parted Lips

Lips which are slightly separated are at the first stage of speaking, which means the person would like to speak to you. Most times, when I'm talking to a woman, I'll be looking at her with my lips ever so slightly parted. For one, it causes my lips to appear a little fuller, and thus more desirable. I'm subconsciously hoping she'll take this as a "yes signal" I'm giving her, that I want to touch her. It will at least draw her concentration to my lips and make her think about them; the next place her mind goes is a kiss, logically.

Licking the Lips

Licking the lips is a deliberate signal signaling desire. It is sexually appealing and is used either during foreplay or as a short tease. Refer back to the eye contact section of the book and hold her gaze. If you are making eye contact, your eyes should slightly narrow when holding her attention. Around the same time, brush your lips with your tongue as if to wet them. Again, don't over-lick them. Just rub your upper lip with your tongue. It's a mannerism that is used to work on her subconscious sexual desires. A woman often does the same thing, wetting her lips while maintaining eye contact. This just further strengthens the fact that she's interested in you and that you should approach her.

Smiling

Smiling means happiness or acceptance. A full smile involves the entire face as well as the eyes. When only the lips are involved, the smile will most likely look forced. Even though she initially liked you, she might change their minds in the end. Think about going into an elevator and making eye contact with another person standing there. You force a smile, and so do they, but you're still a little uncomfortable. However, you should view a forced smile as an invitation to approach while in a social environment.

Laughing

Laughter is a smile which shows even more joy or approval. People can laugh with the people they like and they like you if they laugh at all of your dumb jokes. Being funny is considered to be non-threatening or harmless, and helps break down barriers.

The Face

The face comprises thousands of tiny muscles that are used in unison to build hundreds of expressions and convey emotions of any kind.

Head Tilt

Tilting the head to the left or right at a forty-five degree angle shows interest in you or what you are saying at the moment. When your head is turned, the carotid artery at the side of the neck is exposed; this is a symbol of submission and weakness.

Blushing

A red face may mean the target is hot as the blood comes to the surface. This can happen when feeling humiliation or intense tension in a social environment. For example, when a woman gets excited and shows enthusiasm, her face and/or neck turns red. Everyone will blush in various ways. Some people blush in different circumstances as well. If she is having an orgasm, a woman's face goes red. On a physiological level, triggering a blush is the same phenomenon that happens during sex as when in a social environment. Take her blushing as a token of her interest in you.

Flipping Hair

Flipping hair throws the hair backwards and draws attention. She says, "Oh, guys, you wouldn't want to brush my lovely, long hair!" Long hair can be used as a curtain that covers the eyes to make a person feel more confident in social situations. Flipping hair reveals the face and opens the doors for contact. A woman's hair does more for her than simply enhance her appearance. She can use it as a shield, attract your attention to it or give you signals. All it takes is a little hair-flip.

Stroking Hair

Touching hair is a preening gesture, to ensure that everything is in order and to attract a potential mate. When a woman is stroking her hair, she is making sure that she looks her best. It's also a flirtatious gesture, allowing an attractive person to play with their hair. She will continue to do it and flirt and tell you while you're engaged in conversation, "Look at me, don't you like me, look how pretty I am." She does this as a way to make you interested in her.

Revealing The Neck

This is a crucial move that has several interpretations. A woman with long hair will brush her hair back to expose her face. It is a preening motion that helps the target fix her hair and set it up to look more desirable, as discussed above. This gesture is going to attract attention to herself and her hair and encourage you to touch her. Girls use this gesture as a way to break a barrier. She is encouraging you to start contact with her by getting it out of the way. It is, eventually, a submissive move. When two animals battle, the weaker animal in the animal kingdom will submit defeat by lying down and giving their adversary their face. It's their way of saying, you're ruling over me.

Women are also mindful of their appearance. They test themselves to show their best appearance when they see the object of their desire. In order to attract a potential partner, we always want to show ourselves in the best possible light. A woman will do everything humanly possible to catch your attention, from constantly checking her appearance, to sitting in a flattering place.

Primping

Women also try to attract the people they want by looking their best. If women see a guy that they find sexy, they are going to primp themselves and make sure they look their best and grab his attention. Signs of primping include fixing her hair, checking her makeup, changing her clothes for better fitting ones, and sitting up. You know that the target is interested in you based on what she does as she walks away. Let's say you two hit it off and talk for about thirty minutes. She makes an excuse to use the bathroom. Pay attention to what she does when she gets up. If she's interested in you, she'll run her hands down her clothes backwards. The explanation for this is that she wants to present you with the best possible angle; she wants to show off that "butt" in the most desirable way.

Seated Position

The most attractive sign a woman can send is to sit with one leg crossed over the other. This movement makes the legs look really well toned. A hand on the thigh finishes the setup and it is certainly a call for attention. The body has its own consciousness. Our subconscious emotions are constantly seen in our body language. There are many examples of that, which we have already discussed. We use different parts of the body to show us the way we wish to go. That can be achieved with any part of the body. No matter how hard we try to hide our real intentions, inevitably, the truth comes out.

Pointers

One thing to look for is the way a woman crosses her legs. Crossing her legs toward you is a cue to say yes. She's curious and, most importantly, she needs you to step it up a notch on the flirting front. If she turns her legs towards you and makes contact with you and/or maintains contact with you, this is even better.

Touching Herself

She touches a part of her body and draws attention to herself. This makes the Man think about doing the same. Touching her neck, chest or legs will steer your attention to what she believes is the most attractive part of her body. This is a flirtatious and highly suggestive gesture. Stroking her body in order to bring your attention to it is an even louder signal.

Pointing the Elbow

We prefer to point to people and stuff we are in some way interested in. The most obvious way is with your eyes. The elbow is one of these subtler subconscious ways of pointing at people we are interested in. The most common way of doing this is for a woman to place her hand on her hip and point her elbow in your direction.

Pointing the Foot

The foot of the target shows you where her interest lies. Look around you for women pointing in your direction. They're going to talk to you. Look for a target that talks to a guy you can tell she doesn't care about. Rather than being meek, she'll move her feet away from the guy in the direction she wants to go. That is her "no signal" saying, "I want to walk away from you, quit distracting me."

Pointing Out the Pelvis

The direction of the hips is along the same line. It is more obvious than the feet, and the two together are a sure sign that the target is open to your advances. When a woman aims her pelvis your way, it means that she is open to your advances. You see this a lot in couples. Look at how they kiss. If they are happy, then their hips will be in line and touching when they embrace. A couple that hasn't had sex before, or isn't prepared for sex, will either turn their hips to stop being in a straight line, or lean forward, holding their hips away from each other, showing that they're not ready for sex.

Thrusting the Chest

Puffing up your chest attracts attention. People are likely to be attracted by the sight of breasts. As women push out their breasts, they invite you to come and take a closer look. This position is accentuated by wearing high heels, which bends the spine and forces out the chest and buttocks. The target may also turn sideways or at a forty-five degree angle, exaggerating the signal and showing their breasts' curve in a more flattering position. She can even position herself to produce more cleavage; another way to draw your attention to her most attractive characteristic. She does all of that subconsciously. These signals are designed to attract and turn the interest of the male in the female.

Thrusting the Hips

This is a suggestive move to drive hips forward. It is difficult to force the hips forward without losing balance, so this step is done by reclining against a wall or chair. It forces the breasts out, and draws more attention to both areas.

Displays

A woman who is brazen or confident is going to show the object of her desire precisely what he can have if he wants to make a move and speak to her. She will expose parts of her body in sexy and exciting ways, putting on a personal display, saying, "This could be all yours!"

Showing The Arm

Once a woman shows skin on her arm, she says," I'd like to show you something." It's like showing her face to you.

Opening Her Legs

Women are trained to be ladylike, and so they are taught to sit closed or crossed legged with their hands on her thighs. If the target intentionally or subconsciously opens her legs to you, she is sending an open invitation. The target will go to great lengths when wearing a skirt to keep her legs closed to avoid public humiliation. The type of signal the target sends when she opens her legs to you while wearing a skirt should not be questioned.

Rejection Signals You Should Look For

Rejection is a part of life, so you have to be confident in managing it. The best way we can respond to rejection is by being able to recognize signs of rejection and turn the attraction back in our favor. There comes a particular time when we have to understand that the target is simply not drawn to us regardless of what we do. It can occur every time, but you should depart on your own terms rather than let her turn her back on you and humiliate you publicly.

The Face

The face shows rejection the easiest way. When women do not want to speak to us, they show their intention to not communicate with us in many ways:

- Averting the eyes, so as not to make eye contact.
- Head turning.
- Twisting the body while keeping feet rooted.
- Twisting the body further while pushing one foot in a different direction.
- Turning at an angle, so both feet move in a different direction.
- Completely turning around so their back is to you.

Each of these is an escalating warning sign. Even turning at a slight angle sends out a simple message, "I don't want to talk to you." Turning around absolutely sends out the loudest possible warning, short of telling you, "Go away!" So how are you supposed to beat this? Well, when you note that she moves away gradually, this should be a simple signal to adjust your approach. If what you're doing isn't working right now and you keep it up, it will continue to fail. Change the topic of your conversation, go into a routine, or just excuse yourself and regroup while you're still in good shape and try again at a later date.

Crossed Arms

Crossing the arms indicates disagreement with you or what is being said at the moment. Crossed arms cover the waist, and keep your line of vision away from her breasts. This can also be used as an obstacle and a defense mechanism. She is saying "I won't let you in" by crossing her arms. Before communicating effectively with the target, you need to get her to lower her defensive guard. It can be as easy as handing her something to hold on to, like your drink when adjusting your shirt or putting your hand up for a high five. You should make her aware of it. Tell her you've read in a body language study that when a person crosses their arms, they put up a defensive front. If everything else fails, go into the routine of palm reading. Take hold of her hand and tell her that you have a psychic intuition and want to tell her about it.

Double Crossed Legs

A woman sits ninety-five per cent of the time with her legs crossed; that's natural. In this case, however, we're talking about crossing hands over knees. This posture shows dissatisfaction and a reluctance to open up. To combat this, simply make the target stand up. Ask her to show her shoes to you. Say, "May I see your shoes?" If she puts her foot back down, she will be more responsive and more receptive to your advances. If her legs are not crossed in your direction, that's also a "no sign". She is either no longer drawn to you or you have done something to put her off.

CHAPTER FOURTEEN

VOICE, GESTURES & POSTURE

WE CAN INFER many things from someone's voice: age, sex, educational history, and even attractiveness. Vocal traits help us to determine the character and temperament of an individual.

Think about how many times you have said something like, "She sounds good to me," or "I like how that sounds?"

All you do is to determine if you like or hate others or believe in them or trust them based on the sound of their voices. The nonverbal features of speech form the basis of paralinguistic research and include speed, sound, pitch, voice strength, speaking rate, accent, and stress.

The Importance Of Your Voice

Your voice's volume should not be too high or too low to encourage confidence. Trust is a bidirectional operation. Trusting others is really hard when you know they mistrust you. Being loud gives the impression of a desire to dominate, which can hinder the growth of mutual trust. A voice that is too soft gives the appearance of diffidence or submissiveness, which also impedes the development of a relationship based on equality.

Vocal tone should be neither harsh nor smooth. Harshness feels like an attack to your audience and repels them. Too much smoothness will make them believe they have the wool pulled over their eyes and make them suspicious.

You do have to sound relatively self-assured. It's hard to trust someone who doesn't sound confident in themselves.

Gestures

A gesture is a specific movement of the body which strengthens a verbal message or conveys a particular thought or emotion. Although movements may be made with the head, shoulders, or even the legs and feet, the majority of them are made with the hands and arms.

When you speak, your hands can be great communication devices. But many novice speakers are unsure about what to do with their hands. Some try to put them in their pockets or behind their backs to keep them out of the way. Others unwittingly alleviate nervous anxiety by making distracting and uncomfortable gestures. Waving arms and hands around is a sign of nervousness.

A speaker's movements can give an audience a very specific idea about the speaker. Native Americans invented a sign language that allowed people to converse with each other regardless of them speaking entirely different spoken languages. Sign language also allows deaf people to communicate without speaking.

In communication, the use of gestures varies from society to society. In certain cultures, such as those in Southern Europe and the Middle East, people freely and expressively use their hands when they speak. In other cultures, gestures are used less often and often in a subtler fashion.

The basic gesture that we make, and the meaning that we add to it are products of our cultural education. Just as cultures diverge, so do the perceived meaning of movements. For example, nodding one's head up and down signifies approval or assent in Western cultures but this gesture means the exact opposite in some parts of India. In certain parts of the world, a common gesture used in the United States (making a circle with the thumb and forefinger implying approval) is considered an insult and obscenity.

To be successful, the speaker's movements must be purposeful, even if they are unintentionally performed. They've got to be open to the public, to the audience. Movements also need to correlate with the speaker's words and their meaning.

Why Gestures?

Every good orator uses gestures. Why? Gestures are, perhaps, the most evocative type of nonverbal communication a speaker may employ. No other kind of physical activity will enhance your speech as much as gestures. They:

- Clarify your phrases and promote them. Gestures strengthen the public's appreciation of your verbal message.
- Dramatize your feelings. Gestures help paint vivid images in the minds of your listeners along with what you say.
- Offer the spoken word accent and vitality. Gestures more clearly express your thoughts and attitudes than what you say.
- Help to relieve nervous stress. Purposeful movements provide a good outlet for nervous energy.
- Act as visual aids. Gestures enhance the attentiveness and retention of viewers.
- Encourage civic engagement. Gestures help you identify the answer your listeners are looking for. Gestures are extremely clear. If you address a large number of people, movements provide visual support because not the whole audience can see your eyes.

Types of Gestures

Given the large number of movements which qualify as gestures, all gestures can be grouped into one of the following main classes. Descriptive gestures, which explain or reinforce a verbal message, help the audience understand similarities and contrasts, and imagine the scale, form, movement, position, feature, and object count.

Emphatic expressions, which underline what people are doing, show commitment and eagerness. A clenched fist, for example, indicates strong feelings, such as rage or determination.

Suggestive movements are representations of feelings and ideas and help a speaker create a desired mood and articulate a given thought. An open palm implies giving or receiving an idea, typically, while a shoulder shrug indicates confusion, perplexity, or irony.

Prompting movements are used to assist the audience in evoking a desired response. When you want listeners to lift their hands, cheer, or perform any particular action, doing it yourself as an example can improve the audience's response.

Gesturing above shoulder level indicates physical height, strength, or emotional exultation. Gesturing below shoulder level suggests disapproval, apathy, or condemnation. Gesturing at shoulder level indicates calmness or serenity.

The movements most commonly used include an open palm extended outwards towards the crowd. The meaning of this gesture depends on the palm's location. Keeping the palm upwards means giving or receiving, although sometimes this gesture is used as an involuntary action, with no specific meaning. A downward held palm may convey restraint, secrecy, completion, or stability. A hand held out toward the crowd indicates refusing, repulsion, rejection, or abhorrence. When the palm is placed perpendicular to the body of the speaker, it appears to indicate distance, space or time constraints, parallels, or contrasts.

How To Gesture Effectively

Gestures represent the individual personality of each speaker. What's right for one speaker probably won't work for another.

Nevertheless, the following six rules apply to almost anyone trying to become a creative, successful speaker.

1. React to What You Think, Feel, and Say.

When you give a speech, you naturally express yourself with gestures. Each of us has a natural impulse to punctuate and reinforce our words with expressions, no matter what our personality or cultural background may be. The trick is not to inhibit the instinct by retreating behind a mask of impassivity, which can only generate stress. At the same time, don't imitate motions from a book or from another person. Stay true to yourself and be spontaneous. If you force artificial movements on your natural style, it will be seen by your audience and branded as fake. Of course some people are animated while others are more relaxed. If you use your hands freely when conversing informally, use them freely when giving a speech. If you're a quiet, low-key person by nature, don't change your personality just to match circumstances.

2. Establish the Gesturing Conditions, Not the Gesture.

Your actions should be the natural outcome of your own particular feelings and thoughts. They will come naturally from your attitude toward the message you are delivering.

When you talk, the way you hold your body expresses its own visual signal to an audience. More than anything, it represents your mindset, telling your listeners if you are comfortable, alert, and in command of yourself and the situation in which you are. There are three main types of posture:

- Standing
- Sitting
- Lying down

Obviously, there are many variants of these, and we will only concern ourselves with the first two here. You can read a lot about someone's state of mind based on the different positions of their arms and legs, and the different angles at which they carry their body.

Most people have preferred postures. These are said to mirror a person's state of mind. People who have gone through extended periods of depression, for example, may still maintain a hunched or stooping posture even years after healing and resuming normal lives. Those who experienced bullying or who were forced as children to stand up for themselves, can exhibit a curved, protective posture. Therefore, by becoming aware of your posture, we may be able to change the way we carry ourselves, thus improving our ability to maintain constructive and communicative ties with others.

Your Posture Reveals Your Mood

You can't tell who someone is just by watching their posture, but you can definitely gage their general state of mind—whether they are happy, sad, relaxed, nervous, dominant, or submissive. These are the "signatures" that define our presence and, for this reason, the evaluation of posture is useful in determining the most effective way to approach someone else. Unlike facial expressions, where a greater degree of proximity is necessary, posture also has the advantage that it can be seen accurately from some distance. For instance, positive attitudes towards others tend to be accompanied by leaning forward, especially when sitting down. Leaning backwards indicates pessimistic or aggressive behaviors. Inaccessibility, indifference, or disdain are signaled by the arms crossed across the chest. Keeping them relaxed by your side generally shows responsiveness and a willingness to communicate.

Insiders & Outsiders

As people speak in groups, those who are really in the "in crowd" frequently show very different postural behaviors from those who are not. Outsiders usually stand with their weight on one foot, while insiders lean a little forward with their head turned forward. An effective talk posture has other benefits for a speaker. It lets you breathe correctly and effectively projects your voice. It also offers a strong starting point to push the body in any direction or movement from there. Making you feel both alert and relaxed helps to lower nervous anxiety and reduce frequent, distracting movements.

What is the right posture when speaking? Ask someone else to read the next two paragraphs aloud while you follow the instructions: Stand straight but not rigid, with your feet about six to twelve inches apart and one slightly ahead of each other. Divide your weight evenly on the balls of your feet. Only lean a little forward. You should keep your knees straight but not closed. Relax the shoulders but don't let them slip. Hold the chest up and the stomach down. The head and chin should be high but not uncomfortably so. Let your arms hang naturally from your shoulders and keep your fingers curled slightly.

Now, take deep and full breaths. Do you feel relaxed? Your disposition should be alert but not formal, relaxed but not too much. If you don't find this position comfortable for you, try repositioning your feet slightly until your body feels balanced.

Do not hold the same position over the entire presentation. When you move from one location to another, be sure to balance your body until the movement is over.

Your Posture Reveals Your Body Image

Your posture reflects your mood. The more confident you feel, the more upright and mobile you appear. The less optimistic you feel, the seemingly less open and accommodating you present yourself. Whether you are in the eye of the public or just a member of the public, self-presentation matters. Actors and leaders undergo instruction to introduce themselves to their respective audiences effectively. But the distinction between acting and putting on an act is important. At times, excessive postures and movements work for the sake of clarification or dramatic emphasis. But you have to be credible. Failure to do so will give a negative impression and will not make up for a bad performance by any amount of exaggeration.

A dramatic example of this is drunken behavior. When someone behaves like a drunk, it gives the impression of being out of control even if the person believes they are in control of themselves. The exaggeration of normal postures and movements, while funny at first, quickly becomes humiliating as it escalates. That's because what we're seeing challenges our perceptions of what we find natural. The lurching gait, flailing arms, and loss of balance of a drunk person contrast with the self-controlled body image of a sober person.

Trust is visual. The girl who walks down the road staring at the ground with her arms tightly wrapped around her body indicates she feels defensive and desires to remain unseen. Her subtly bent stance and closed body language offer a glimpse into her low self-esteem. In contrast, women are constantly bombarded with promotional photographs showing smiling girls with upright postures and relaxed expressions, implying that this is the role model that confident women should aspire to become.

The truth is that the way we imagine ourselves shows how we feel about ourselves. Some people who are said to have "presence" exude confidence (even if it is an act) and show less changes in attitude and gestures than most of us do. This quiet calm is often synonymous with rank and respect, as if they had that certain "je ne sais quoi," the elusive element that distinguishes between being special and being ordinary.

There are other posture giveaways:

- Folded arms suggest isolation, defensiveness, self-protection, and closure. Self-wrapping is particularly prevalent among women.
- Hunched shoulders, where the shoulders appear to hunch up and the palms of the hands face outward, suggest confusion, perceived danger, impotence, and inadequacy. The akimbo arms where you stand hands-on-hips with elbows turned is a superior stance, suggesting superiority. It is often used, for example, in corporate settings, in the presence of individuals considered to be of a lower status. Walking tall gives a feeling of uprightness, integrity and faith in oneself. It is a way of showing you're feeling good about yourself and you're not afraid.
- When the head is held by the index finger pointing over the cheek on one side shows positive values.
- When the foot of one leg lies on the knee of the other with the hands clasped behind the neck and the elbows out indicates dominance. Men do this often to create an impression of trust and authority. Postural conflict often occurs when people intentionally take different roles from the ones others assume they have. This typically happens to mark the limits of contact, or

place space between one person and another. The arms and legs are placed in this way to indicate intruders are not welcome.

- Posture related to hands in pockets, folding arms, and crossing legs at the same time as another person performs these actions suggests a high degree of connection.

CHAPTER FIFTEEN

NEVER UNDERESTIMATE THE IMPORTANCE OF BODY LANGUAGE

FIRST OF ALL, what do we mean by body language? The term refers to various forms of non-verbal communication in which a person, through their physical behavior, can reveal clues as to some unspoken intentions or feelings. Such behaviors may include the general body posture, gestures, facial expressions, and pupil movement. Because body language is usually made up of unconscious reflexes and it is difficult to control, it can provide accurate information about a person's attitude or state of mind. For example, by paying attention to someone's body language, you should be able to know what they're feeling, whether it is arousal, aggression, attentiveness, boredom, or a comfortable state, like enjoyment and fun.

In communication, body language is as critical as speaking, listening, reading, and writing. Nevertheless, it may be argued that it is more relevant because less than 10 percent of what we convey to others is in the form of words. It is only fairly recently that research has centered on language, behavioral, and non-verbal elements. We learn more about human communication today than at any point in our history, thanks to groundbreaking research in multiple fields, from zoology to paralinguistics. Work in programming for chronemics, haptics, kinesics, proxemics, and neurolinguistics has opened our eyes to the vibrant world of signals and indications in which clues, motivations, thoughts, emotions, and perceptions are communicated through subtle gestures, signs, and meaningful movements.

We use body language to express unspoken feelings, and we believe that others can understand our meaning. Much of this happens on a subconscious stage and we might not even be aware that our facial gestures, hand motions, winks, blinks, smiles, and sighs send out messages of approval, criticism, desire or dislike. The argument is that for sense to be understood by others, language does not need to be in the form of words. The manner in which you use your body is like pointing. Without it, it lacks meaning and focus.

It is only when we study our body language more closely that we begin to understand what it is that makes us tick. Things that we have forgotten unexpectedly become apparent in the course of our busy lives. A smile, an eyebrow lift, and a focused gaze take on new meaning when the face is used as the carrier of unspoken thoughts, unstated behaviors, and hidden passions. A bent head, arms folded, and legs crossed tell us whether we succeed or fail to persuade. The way we stand, protecting our personal space or allowing ourselves to be touched, sends a message about how comfortable we feel, and our willingness to communicate with other people.

In the pickup game and in everyday life body language is important. Only 10% of what you're saying comes across in your words, the rest is body language. What you are saying is directly tied to your body language. When you show positive body language, the conversation is also likely to be positive. You can't pair negative body language with nice words without coming across as ungenuine. Rather than sounding bland or rehearsed, the conversation will flow when words and body language match. This will also make conversations more fluid.

Whenever I walk somewhere, I walk purposefully. I have an air of confidence and a touch of cockiness. I walk like I'm someone else. Some would say that I am walking around like I think that I am tougher than anybody else. I walk the same way whether I'm heading into a club or my work. I'm walking straight with my head up, my chest out. I smile at people, sometimes I laugh. I have more fun than anyone else. I am walking with a purpose, just like I own the place. When I am in a group, I do the same thing. With a steady gait, I walk tall. All the things I'm doing are sending off signals that I'm comfortable and I'm interesting, I have something to give, I'm having fun, and I'm fun to be around. I walk in, and everyone in the bar wants to make my acquaintance. This is the power of body language!

Let's break some of this down. It is nice to go places with women and to be seen with women. You get other women interested in you. In other words, other women will think, "All those girls are hanging out with that guy, he has to be really cool." When you walk into a bar with an attractive woman, other women will notice you. I like to take it one step further by smiling and linking my arms with my date. On top of that, we joke around and seem to have a great time. So, any girls I may later meet at the bar will likely think, "This guy must be really interesting, he's got girls all over him, they're laughing, he's fun, he's got something to give. I want to see him!"

Some Men who are on their journey to becoming an Alpha Male may be still scared by the competition. They're afraid that if they tell their friends about body language, the competition will be too much. Although that's true to some extent, by being in a cohesive group you'll get better outcomes than if you're on your own. People hang out in communities. Each group has a leader. Whenever we're socializing, there are not only Alpha Males, but also members of each leader's pack. These members of the pack will look to the strongest, most dominating Alpha Male. When hanging out with friends, I make it clear that I am the leader of our group, while they make up my "pack." I use subtle signs of dominance to show outsiders that I am the leader. This makes patrons become aware of my Alpha Male status within the group. I stand when my friends sit. When I talk to them, I might put my hand on their shoulder, or if I tell them a joke, I give them a pat on the back. These are subtle signs of dominance over others.

When I hang out with my friends, I stand approximately one shoulder-length away from them. You want to take space in your party to show you're the Alpha Male. Stand in a relaxed way with your head back and your chest out. Don't place your hands in your pockets. That is a sign of nervousness. Don't hold your drink in front of your face. This makes you look inaccessible to conversation; you just put a barrier up. Take up a reasonable amount of space and send out messages that say, "I'm available and accommodating." Instead of standing pigeon toed, point your toes out slightly. This may seem like a small thing, but it is not. Women notice stuff like this. I like putting out an air of confidence, so I move my hips forward. Depending on what I wear, I lock my thumbs in my belt or pants pockets, and let my hands hang down my legs. This is a relaxed pose that appeals to the erotic subconscious of a woman.

To be an Alpha Male involves a certain look. You don't have to be the best-looking guy, the tallest guy, the fittest guy, or the funniest guy. Your body language needs to send out the right message, however. This message is quite sexual and it helps you become the center of attention without even trying too hard. People around you all want to know what you're about and why you're successful.

Body language is absolutely essential in all areas of your life, not just the realm of dating. Ninety percent of how people interpret you will come not from the words you say, but rather the body language that you use. A simple sentence can have a number of different meanings depending on your body language. In short, it isn't so much about *what* you say as it is about *how* you say it.

Positive body language is key to building confidence. If you find that you struggle to converse, stumbling over your words and coming across as stilted or indecisive, take a second to sit back and imagine how you physically act during conversations. Chances are that you're pretty awkward, and for a simple reason: you care *too much*. While it's always good to be visibly invested in an interaction, you never want to seem overcommitted. It makes you look clingy, desperate, and sometimes even a little scary--in a creepy, stalker-like way, not an impressively intimidating one.

One place to start is your style of walking. A straight back, prominent chest, and high head all exhibit confidence, signaling that you're comfortable in your environment, and that you're having fun. This will then subconsciously spur people to want to approach you, so that they can join in on that fun. It might feel impossible to present yourself as extremely confident and calm, especially if you feel the opposite way on the inside. Just remember that nobody can read your mind. All anyone has to work with is the image that you present to them--make it a good one!

It's always a huge bonus if you're accompanied by women, whether they be partners, friends, or even family. Women tend to be cautious around Men they don't know, and with good reason--they have no way of knowing whether any given stranger has violent or predatory intentions. If you surround yourself with women, you're showing off the fact that you're trustworthy, and that women enjoy spending time with you. You can further emphasize this by making an effort to smile, and by expressing physical closeness through gestures like hand-holding and arm-linking. Last but not least, make sure you're having a good time with your female companions! If women see other women having fun, they automatically imagine themselves in the position of your acquaintances. They'll want to get to know you in the hopes that they'll also be able to have a great time.

When a guy is working towards becoming an Alpha Male, he sometimes feels defensive of the tricks that he's learned. This is natural instinct; an alpha, by definition, is someone who stands out from the pack, and it makes sense to worry that you'll blend in with your friends if they start to learn your techniques. Consider, however, that there are different levels of alpha. Your friends' group may consist mostly or entirely of Men who present themselves as Alpha Males, but that doesn't mean that you're all equal. As a matter of fact, being surrounded by other alphas can serve as an excellent opportunity to show off just how superior you really are. Your whole pack may be confident, attractive, and powerful, and yet *you* are the leader among them. How impressive is that?

There are a few basic physical gestures that can serve to show that you rank higher than your friends. Try standing up while everyone else is sitting down, or patting them on the shoulder when the moment is appropriate. Both of these put you in a position that's physically higher than your counterpart, signaling that you're the dominant one in the interaction. Many people make the mistake of assuming that the act of being alpha is solely a competition, in which every player should be wary and cutthroat, but the opposite is actually true: being alpha is about loving, respecting, and protecting your pack. Strong male-male relationships are at the core of any true alpha's lifestyle.

There are some other strategies that you can also use to establish your place at the top of the food chain, so to speak. Keep your feet apart with your toes pointed outward, at about the width of your shoulders; don't be afraid to take up space. Your hands should stay out of your pockets, preferably with their thumbs hooked around your belt loops. Don't cling to your drink, either. All of these actions make you look insecure and closed-off--both being characteristics that women find repulsive. You want to be exposed, and to be visibly comfortable in that exposure. An alpha has nothing to worry about; nobody is going to challenge him--and, if someone is foolish enough to do so, he'll have no problem putting them in their place.

You can further supplement your posture by adding small indicators of your sexual availability. Obviously, you don't want to be shoving your crotch in women's faces--if you're *overly* sexual, you'll seem both crude and desperate. Subtlety is key here. Keep your hands down by your legs, push your hips forward slightly, and tilt your fingertips in the direction of your crotch. This will work on a subliminal level. Instead of thinking, "God, that guy's so horny and eager for sex; he must not have gotten laid in a long time," women will find themselves seeing you in an erotic light without even knowing why. They'll be the ones who are eager to come on to you, rather than the other way around.

Remember that being an Alpha Male is all about sending a message that you're the right man for women to be pursuing sexually. No matter whether you're short, average-looking, overweight, or frankly just charmless--or, for that matter, all of the above--you can and will be able to establish an alpha status by utilizing body language. It's all about sending a message that triggers women's mating instincts. You absolutely don't want them to know how hard you're *trying*. Let your body language express that there's nothing fraudulent about your identity. You don't just want to be an Alpha Male; you already are one.

A Better Understanding of Body Language

This universal language is physical communication between humans (and between humans and animals). This is an explanation that can easily be understood by everyone. Unlike TV, there's no need for a decoder to put words on what you unconsciously just know. This natural skill will be of great help to you.

But most guys have no idea what's going on with their body at all. They do not even know that the way they walk or the way they touch people shows a great deal about them. It's the root of their problem with dating. Their failures have nothing to do with the fact that they are small, fat, or they have a big nose. Good body language can get over any small defects. We all have different bodies and see our own issues. What actually matters is what we do with our bodies. The body of an Alpha Male is under his control. You have to be able to comprehend that if you don't have an awareness of your body, it will be very difficult for you to succeed in any field, not just dating.

Your Sensual Acuity (Sensitivity Degree)

Sensual acuity is the ability to understand what's happening in other people's bodies, not just yours. This chapter should help you develop your sensual acuity because you need to know how to better communicate, which is that you need to enhance your interpersonal skills.

Also, you have to keep yourself under control. How to take control of your body, however?

Begin by settling into your chair. Once you're comfortable, close your eyes and focus on your breathing. Take one deep breath, in and out. Then repeat this. Become aware of how your breath fills your whole body, all the way down to your feet. Let all of the energy seep out of you until you're completely relaxed.

Next, focus on each part of your body, starting from your toes. Make a conscious effort to *feel* the energy flowing through you: up your legs, along your buttocks, then to your lower back, stomach, arms, shoulders, neck, and face. Take your time--it's imperative that you don't rush yourself. If physical stimulation helps, you can gently massage each body part as you direct your focus towards it. Once you've worked through every inch, open your eyes and reorient yourself to your surroundings. You should feel much more comfortable and alert.

Practice doing this every time you head to a club or go out on a date. You can make incredible progress by staying in contact with your body all day and all night long.

Spatial Awareness

You need to get spatial awareness as well. That is, you need to know your personal space, and learn how to blend in. The personal space of most people is small and this is a bad thing. When your personal space is tiny, it is psychologically very difficult to interact with someone. Personal space is like a social bubble that stands around you. It is a three-dimensional bubble, moving between left and right, forward and rear, top and bottom. The next step is to learn how to feel the size of this bubble and use Alpha Male postures to make it grow. Your body language can create a massive difference in how people are reacting to you. You will learn how to increase your presence and your relationship with space throughout this book. You're actually going to get very different feedback from women once you increase your spatial awareness.

The Mental and Physical Process of Body Language

Before language developed, body language was the way to understand what others are trying to convey. Body language is still the primary means of communication nowadays. It is instinctive and is the easiest way of speaking to women's primal, instinctive mind without interference. This goes beyond the rational mind. Our bodies ' shape and size and the way we present ourselves exert considerable influence on how others respond to us. Just think about the power of the fashion and the fashion industry to realize how obsessed with our looks we are. What's more, we assume we're definitely in charge of how we look. There's no denying we go into a lot of trouble to make ourselves presentable to the world. But why do we do this and what does body language have to do with our looks?

Creating an Impression

As we have already seen, our initial contact with other people is by looking at their bodies. Before we even make eye contact, we look at their bodies. The first things we note are the clothes they wear, their body shape, and what they look like. In most cultures, clothing adorns, wraps, covers, and advertises our bodies and has a significant value in communication. They show our self-consciousness, temperament, wealth, status, and job. Through the way we dress, we define our age, gender, individuality, or sameness. You can tell a lot about someone by looking at their choice of clothing and how they wear it. For instance, introverted people tend to choose quieter or more muted colors, whereas extroverts choose brighter and more contrasting colors. Things like jewelry and other items people wear can also tell us a lot about their personalities.

But there's always the desire to look good. Generally speaking, feeling good means looking good. This is why we are putting ourselves under pressure to find clothes that complement our body shape. I'm sure you've heard suggestions about wearing darker shades for pants and lighter ones for tops. Similarly, you've probably been told to wear vertical stripes rather than horizontal ones to make yourself look slimmer. The point is that you feel more self-confident and create a better impression if you can hide the parts of your body that you're uncomfortable with.

Consequently, appearance provides useful hints to what people are like. Sales executives and people in the media take utmost care about their looks because they know that appearances matter. However, make sure that you don't overdo your clothes and fashion statements. Looking good is easy but if you go overboard with your choice of clothes or grooming, it may have the opposite effect than what you're trying to achieve and make you look fake. For example, studies have shown that students are more likely to consider what a teacher says if the latter is dressed in a traditional way, rather than a casual one. Even juries judge people on their looks. Well-dressed, attractive women tend to receive lighter sentences when their offense has something to do with their looks, such as fraud, for example.

Body Confidence

If you don't feel good about your body you run the risk of disclosing this to others nonverbally. Having a good physique helps and there's no question that self-confidence emanates from a sense of attractiveness to others. However, being over-weight, for example, shouldn't make you feel bad about yourself. What matters is that you are comfortable inside your skin; that you like yourself just the way you are.

Changing your appearance is easier than changing your body type, but with growing focus on health and fitness, losing weight and dieting, both Men and women go to great lengths to' stay fit. In an age when body consciousness dominates the advertising media, we are forced to examine more than ever our shape, size, and appearances. We are bombarded by images of perfection. Women are particularly subjected to this. Look in any women's magazine and you'll see that they are told all the time what they should look like. This has the effect of making people compare themselves to ideals of beauty all the time. If your hair, skin, teeth, and even your choice of personal hygiene products don't reflect what's in, you're made to feel like there's something wrong with you. Never mind the fact that these ideals of beauty are photoshopped to look perfect in a way that no actual person could. They are powerful because they are pushed by the media.

Going to such lengths to change your body's shape and size is all about meeting the expectations of other people and getting them to respect you more. For example, people who lose weight also report an increase in self-confidence, a greater sense of well-being, and an improvement in their personal and social lives.

Putting on weight can affect your mind, as well. People who put on weight during middle age can get quite depressed, particularly if they lack the desire to do something about it. On the other hand, people who are thin to the point of anorexia, often have a poor self-image, believing that they are overweight even when they look like they're starving to everyone else. This is because sometimes emotional and psychological factors get in the way you see yourself. Not being able to stop eating or refusing to eat for fear of putting on weight reflects a negative mental state. If you're suffering from an eating disorder, make seeking professional help your utmost priority.

Body Shapes

The fact that we identify Men by their body shape and appearance is taken for granted. For starters, Men tend to be heavier and taller. They have broader shoulders, narrower pelvises, longer limbs, bigger necks, lungs, and cores, stronger skulls and sturdier jaws. Therefore, they are better protected from physical attack. They also have more body hair and deeper voices than women.

On the other hand, women don't grow beards, they have smoother skin, shorter waists, breasts, a wider pelvis (hence rounder buttocks), and more of a hip sway while walking. The pelvis provides a space at the top of the thighs that was designated by Desmond Morris as the "crotch gap," a sensible natural arrangement for their position as child bearers.

You may wonder why it would be important to be able to identify gender differences in this day and age. A lot of the time, they really don't matter. Androgynous Males and feMales have long been depicted in books and movies. A blurring of sex roles is tolerated in the Western world. But while people's sex may not be relevant during their daily experiences, it is important in forming relationships, whether straight or gay, and especially if these relationships will end in procreation.

We are looking for things we find attractive inside each other. This doesn't mean we're not also attracted to things that are on the outside. However, don't set out to find perfection in your desired partner. Research has shown that people who are taller than average are often seen as smarter and more attractive, as are those whose body shape is more muscular and more fit. FeMales whose bodies are slender and curvy, underlining their femininity, are often viewed by Men as attractive and desirable because they unconsciously fit the ideal breeding partner's image.

An Alpha Male's Body Language

Size

An Alpha Male shows dominance at all times, and one way to do this is by making himself seem physically bigger than everyone else. Animal instinct tells us that larger Men are more powerful than small ones, and therefore women find them more sexually attractive. This doesn't mean that you need to be a thickly muscled ape in order to have any success with women; you just need to learn how to appear bigger in your own frame. There are a number of tricks that you can use to accomplish this.

Standing Tall

Picture a typical business meeting. The boss is at the head of the table, while everyone else sits around it. When the boss speaks, he's the only person standing. This indicates that he's the person of authority in the situation.

Now, think of a waiter at a restaurant. Though they'll usually be standing upright, they often bend down to eye level or lean in close to take your order and deliver your food. This signals inferiority and servitude. Waiters tend to play this up in an effort to get more tips, since customers generally appreciate feeling that they're the ones in power.

Ultimately, how tall you seem to be has very little to do with your actual height. Of course, if you're 6'4", there's no hiding that fact--but if you're on the average or smaller side of things, you shouldn't feel hopeless. When you're out with your friends, make an effort to stand while everyone else is sitting. This directs attention towards you and frames you as the alpha of the group. Girls will notice you more easily, and will be curious about what makes you superior to the other guys around you.

Make sure to never slouch, even if you're a taller guy. It makes you look lazy and sloppy. Never be afraid of showing off your full height; girls go crazy for tall Men!

Chest Out

A common gesture among Alpha Males is an outward chest thrust. This shows off their strong pectorals. To women, this screams, "Look! I'm big and powerful, and I'm capable of defending you." To other Men, it signifies dominance and tells them to stay out of the way. You can exaggerate the breadth of your chest by turning your body at an angle and showing off your side profile. You don't need to put in hours at the gym to impress women with your pecs--it's all about the way that you stand. If you assume a powerful pose, women will subconsciously recognize you as strong and protective.

Shoulders Back

You can further accentuate your chest by pulling your shoulders back. Sagging shoulders and poor posture convey laziness and weakness. This is a powerful tip regardless of body type: pulled-back shoulders make smaller Men seem bigger and portly Men appear more comfortable and confident in their skin.

Elbows

Elbows can also be used to make you appear larger than you really are. Think of how male birds fluff up their feathers in order to appear bigger and more powerful. You can do something similar by resting your hands on your hips and bending your elbows outwards.

Shoulder-Width Stance

Holding your feet shoulder-width apart enables you to take up more space, making you look wider. It also exposes your crotch, signaling that you're open and accessible rather than closed-off. This demonstrates a lack of fear, whereas closed legs cover the crotch, suggesting a fear of assault.

Toes Out

When you point your toes out, you're telling those around you that you're approachable and ready to talk. Pointing them inward, on the other hand, shows that you're cutting yourself off, likely because you feel threatened by the environment. You never want to come across as defensive or give the impression that you're hiding behind personal barriers.

Strength

Studies have shown that women's favorite parts of the male body are the hands, the butt, the chest, and the arms, with 40% listing the buttocks as the top choice. In general, women seek an athletic body shape. If you pair this with a tight ass, you can't go wrong.

Male bodies originally evolved to excel at hunting, chasing, fighting, and killing for both food and protection. Though society has come a long way since the time of the hunter-gatherers, women are still attracted to Men who look like they can provide these basic needs. You don't need to be gigantic, but you should be in shape. If you don't already exercise on a regular basis, you need to begin doing so. If you're skinny, start weight training. If you're overweight, running or walking will do the trick. Even if you only exercise for ten or twenty minutes a couple times per week, you'll see major results. Anything is better than nothing!

Wide Shoulders

The combination of wide shoulders and a narrow waist creates a sporty-looking V shape. If this doesn't describe your current body type, don't panic--there's always a way to make the most of what you have in order to put yourself in the most desirable position possible.

Muscular Arms

Muscular arms are one of the key indicators of physical strength. They show women that you can protect them, giving them a sense of security. They also like having something to hold onto while the two of you walk around together. If you already have big arms, wear shirts that will show them off. If you've got beanpole guns, on the other hand, stay away from baggy shirts; they'll make your arms look even smaller. Contrary to what most people think, a tightly fitted shirt will actually make small arms look bigger. You can also go with a long-sleeve button-up.

Tight Butt

A nice butt is every woman's dream. At a football game, you can ask just about any girl what she loves most about the sport, and 90% will say that their favorite part is the uniforms! Women are attracted to tight, muscular butts because they signify better sex performance: a fast thrusting motion will transfer sperm more efficiently. Emphasize your assets by wearing tight-fitting pants that show off the curvature of your butt.

Muscular Legs

Muscular legs symbolize strength and stamina. They allowed our ancestors to run fast and to chase and hunt game over long distances. As in the case of many other characteristics, women have evolved to favor Men who can display these capabilities.

Attitude

The Alpha Male's attitude is what lends them their special swagger: the gaze in their eye, the thunder in their voice, the prominence of their walk. It's the thing on which women can't quite put their finger when they ask themselves, "Why am I so drawn to this guy?" If you have the right attitude, you'll have the right confidence.

Thousand Yard Gaze

The eyes of the Alpha Male are crucial for hunting, attacking, and protection. In modern times, they can be used to lure a girl from across the room, or to stare down any potential rival. As you scan a room, move slowly, doing your best to make eye contact with your target. When it comes to body language, eye contact is critical; it exhibits trust and confidence. No matter how well you present yourself, women will see right through you if you can't establish yourself via eye contact.

When you do meet a woman's eyes, hold her gaze for an extra second. This will help begin to build sexual chemistry. Put on a smile to show her that you're not only confident, but also genuine. You don't need to do this with every cute girl you see, but if you do manage to catch her eye, make sure to maintain contact instead of looking away quickly. If you're shy, this can be difficult, but it gets easier over time. You can start practicing by looking friends, family, and coworkers in the eye while you're talking to them.

Your gaze is also a very powerful weapon among other Males. When you see a potential threat, such as when another guy tries to make a move on your girl, try squinting slightly and staring directly at his forehead. Squinting your eyes helps you to focus on the threat while also lowering your eyebrows, resulting in a threatening look. Staring at someone and then looking down is a sign of defeat. By looking at your target's forehead instead, you're communicating that you don't value him, that you're stronger than him, and that this is your territory. Needless to say, it's very daunting to be on the receiving end of this look.

Chin Up

When you hold your chin up, you keep yourself from looking down and appearing submissive. It allows women to see your facial expression more clearly, showing that you have nothing to hide. You're proud of what you have, and not afraid to show yourself out. Sticking out your chin displays confidence by making yourself vulnerable to attack. Think of it as silently communicating, "Go ahead, take your best shot. You can't knock me out!"

Shaking Hands

In a one-on-one interaction, a basic handshake is enough to decide who's superior. There are three different ways to approach a handshake, each of which sends a different message. If you stick your hand out with the palm up, it indicates submissiveness. Holding your hand sideways will show that you consider yourself to be on equal ground with the other person. By holding your hand out with the palm downwards, however, you're displaying superiority.

If another Man tries to show his own superiority when shaking your hand, you can trick him out of it by stepping forward with your left foot. This will cause him to pull back his hand in order to make room for your advance, turning his palm upright in the process.

Adjusting the Crotch

A Man will adjust his crotch when his junk feels uncomfortable. This is usually done subconsciously, or with very little thought. If you do it on purpose, however, it works as both a sexual display and a presentation of power. To Men, you're saying "My dick is bigger than yours!" To women, you're inviting them to look: "Hey, dames! Check out my rooster!" As ridiculous as that sounds, it can have a powerful impact on a woman's subconscious.

Hands at Your Sides

Keep your hands at your sides and your palms facing outward at all times. This is a sign of transparency, as well as an invitation for anyone to approach you. Folding your arms across your chest shows that you're shut off. Wringing your hands together displays anxiety, and holding them in front of your crotch conveys panic. Even something as innocuous as holding a drink at chest level should be avoided, since it forms a barrier between you and your environment. By setting aside your drink, you're showing that you're relaxed and comfortable with your surroundings.

Non-verbal Cues That Scream "I'm non-dominant!"

What do you think women are most attracted to in a Man? It's the illusion that you're a dominant Man. This doesn't mean that you get a pass to act like a caveman. You can express your dominant male status simply by acting the way dominant Men do, deliberately manipulating the nonverbal signals you send out, and creating the impression that you are an Alpha Man.

This is called the theory of connection. Within a woman's mind you identify with attractive masculine traits, while dissociating yourself from unnecessary "nice guy" traits. This is the way magicians act. The magician carefully manages how they are viewed by the audience while on stage. By diverting the attention of the audience to items they equate with magic— like a spinning wand— the magician prevents the audience from seeing the thing that would make the illusion fail, namely the fact that they use their hand to do the trick!

Similarly, you may use perception management to influence what a woman thinks of you. And here's some really good news: you'll eventually grow to become an Alpha Male by adopting the right mindsets discussed in this guide. Today, you can start moving in that direction by adopting an Alpha Male's behavior. Let's talk about superiority, the social power which comes from being assertive. As you go through the self-improvement process, you'll finally internalize this book's ideas and become an Alpha Male. Right now, by using your voice, your eyes, your actions, and your attitude, you'll learn how to perform like an Alpha Male, giving the impression of superiority.

The number one nonverbal signal that lets people know that you are an Alpha Male are your eyes. A powerful Man doesn't hate looking at people directly. When you avert your eyes, you express submissiveness, self-consciousness, guilt, and a sense of low status. There's no limit to how much eye contact you can make when you're the one who is talking. Research has shown that the more eye contact the person speaking makes, the more listeners perceive the person as being dominant.

Moreover, the opposite is true when you're the one who is listening: the less you gaze at the other folk while they talk, the more dominant you are. Were you wondering why your mom used to say to you, "Look at me when I'm talking to you?" when you were a kid? It was a way to reinforce her superiority over you. Of course, you don't want to go crazy and stare at a woman to make her uncomfortable. If you are seen to be too dominant then your likeability begins to suffer. You need to find a balance.

Your voice is yet another sign of your superiority. Interactions and communication are dominated by Alpha Males. We always talk in a cutting voice and do not fear interrupting the other person. Research has shown that you can give the impression that you are not assertive when using a calm, quiet voice.

Try letting your words flow as you speak and don't be afraid to speak your mind. Individuals hesitating and hedging are viewed as less effective than those who do not. Note your attitudes and mannerisms. Try to avoid the following beta male behaviors and patterns of speech:

1. Using "oh" and "um" between sentences and words. Studies have shown that people view others who act like this as lacking in faith and being weak. It is a form of nervousness. We usually say "um" because we are afraid the other individual will be disturbed by us. Do not be afraid to pause for impact, however. When you pause between important points, you will feel more confident and people will remember what you are saying.

2. Talking too fast. It gives the impression you feel anxious and have little faith in yourself. A natural, comfortable speaking rate will vary from 125 to 150 words per minute within a moderate range. So, slow down!

3. Talking with a monotonous voice, also known also as mumbling. Individuals with a narrow range of pitches are regarded as unassuming, uninteresting, and untrustworthy. So, change your tone and you'll be viewed as an alpha, outgoing Man.

4. Taking too long before answering a question. This suggests that you think too hard to reach an answer, which makes you seem indecisive. It also seems as if you are trying too hard to gain the respect of the other person.

5. Keeping your posture stiff and your limbs close to your body. An Alpha Male is relaxed enough to stretch out his arms and legs. If you hook your thumbs in your back pockets, it can help to open up your body language.

6. Holding your hands up in front of you. This is a defensive move. Instead, you should remain open and vulnerable because you have nothing to fear. Relax your arms. Nobody's going to dare to attack you, so you have no reason to cover yourself.

7. Fidgeting with your hands or toes. It's common for Men to fiddle with sugar packets and straw wrappers when they're sitting across from a woman, but you should avoid this; some women find it incredibly irritating. The same rule applies to drumming on the table with your fingers. Just don't do it.

8. Touching your face while you're thinking. This shows that you're concentrating too hard, either out of nervousness or indecision. Instead, hold your hands together in a steeple formation before your chest or neck. This is a technique commonly used by lecturers to convey trustworthiness. Another option is to keep your hands on your hips.

9. Folding or crossing your arms. It is actually possible for folded arms to be an indicator of alpha status--for example, think of Brad Pitt in the movie *Fight Club*-- but, in general, it should be avoided.

10. Maintaining a hunched or rigid stance. The Alpha Male should be confident at all times, whether he be sitting or standing. Loosen yourself up and disperse your weight.

11. Looking downwards. By holding your head high, you're looking down at the losers around you. You're also exposing your neck, which shows off the fact that you have nothing to fear. Remember to maintain consistent eye contact during conversations.

12. Making nervous facial movements such as lip-licking, pursing your mouth, twitching your nose, and chewing

your tongue. An alpha has no reason to be nervous, so his face should always be calm.

13. Smiling excessively. Experiments on primates have confirmed the fact that beta Males use their smiles to signal harmlessness and prove that they aren't a threat. Alpha Males only smile when there's a reason to do it-- and, of course, they're very much a threat when they want to be.

14. Walking faster than usual. Instead, you should do the opposite and slow your pace down to a swagger. You're an alpha; nobody is chasing you, and you don't need to hurry to satisfy anyone else. Try to walk as though you just experienced a huge success that left you feeling on top of the world. You'll find that you move with a casual bounce in your step. This should be how you aspire to walk whenever you can.

15. Slouching. You don't have to keep your spine ramrod-straight to the point where it gets uncomfortable, but you should still rise up to your full height. This is another area in which Brad Pitt particularly excels.

16. Rapid blinking, or closing your eyes in frustration. Just relax your eyelids and let them drop a little bit. You don't want to come across as overly exasperated or cynical, nor do you want to appear anxious.

17. Shifting your eyes back and forth when you talk. This is a classic signal of beta status. Gaze at the face of your conversation partner. This is a nonverbal way of expressing that what you're saying is important, and that you're worth listening to.

18. Constant eye contact. There are some books of dating advice that tell you to keep eye contact nonstop, but the truth is that it makes you look weird, insecure, and socially inept. Instead, let your eyes unfocus. Try looking

through a woman rather than looking *at* her. The ideal amount of eye contact is about two-thirds of the duration of the conversation, and you should use it when she tells you something genuinely interesting. Otherwise, focus on other things: her shoulders, her hair, and things happening in the space around you, and so on.

19. Looking down before answering a question. If you need to look away in order to think before replying, angle your gaze up and to the left. Studies have shown that women gain more faith in you that way.

20. Not touching a woman. You shouldn't be afraid of physical contact! Any visible nervousness that you display when approaching a woman can be detrimental to your relationship with her. The alpha move is to hold her hand to guide her around. Be gentle; using excessive pressure shows vulnerability. Since you're alpha, it's a given that she's going to follow you. There's no need to be anything but friendly and tender.

21. Turning your head up quickly when someone calls for your attention. You should instead use the same movements that you would in a home environment. Keep everything slow and comfortable. You're always alpha, so you should behave the same way that you do on your home turf.

22. Using overlong words and sentences. Alpha Men's speech patterns are short and to the point. If you're tempted to speak in a lengthy manner, break your sentences down into smaller, more concise statements.

Don't feel bad if you occasionally slip up and send some of these nonverbal signals. No one is perfect and there's no use in beating yourself up about it--especially if you're in the middle of a conversation with a woman. Let your mistake go and keep moving the conversation forward. If you overthink things, you begin to doubt yourself, and when you doubt yourself, you end up feeling insecure, anxious, and reluctant to continue. Instead, focus on staying nonchalant and sincere at all times. Self-awareness is enough in and of itself to help you avoid the accidental expression of unpleasant messages.

Perhaps we don't know to what degree this "silent language" works for us humans, how it opens or closes contact and makes or breaks ties. It is because, during conversation, we don't actively think about how non-verbal signs relay information about our state of mind. But why should we, then? We don't think about why we're either walking or talking, we're just doing it.

Now you know so much more about body language that you will start to understand how your life can change. If you know how to read the facial expressions of others or their movements and postures, you have a greater chance of engaging positively with them. Tuning in to their actions helps you to understand their thoughts and emotions and to make you more generally receptive to them. Your increasing knowledge of your own body language also allows you to view yourself in a more favorable light.

It's no use to kid yourself that it doesn't matter how you present yourself. How you act, how you socially express yourself, how you match with others, and how you accept them and talk to them affect how others view you. Attention to body shape and fitness and basic appearance improvements can have a huge effect on how individuals react to you. Being conscious of your voice's pitch, tone, and speed contribute to your effect on people.

Basically, all this comes down to how you want to be viewed. Being a star doesn't mean owning a yacht, or becoming a TV celebrity, it's about self-respect and the ability to better yourself. The secret to personal development is self-motivation, and the more abilities you have to reach your full potential, the more effective you will be. Ideally, you now have the knowledge you need to learn about the art of body language. By using what you've learned to improve your self-confidence, you'll begin to reap the rewards in your relationships, at work, and in your everyday interactions with others.

CHAPTER SIXTEEN

PERFECTING YOUR DAY GAME

AS MOST GUYS consider themselves to be good with women, they are thinking about their social lives and picking up hot girls when they're out and about. Nevertheless, they face some difficulty in this scene as well, mainly because of things that are outside their control. Most people only go out two or three times a week and spend less than three hours in a bar or pub. This means that the opportunities to meet new people are limited. This chapter deals with the rest of the week, giving you ideas for opportunities to meet new people in normal situations. It also provides information for people who don't like the pub and bar scenes.

Picking up women in normal situations is different than going out for fun. There's a different mood among women when they're out for fun. They go out to meet someone, talk to people, drink, and have a good time. Conversely, when they are locked into their routine, as they are during the day, they're different. They don't think, "That guy by the bus stop is cute, I hope he's coming over to talk to me." No, at that point they're worried about what's going on in their lives. Even if you were to try to chat up a woman who's going about her day, she'd likely not be interested in talking with you.

In normal situations, don't try to pick women up. Instead, try to get a date. You should focus on the future, not the present.

Girls can be shocked, depending on where they are at the moment, that someone wants to talk to them. At first, it may feel awkward. Once they get to know you, they're going to start realizing what a nice guy you are and they will begin to open up to you. It's best to be as straightforward as possible. When you see a girl on the street, go up to her and ask her an indirect question like, "Excuse me, have you seen, or do you know where..." Then stop yourself and say, "Wow, you're very cute, I really need to get your number, my name is..." You want to keep the conversation to five minute tops. Tell her that you have a place to be but it was nice to meet her and that you'll call her to decide on a date later.

When you're on the beach or at the pool, walk up to a group of girls and ask them to watch your stuff when you're taking a dip. This is a good way to show off your toned body. Go for your swim and say, "Thank god my stuff is still here, I thought you were going to steal it," with a smile. From there, introduce yourself and start flirting.

Finding a girl just out and about during the day plays into the girl's fantasy of meeting her dream guy. It creates a story that the girl can tell her friends about proudly. Instead of being some random dude she met at the pub, you're the nice guy she met while at work. This makes her feel good. Whether you're going up to a girl walking on the street or working in a shop and telling her how pretty she is, the secret is that you made her feel good. That is pretty sweet.

The day game is about creating the right mood. You must be capable of playing off your present position and read a girl's body language to see whether or not she is in a rush. It's as simple as taking a seat next to the girl while she is sitting on the park bench. If you're in a store and you're walking by a pretty girl, ask her opinion on what to buy. Say something like "Oh, do you think this looks good on me? You really think so? Well, you're my personal assistant now, and the job today is to help pick up a new wardrobe."

If you see a girl in a shop, grab an item off the shelf and say,"Hey, have you ever made... I've got a special opportunity come up and I need it to go well ..." If she asks what that special occasion is, tell her "I've got a dinner date with you, of course. Hi, I am... " It's all about adjusting and using what you have around you. If you're playing Frisbee with a buddy at the park, chuck it in the direction of the girl, "Sorry about that, throw this away, let's see what you've got." Next thing you know she's participating in a game with you. Being straightforward and frank is the most important thing to remember on game day.

You must be also capable of doing these three things:

- Interrupt a girl's routine
- Make her chat
- Build sexual chemistry

If you can achieve these three things, you'll be good and you'll be able to get the girl's number and set up a date for later.

In the previous chapter, we discussed different types of body language and how to interpret them. It's essential that you respond appropriately to any bodily signals given to you by a woman. When she gives you one of the "yes" signals that we've mentioned, you need to reciprocate it to show that you're interested in her. Likewise, if she signals a loss of interest, you need to adjust your body language to regain her focus. Let's look more closely at some "yes" signs that we've mentioned before.

Eye Contact From Across the Room

We've already talked about eye contact a lot so we won't get too far into it here. However, eye contact is the most common body language signal that you'll get from across the room. As we said before, this is the first sign you'll get that a woman is interested in you. Again, hold her eyes for a few seconds after you have made eye contact. By maintaining eye contact she gave you a yes signal. You reciprocate by maintaining eye contact, too. Now get your butt over there and start talking with her.

Facial Expressions

Most of the time that you make eye contact with a woman, she'll give you a smile in return. This is a definite "yes" signal. She also might part or lick her lips. This is a way to bring her mouth to your attention, indicating sexual interest. Don't return this gesture; on a guy, it comes across as creepy. Instead, smile again, then walk over to her. You might catch her laughing with her friends while still looking in your direction. Her laughter means the same thing as her smile, and you should mirror it--while giving her attention, make sure you're still having a nice time with your friends. By continuing to laugh and joke with your buddies, you're showing her that you're fun and interesting and that people enjoy being around you. You're also letting her know that you're thinking about her even while having a nice time with your mates.

Body Positioning / Touching Herself

If she tilts her head, this is another "yes" signal. So, if a woman makes eye contact, grins, and turns her head all at once, she's given you three "yes" signals in just a matter of seconds. She's definitely interested, so don't just stand around like a loser-- make your move! She might also throw her hair behind her back or fasten it in order to expose her face and make herself more attractive to you. This also needs to be reciprocated, but of course you can't just toss your hair back in return. Instead, try adjusting your collar or running your hand over the back of your head. Drawing attention to the neck is another common way for both Men and women to display sexual interest. If she's displaying several of these signs, give her a smile and start moving in her direction.

After the Approach / Initial Communication

Some of the "yes" signs that a woman sends from across the room will also appear once you engage her in conversation.

Eye Contact

A woman who is interested in you will maintain good eye contact throughout the duration of your interaction. It's critical that you do this, as well. Every moment that she shows interest in you, you need to display that you feel the same way about her.

Facial Expressions

A woman might continue to smile and laugh while you're talking to her. This shows that her interest is growing, and serves as a way to create sexual chemistry. Once again, you can do the same thing: smile while she's looking at you, and give a little chuckle if she makes a joke--but don't go over the top. If you seem overly invested during a first casual interaction, she'll be turned off. A good rule of thumb is to try to match her level of interest at all times. This keeps the two of you on even ground and stops you from coming across as either too forceful or too aloof.

Body Posture / Touching Herself

Some more "yes" signals are playing with her hair and drawing attention to her face. If she likes how things are going, she'll continue to do this. Don't take this as a sign to start coming on to her more overtly; this means that what you're doing is working, and you should continue to do it. Look at the way she holds herself while talking to you, and try to mirror it. If you're talking side by side and she turns slightly to speak to you, do the same towards her. This body language shows that she's relaxed in your proximity, and that she's opening up to you. You, meanwhile, show that you welcome her into your personal space, and that you're comfortable and confident while being physically close to her.

While sitting, a woman may also cross her legs in your direction to show increased interest. If this happens, try to find a way to make physical contact with her. For instance: if she crosses her legs towards you, you should turn in a little bit and move one of your legs so that it touches hers.

Accidental Contact

If a woman's attraction to you continues to develop, she'll find a way to make physical contact with you. One common way of doing this is to touch your forearm or thigh while she's speaking to you or laughing at something that you said. As we previously established, whenever she breaks the contact barrier, you should respond in a similar fashion. In my experience, if she speaks and touches me on the forearm, I'll respond and touch her on the back of the arm, right above the elbow. Try to touch her in a location similar to where she touched you in order to make sure that you aren't overstepping any boundaries.

If you're conversing in a noisy location such as a bar or nightclub, you'll probably have to lean in close while talking to make sure that she can hear you. This makes it easy to place your hand on the small of her back. Remember to keep your movements natural and non-threatening at all times; if she feels threatened, you're out of luck, and your best course of action is to leave her alone and try approaching someone else.

Touch Barrier Shattered / Extended Eye Contact Communication

At this point in the conversation, you should know where you stand with a woman. If she's interested in you, she'll have made it explicitly clear by giving you her number or even a kiss. This is the moment to focus on inciting sexual chemistry. Stay on the lookout for "fuck me" eyes. These are characterized by deep eye contact, parted lips, and excessive touching. Everything about her body language will scream "I want sex right now--take me home!" If this is what you're looking for as well, then that's your cue to head out with her. If you prefer to take things slowly, make sure that you have her number and either continue to flirt or call it a night.

Facial Expression

If she's interested in advancing your encounter into something sexual, she'll typically be making an effort to draw attention to her lips at this point. If she's biting her lip, it could mean that she wants to touch you, but it could also signal that she isn't quite ready. You should also take note of where her eyes are directed. If she's gazing at your lips, this likely means that she finds them enticing and kissable, and that she's imagining how they might feel against hers. If she's been giving continuous "yes" signs and proceeds to bite her lip while making eye contact, it's the perfect time to move in for a kiss.

Body Position / Touching Herself

Once you've been talking for a while and some physical chemistry has developed, a woman's body language will become more sexual. She could open her legs to signify that she's sexually available and welcomes you. Treat this as you would treat any sexual advance; tell her, "Would you like to move over there where we can chat," "Would you like to go somewhere quieter," or "Would you like to go back to my house?" All of these questions can shift the conversation to a more intimate setting.

She might start pushing her chest in your direction or positioning herself in a way that emphasizes her cleavage. Remember that all of these things happen subconsciously, meaning that her sexual interest is deep and genuine. She's operating with animal instincts in the hope that you'll be drawn to her. You can return the sentiment by adjusting your tie, smoothing your shirt, or pulling back your shoulders to inflate your chest.

If the two of you are standing up, she might place her hand on your shoulder and lean in very close. If you're sitting, her legs will be touching or entwining with yours at this point. After you've been engaged in conversation for a while, try positioning yourself so that her legs are between yours or vice versa. It encourages both of you to touch more, and also creates a physical entanglement that suggests further sexual activity. When she makes an effort to close the distance between you, make sure that you don't shy away. Once the touch barrier is broken, it's crucial that you keep moving forward in your interaction--the more touching you do now, the more touching you'll likely be doing later. Try to maintain an atmosphere in which she can relax, so that she's more comfortable with touching you.

Accidental Contact

At this point, there's really no such thing as accidental contact. Once the initial barrier has been broken and she's comfortable being touched and kissed by you, unintentional grazes turn into deliberate, prolonged contact. While she may have touched your arm while laughing at a joke before, she'll now fully clasp your hand in hers. She's shifting from passion to outright desire and wants to move forward with things. It's important to show that you share her attraction, and that you reciprocate it. As an example, I recently went out with a girl who seemed to know every guy in the restaurant where we were eating. She and I were trying to chat one-on-one at our table, but different guys just kept showing up. When this happened, she would catch my hand and give it a little squeeze, as if to say, "I'm not trying to ignore you--he's just a friend, and I really like you." I reciprocated by giving her a squeeze back, or sometimes by gently gripping her shoulder. This says, "It's okay, I understand--I know you're into me, and we're going to get plenty of alone time later on." This appealed to her subconscious, thereby advancing our sexual chemistry.

Dealing with "No" Signals

At the end of the day, there's always a chance that a woman will send you negative signals instead of positive ones. In most situations, this means that you should just move on. On special occasions, however, there may be messages that you can send to re-engage her attention. Here are some examples of body language signals that express disinterest, along with how you should respond to them.

Eye Contact From Across the Room

There are two ways that a woman can express disinterest via eye contact. The simplest way is to avoid it entirely. If she doesn't look in your direction, or if you can't seem to lock her eyes, she's definitely not interested in you. In this situation, you'll probably want to move on. Remember, though, that you're unlikely to end up here if you walked into the room with the relaxed swagger that we addressed in previous chapters. When a woman doesn't want to give you a second glance, you're probably acting too much like your normal, shy self. Try re-evaluating your looks and mannerisms before trying again with another woman.

Another way that she *might* express disinterest is by looking down when you try to make eye contact. This gesture, however, can be difficult to interpret, she may just be shy. Shy women will often hold eye contact with a guy for only a second before looking away, which by no means indicates a lack of attraction. The trick here is to be mindful of what else she's doing. What messages is she sending via other types of body language? If she continues to sneak glances at you while laughing and conversing with her friends, you likely still have a chance with her. If her body language is quieter and more closed-off, however, repeated looks in your direction could mean that she's creeped out by you. Do your best to evaluate the situation, and respond accordingly.

If you mess up with one girl, don't worry. The great thing about casually connecting with women is that you'll always have a chance with the next one. If you maintain positive, enticing body language, you're guaranteed to spark a girl's interest sooner or later.

Body Positioning / Touching Herself

As we said before, a woman who's interested in you will turn in your direction, indicating her availability. The inverse of this is that, if she lacks interest, she'll try to turn her back on you, making it impossible to interact. If she makes brief eye contact, then pointedly shifts in a different direction, you're done; everything about her body language is telling you "no," and your only option is to move on. She is completely shut off to you.

After the Approach / Initial Conversation

This is where it can get tricky. When it comes to conversation, "no" signals aren't as cut-and-dry, in part because you know that she was at least initially interested in you. If you get a "no" signal at this point, you may still be able to salvage your chances and turn it back into a "yes."

Eye Contact

If her eye contact starts to stray away from you, she's probably scoping out the room, looking to see who else is available at the moment. When this happens, you need to do something to actively re-engage her in the discussion and restore her trust in you. There are a number of different ways that you can do this. It's still too early in your interaction to pull anything totally crazy, but you can still try to pose an interesting question that will get her talking to you again.

Facial Expression

When a woman's mind is wandering, her face is likely to be blank or sleepy looking. The same technique that you can use to restore eye contact is also applicable here. All you need to do is find a way to reel her back into the conversation.

Body Positioning / Touching Self

Obviously, when a woman turns her back to you, you can safely assume that the conversation is at an end. However, there are subtler signs that you should also be monitoring. Pointing her feet, legs, arms, or hands in a different direction can also show that she wants to get away from you. If she starts to pull away from you like this, you should do the same. Her body language is telling you, "I'm not really feeling this anymore." In response, you're saying "I see that you're not interested, and that's all right with me." This tends to prompt her to react in a favorable manner. If you give the impression that you're no longer interested, she might make an attempt to win you back. Nobody likes to feel like they've turned somebody off--women included. She wants to end the interaction on a good note, rather than worrying about something that she may have done wrong. On the flip side of this, if she doesn't start sending "yes" signals again after you back off, then she definitely isn't the one for you. Try again with somebody else.

Accidental Contact

If she's not interested in you, there will be no physical contact at all. We can do a lot of things to position ourselves in a way that makes it easy for women to casually or "accidentally" touch us. By completely avoiding this, she's clearly making a conscious effort to avoid physical contact. This doesn't mean she isn't attracted to you; it just means that you haven't advanced your chemistry to the point where she feels comfortable touching you. Slow down and refocus on building intimacy between the two of you, then try again once the time is right.

Touch Barrier Broken / Prolonged Talk

A woman won't simply stand up and walk away if the two of you have been having a nice conversation for the past hour. You're clearly both enjoying each other enough for a prolonged interaction, and you've probably managed to develop some strong sexual chemistry at this point.

The only exception to this is if you said or did something that made her feel angry. If she gets annoyed and storms off, you can either let her go or track her down and try to regain her affection. If you go for the latter option and she continues to send "no" signals, it's time for you to give up. A positive "yes" response from her, on the other hand, means that you might still have a chance.

Sometimes, the act of turning and walking away is a test to see how far your interest in her will go. Never pressure her when she's clearly uncomfortable, but also keep in mind that all may not be lost just because she seems to be moving on.

CHAPTER SEVENTEEN

THE DATE

IT IS JUST a matter of time before a woman wants to take things further and sleep with you. The only thing that worries us is how long this is going to take, and what we can do to speed things up? Well, we already know tricks to create sexual intimacy. Yet at the end of the day, each woman has her own unique idea of how long she wants to know you before she agrees to let you take it to the next level. This is not necessarily the amount of time we would consider "normal," as in hours and days. Instead, it is a measure based on her internal clock, which only makes things more complicated.

The time frame she feels is appropriate to wait before you have sex can be influenced by several different factors. For example, it can be hard for a very religious girl to move to the next stage with you because that would contradict her faith and her views on sex. When you're not of the same faith, you don't match the ideal archetype she has in her mind of what a mate should be and she'll be hesitant to sleep with you. It can be difficult for a virgin girl to open up to you sexually because of her own feelings of vulnerability and lack of experience. She may want to wait for the right moment, like in romance movies, to lose her virginity to "the one." On the other side, we have the girls with whom everybody except you has slept, and that's when we begin to apply the book's basic principles. This girl will be willing to sleep with you at a moment's notice. This has nothing to do with possessing all the qualifications to be the ideal friend, it is just a matter of being next to her when she decides that she wants to go home and have sex. Then we've got the girls who are out on vacation, out of town, or out for summer flings. We can meet girls who are on vacation when we go on a trip, when we mix with the local people, or in any scenario where both parties know that there can be no long-term relationship because you'll just be around each other for a couple of days. Such girls are also interested in having sex because time is short and the standards of a relationship are not there. She may have sex because she doesn't have time to get emotionally involved with you. She's ready to lower all of her defenses and have a good time.

Let's go back and see how this concept of time is important to a woman, and how we can manipulate it. The best way to think about it is not in terms of minutes. Let's take the following example, with which we should all be familiar. We're out at the bar to find a girl we like, we get her phone number, we call her up and make weekend plans. We're going to take her out to the park, maybe go out for ice cream, have some fun, chat, and that's it. We initiate some interaction on the second date, like friendly touching and we go out for dinner. If things are going well, we get a hug. We go bowling on the third date, walk around the park. There's sexual tension and we build the momentum to get our much-deserved kiss. Things are going gradually until three months later when she eventually lets us in and we get to sleep with her.

Sounds familiar? Well that's a fun story to tell the grandchildren, but it doesn't keep up with the standards of those reading this book. We want immediate results. We wish to do what takes three months to accomplish in two or three days. Why are we doing this? It can be seen as time distortion. See, when a woman thinks about a guy she's dating, she doesn't recall particular dates but she remembers various circumstances. When you've taken a girl out to the coffee shop, the park, and then out for some ice cream, she doesn't just remember a date, but three different and distinct encounters. Coffee is one experience, the park is the second experience, and eating ice cream the third. It may well be three different dates for her.

And how is that applicable to us? By taking the girl to different locations, she'll begin to let us in faster. One date amounts to three. It'll amount to six if we do it for two days in a row. After a week, she will feel as if she's known you for more than a month. Using this strategy, I've found that the average girl would sleep with you after a week, if you stick to it. Not all dates have to involve money. Look at the list below to see some free or low cost potential dates. Most often, it is the thought you put into making such a great date for her that counts. Some activities you can do include:

- Happy Hour, when there are half-priced food and drink specials in restaurants and bars.
- Spending time in nature and nearby walking trails.
- Spend a day at the lake or at the beach. Make a fire.
- Explore the place. Visit the city downtown and dine in one of the nearby mom and pop restaurants.
- Plan a picnic. Visit the local park, drive out into the woods, or set up a backyard blanket.
- Build a bonfire in your backyard. You just need some firewood.
- Visit your favorite hangouts from when you were a child, like a roller skating rink or a pizza joint.
- Go camping. Some parks' fees are under $20.
- Swimming at the nearest swimming pool, lake, or beach.
- Watch your favorite show together.
- Write each other notes to make memories.
- Take her out in the country for a scenic drive.
- Go wine tasting. Many wineries charge a nominal fee for a tasting. You can take a walk around the vineyard as a bonus.
- Visit your local art gallery. Some galleries have free admission at least one day a week.
- Go watch a performance at your nearest college or high school. Entrance is usually free.
- Paint a mural together.
- People watch on a bus or a busy street.

The First Date

The thing about first dates is that you're still in the initial stage, where it's necessary to develop sexual chemistry. That being said, you need to do something where you can talk to each other and get to know each other, but be flirtatious and have fun at the same time. We do dinner and a movie a lot of times. I don't know why anyone should. It's safe, it's easy, but come on, be imaginative, don't be boring. We already know you need to be original when approaching a woman. You need to stand out to her. You have to be different from the other 10 guys who hit on her. And why are you going to take her on the same first date she has been on so many times before? No one in there would ever want to have dinner and a movie as their first date. When you're past the initial stage of building sexual chemistry, there's nothing wrong with dinner and a movie. If you're aware it's in the bag and she's going to sleep over, then sure, take her anywhere you want, but not on a first date.

A Cooking Class Or Seminar

Cooking classes are great for a first date. A cooking class is a place where communication is unlimited. You don't have to think about planning anything or entertaining your date. The evening's events are scheduled for you. What you need to do is flirt.

A Fair Or Carnival

This is perfect if you live in a small town. It might sound silly, but if she's from a similar environment and grew up attending these events, then she's grown up doing this and you know she's going to like it. It's just like the other choices on this list, a place where you can let go and have fun. You can do a variety of different things, go on rides, play sports, get your pictures taken. You can both have a great time.

A Museum Or Art Gallery

When you know that art or literature is one of your date's passions, take her to a museum or art gallery. You can visit for hours. She'll love it. Maybe you don't know anything about art, but that is a bonus. It will encourage her to spend hours telling you about it, teaching you about new things. The main thing is that she'll enjoy it. Plus, it's low cost and you have plenty of time to work on building chemistry.

A Park Or Beach

A little preparation is required, but this can potentially be a very cheap and fun date. If you go to a park, get there about an hour before sunset. Take something like a Frisbee or a ball. You may have a good time just walking and chatting, but you'll have a ball to throw around if you need a game to play. Have a small picnic at sunset. Alternatively, go to the beach. Build a fire when it begins to get dark. Bring hot dogs and marshmallows, or something else. She might tell you she's not into hot dogs, but you may convince her to try one. Enjoy the beauty of nature and show some affection.

The 2nd & 3rd Dates

You will know the target pretty well after the first date and if you haven't started holding hands, hugging, or kissing, now is when you want to start working on it. These subsequent dates will allow you to get closer to those opportunities and make the connection you need.

SUPREME ALPHA MALE BIBLE. THE 1NE.

A River Walk, Park, Or Flower Garden

Those places are perfect for second and third dates just as they are for a first date. These places are not expensive. You can walk around and develop sexual chemistry. Walking is also an ideal way to hold her hand. It may sound easy, but it is the first step towards being intimate. Try to convince her to go rollerblading while you're in the park. That's not a first date activity, but it's great for a second date. You are having fun and standing out from the other guys she's dated. You are showing her that you can take risks. A little sweat is good because it physiologically breeds sexual feelings due to the influence of pheromones and physical activity. Don't go out and get all dirty and crazy, though. You can pack a picnic dinner if you do this in the afternoon and relax afterwards.

Pizza & Mini Golf

It is a perfect choice for every date, even first dates. You have a fun game you can play. Mini golf is a great way to have fun. If she has fun, you develop chemistry. Plus, when you play games, it's almost like you're letting your guard down. She's going to realize that and it's going to help her to let her guard down as well.

Close the Deal

This is a phrase used in sales. That is the mindset that you need to follow to be successful with women. Often, you will see a guy do something right. He reads the signals from the target, then makes his move, and introduces himself. He develops sexual intimacy during the night through body language, joking, and playful flirting. He did all right. His target is eating into him, but when the lights come on and the time has come to go home, he goes home empty handed, without the girl, without a farewell kiss, and without a phone number to call the girl for a date.

After studying these techniques, beginners are surprised at how easy it is to speak to and develop sexual attraction with women. They get so wrapped up in the moment that they forget the most important part. They fail to close the deal. That is a common mistake made by many beginners. The ability to close the deal on a regular basis is what distinguishes a beginner from a true master.

Then, there is the guy who probably does things right as well. He knows that the goal is his. He sees the signs and she's seeking more, so he freezes. He is trapped by fear. Fear of rejection, fear that she doesn't feel the same way, fear that she'll laugh in his face, and fear that he'll be a bad kisser in bed. This fear takes over him and he never makes the move. He is not getting the girl. These are extreme cases, but they happen every day.

Closing the deal has a different meaning for different people. It's a way to measure your performance and it is a benchmark for evaluating your success. There are four distinct ways of closing the deal that you may use with the target. You can close the deal with a kiss, phone number, sex, or a long-term relationship. The one you use is entirely up to you. Some guys want to create a little black book full of hundreds of numbers and others are satisfied with only a phone number. Many guys enjoy going out with as many girls as possible. Others want to use this book's lessons to pursue positive, long-term relationships. Your personal target will determine the sort of closure you're seeking or it may be a mix of all four.

Closing the Deal With A Number

Closing the deal with a phone number is nothing more than getting your target's number. Most guys make the mistake of thinking that getting a phone number is going to have to wait until the end of the night or conversation. Should it, then? You don't know what could happen during the conversation. You could be enjoying a drink with the target one moment, and before you know it, one of her girlfriends is having an emergency and she's gone before you can ask her for the number. It's quick to get a phone number. All you have to do is ask. Having the phone number of the target early in the night is helpful in more ways than one. If you're bad with names or can't remember her name, when she gives you her number, she'll write it down. If you don't have a sheet of paper and a pen, give her your mobile phone to type it in, so you can find out her name without saying you've never known it.

The easiest way to get a number is to ask for it right away. You can say things like; "I'm having a nice time talking to you, can I get your number?" Or you can say, "Can I get your number so I can call you?" Most people do not like being that straightforward. Here's a bit of a trick to use. After you've been talking to a woman for a while and you've developed intimacy and sexual chemistry, tell her, "I'm having a nice time with you, we should do this again." Or, "You're a lot of fun, we should plan to go out next week." In most situations, she'll say, "Sure, that's going to be interesting" and offer her phone number to you. You don't ask for her number explicitly; she decides to give it to you.

Another idea is to ask the target for her email address. It has quickly become popular for all communication to take place online, although this is not as intimate as a phone call. Since an email address can be considered less private than a telephone number, if the target is resistant to giving out her number, ask for her email instead. She'll likely not be as resistant. When emailing her, write to her, "Write down your phone number, too!" This is what is commonly known as bait and turn.

Giving your number to the target isn't closing the deal. Giving your phone number is giving her all the control in the relationship without having anything in return. You're the one waiting by the phone, wondering when she'll call. This is not the way an Alpha Male behaves. Let nothing be left to interpretation or confusion. If she doesn't give you her number, get up and walk away. Nothing more can be done. Say to her, "It was great to meet you." Stand up and find your way to the next accessible person. Either of two things is going to happen: either she'll call you back, not wanting you to leave, and give you her number, or she'll let you go, saving you the time wasted talking to a girl who isn't interested in you.

More often than not, if you're able to convince her that you're going to walk away, she's going to cave in on your demands. That's because you've just shown your worth; you don't have time to play games and if she isn't careful, she could lose you. You might find girls calling your bluff every now and then, but the main thing is that you didn't waste any more time with her. You've moved on to another target, maybe one that will give you her number, or even better, a woman planning to take you home this evening.

There is a way to completely stay out of this situation. Give her your number when she asks for it. When she finishes inputting it into her phone, tell her, "Call me now so that I can get yours." You can also say, "Call me now to make sure you have the right number." You're going to have her number now and you didn't even have to ask for it.

Closing the Deal with a Kiss

This is the next step. At some point during your meeting, the goal is simply to kiss your date. Usually, closing with a kiss requires a deeper connection to the target than you would need to get her phone number. You have built up a high degree of sexual attraction, formed a strong relationship, and taken things to the next level. Depending on the degree of sexual chemistry you have developed, a kiss may be innocent, casual, or passionate. Depending on your priorities, closing the deal with a kiss may either be the end-state, or even better, the start of a new relationship.

Unknown to most, closing the deal with a kiss is basically easier than getting a girl's number. A touch is innocent and natural, unless you want to French kiss her. Be straightforward and tell her in a gentle voice, "I want to kiss you now." If she hesitates, move your face in front of hers. Pause when you are a few inches from her face. Take a last glance at her. If her eyes are closed, her lips split or her eyes flicker back and forth, you've got her approval. When she shifts backwards, her head calls off the kiss. Asking for forgiveness is better than asking for permission. You create excitement in the mind of the target as you slowly push your face in for the kiss. The more you draw in anticipation, the better the kiss. A fast kiss can come as a surprise, but a deliberate, purposeful kiss will seal the deal.

Let's presume you're about to end a date. You know you've achieved sexual chemistry and you're pretty sure the girl's into you. You just want to kiss the girl but you don't know how to do it. The entire ride home you're worrying about it, and then you have an idea of how it's going to go. You will walk her to the door and she will pause to encourage you to step in while you tell her good night. You're all set to go for it as you head to the entrance, only she won't hesitate and you're left without your kiss at the threshold. That's poor performance if she was up for a kiss and you didn't make a move and you probably won't get another opportunity. You wasted a chance here because real life does not work like in the movies. Instead of this wasted opportunity, as you walk to the entrance, take her to the side. Look at her eyes, and pull her toward you by the elbow. Then kiss her. It's so easy. You can do it anywhere you want. Take her by the hand, look into her eyes, and move in for a kiss, slowly. You've just created the moment.

Closing the deal with a kiss is dependent on your personal preferences. I would kiss a girl if I'm planning to have sex with the girl that night. Otherwise I'm happy with getting her number and setting up a date later that week. Without the kiss, you can build just as much sexual chemistry, and it helps build the attraction for the upcoming date. Once again, closing with a kiss is all about timing. There's no reason to wait till the end or for the perfect moment. If a kiss is all that you want, then let the excitement build up and taunt her before you create the opportunity. If you're just going through the steps to get her into bed with you, try to kiss her first. This is critical and sets the tone for the remainder of the night.

Closing the Deal with a Relationship

The final form of closure is a relationship. Although having casual sex is awesome, as is going out with a different girl every night of the week, you're simply not able to build the same kind of bond as you would with a steady girlfriend. In the end, dating is nothing more than being able to figure out the attributes that you want in a woman before you settle down. From looks to personality, personal ambitions, and family values, you need to match seamlessly. Dating is a method of discovery where, using first-hand experience, we find out these traits. What you may think you're drawn to turns out to be a big issue until you get it. It's key to dating. Imagine it as a subject of study or as a science experiment for you. The only way we can truly recognize the characteristics that we find desirable in a partner is by trial and error. We need to find out for ourselves.

It's easy to start a relationship; just keep your expectations clear and honest. There is no need to lie or make up lies for different girls that you're dating. You can have one, two, even ten girls involved. There will be no problems for as long as you are honest with each one. When a girl asks you to be exclusive with her, then you will have to weigh that option, but that right there should be a sign of things to come. If she wants to manipulate you now, she is going to manipulate the relationship. The best part of telling the girls that you date that you see other people is the amount of rivalry that this generates. They want to be the only one you are going out with and they will do whatever it takes to make you see that.

When you agree to be exclusive with one girl in the end, talk to her about it. Just because you lost contact with all the other girls doesn't mean that she did the same thing with the other boys. Some guys would believe that if she spends all her time with them sharing her feelings, she's only into them. They are then surprised to find out that she's seeing someone else. Only let her know if you like her. Tell her, "These last few weeks I really enjoyed dating you. I'm willing to put it out in the open that I am willing to date you exclusively, and I wish you to do the same thing." If she says no, then continue to show her the attributes we've taught you and she will be able to tell that there's no other guy that compares to you. Continue to date other ladies to sharpen your skills if things don't work. If it is supposed to happen, it is going to work itself out. Whatever you do, don't grow "oneitis" for this girl because she doesn't feel the same way about you. This is when you're not going out and meeting other girls while waiting for the girl to come to you. It only exposes you as vulnerable and shows you lack Alpha Male qualities. This would push her away from you much further. Dating is a game, so if you want to come out on top, you have to be willing to play and fight dirty.

The most critical of the three types of closing the deal is getting the telephone number. It is the only sure way of getting a hold of the target at a later date. You need to be able to get hold of her somehow if you want to set up a future date. Going to her workplace to pick her up each date or regularly running into her at the bar won't cut it. The first or second time it might be ambiguous, but if you do it more times than that, it shows the target that you have something to hide and becomes a red flag.

Closing the deal may be a sequential process to some degree, but not all four phases happen in sequence. If your aim is to have a relationship, then you'd start by getting her number. Get a kiss the next time you have a date, and then agree to have an intimate relationship after a few more dates. You've done A and B and are getting to D. Whether you have a friendship or not, sex is not a deciding factor. If your main objective was to have sex with the girl and nothing else, including a one-night stand, you can skip the phone number and start with a kiss. The kiss will lead to more, and finally back to the bedroom where you can close up the deal with sex. We were just going through phase B in this case to get to C. You can't switch directly to a near sex situation without having to get a phone number, without a kiss, or close friendship. You could never have started in the first place if you don't intend on ending, so always close the deal.

CHAPTER EIGHTEEN

THE FUNDAMENTAL KEYS OF SELF-DISCIPLINE & GOOD HABITS

WHILE YOU CAN NEVER BE 100% confident that you will achieve your goals (doubt is always there but never voiced), you can also take some steps to become more self-confident and disciplined. The trick is to see what others have done to achieve the same goal, and imitate them. By following a proven plan you will get rid of a lot of uncertainty that comes from taking a seldom traveled route. Nothing comes in your way of achieving what you want when you are following in the footsteps of hundreds or thousands of people who have followed a specific plan and succeeded with it. If your aim is to drop weight, follow a diet and take lots of before / after photos and stories.

If you want to start a business, learn from successful entrepreneurs who have supported hundreds of new entrepreneurs. If you want to develop a certain difficult skill, learn it from someone who has a great deal of teaching experience (and hopefully, a lot of learning experience in general, so they can better contribute to your situation). The experience you gain from someone who has accomplished the same goal will cause your self-doubt to disappear. After all, you can follow a known route and not just wander like a child lost in the woods.

You will have the basic tools to start building an iron-like determination to keep going no matter what the circumstances are. When you combine this confidence with dedication and the proper mentality ("this too will pass"), you will achieve anything you set your mind to. In the long run, the reflections discussed in this book will be useful. The goal is to strengthen your baseline of self-discipline and not just give you a momentary sense of self-control because you are overcoming a little bit of temptation. With these simple concepts in mind, let's move on to more specific exercises and routines that you can incorporate into your life to build up your own discipline. Please note that the aim is self-discovery, namely, to help you find out what works and what does not work for you in building self-discipline.

Having self-discipline is not just about doing something regularly, it is about controlling, modifying, and adjusting your actions constantly to the changing conditions and circumstances of your life. Self-discipline, therefore, is about training yourself proactively and actively to follow a specific set of guidelines and morals that will help you shape and align your thoughts and behaviors with the task at hand. In view of this, the value of cultivating self-discipline is quite obvious. It can not only boost your productivity, but also increase your self-confidence. Self-control offers you a greater sense of control while you work on projects and assignments. This will help you stay focused longer. In fact, you build a higher level of tolerance and may eventually get more done with seemingly less effort in less time.

What Does It Take to Develop Self-Discipline?

Self-discipline is not something with which we are born naturally. It's something we learn and takes many years to develop. It's basically very much like a muscle that gets stronger when we exercise it over time. Nonetheless, for you to start practicing self-discipline, you need specific factors to come into play. Some of these factors come from inside you, while others come from outside sources. Let's look at those variables below.

You Need A Reason Why!

To develop the self-discipline necessary to become an Alpha Males requires a strong will to achieve that specific goal. There is very little potential for self-discipline without a strong desire. Self-discipline needs fuel and that fuel usually comes as encouragement or motivation. To power self-discipline you need one or the other. Otherwise you'll struggle to remain focused over extended periods of time. All of this boils down ultimately to having enough compelling reasons to pursue any mission or project you commit to. Ask yourself:

- What do I want?

- Why do I want it?
- What do I need to follow through specifically and get this done?

The more compelling reasons you can find, the more momentum you'll be able to gather in order to drive your self-discipline forward.

Self-Discipline Requires Unwavering Commitment and Responsibility

Now, of course, there are never enough explanations. You'll also need an unwavering commitment to do whatever is necessary to achieve your goal. Naturally, this is not easy. Long-term dedication takes discipline, and usually, this isn't something that most people have on their own. What these people lack is being honest with themselves. A long-term commitment to something includes either keeping ourselves accountable or making ourselves responsible for our acts. The latter can be done through someone else. However, when they work in tandem, you get the best results.

Self-Discipline Needs Punishments & Incentives

As we achieve our target, our motivation levels ebb and flow. You will feel extremely inspired at certain moments, while at other times you will find yourself struggling to get through specific tasks and activities. It may be helpful to put some incentives and bonuses in place to avoid falling into these loops. Punishments and rewards can be used throughout the day to help direct your behavior. For example, you can reward yourself for making specific decisions or taking part in certain types of behaviors. You can also punish yourself for indulging in other habits or making poor choices. Those penalties and bonuses will add another dimension to the furnace which will keep the self-discipline fuel burning all day long.

It All Comes Down to Your Particular Values

If you lack self-discipline in any area of your life, it's mostly because you don't keep yourself accountable for upholding a set of standards. The personal standards you are following keep you on track when working towards your goal. They're kind of like unspoken rules that govern your daily choices, decisions, attitudes, and acts. With that in mind, let's outline what performance standards you are going to uphold when pursuing your target. Tell yourself:

- What personal standards am I going to uphold?
- What kind of attitudes and decisions do I accept?
- What decisions and habits am I not going to accept?
- How do I get things right when I go off track?

Essentially, all of this comes down to making clear compromises with yourself. Agreements about what you are going to accept and what you will not embrace are the foundation of self-discipline. It then demands that you keep yourself accountable for living up to your own expectations. All of this amounts to monitoring and adjusting your behavior whenever you go off track. That's pretty much what self-discipline is about, in a nutshell. There's one more layer we still need to explore, though and then the world is yours.

Creating A Competitive Environment

The final layer allows you to create a competitive environment that will move you forward towards your objectives. Now, that doesn't necessarily mean you're competing against other people. Of course you can put yourself in the frame of mind where you try to outwork and outperform others. That is certainly one way of disciplining yourself. But there's another way to do that, too. Competing with the best version of yourself is the other way to do this.

Measuring your current performance against past performance can be a helpful way to help you stay focused, inspired, and disciplined. It might, in fact, be the one of the key ingredients that continues to fuel your self-discipline when things don't go completely according to plan.

6 Steps to Developing Self-Discipline

Now that you have some insight into what self-discipline is all about, let us break down a series of seven steps to help you practice self-discipline. You can, of course, use this loop anytime and anywhere. Nonetheless, please bear in mind that it may take some time to get into the habit of applying it regularly to your life, as with any change of habit. So be patient with yourself and improve your self-discipline by playing the long game.

Step 1: Defining What You Want

The first phase of this process is to get a really clear idea of what you want to achieve. Self-discipline will only persist when it is channeled toward something concrete. Let's direct it, in this instance, towards the desired outcome you have in mind. This outcome may be a target you want to achieve; a habit you may want to build, or any other form of improvement you may want to make. To gain clarity about what you want, ask yourself:

- What do I want to do, be, have, or accomplish?
- What kind of new habit would I want to develop?
- Which behaviors do I want to change?
- What's the one thing I want to be concentrating on right now?

Step 2: Explaining the Required Changes

Now that you have some insight about what you want, it's time to explain what kinds of habits and behaviors can help you achieve this desired outcome. In other words, what kind of person do you need to become for your target to be achieved?

Every target we set brings with it an accurate collection of behaviors and habits that are naturally interwoven with the purpose we want to achieve. Clearing this field up will help you figure out what it takes to achieve the desired outcome. Think of your goal with that in mind, and ask yourself:

- What specific behaviors do I need to improve in order to achieve this objective?
- What unique behaviors do I need to follow in order to achieve that objective?

It is important to keep your core values also in mind when answering these questions. The attitudes you practice and the actions you take will reflect the core values you hold. Essentially, that's the only way you can make sure you stick to your goal over the long run. Second, the path towards achieving their desired goal almost always changes people in unexpected ways. We are learning and growing along that road as we strive to achieve a goal. It helps to transform the way we view ourselves, how we see others, and how we interact with the world around us. What this basically means is that in some ways you will have to change and adapt to achieve the goals of your life. In other words, you have to become the person who deserves to have this purpose in his / her life. Ask yourself:

- With that goal in mind, which person do I need to become in order to achieve it?
- What traits will I develop?
- How do I need to focus on myself, my life, and my goal?

Answering these questions is an important self-discipline that rises from the level of certainty you have about something. When you have more confidence about your ability to achieve something, mustering self-discipline is simply easier. But when there is a lack of certainty, then it's possible to get sidetracked and frustrated along the way.

Step 3: Finding Suitable Role Models

Now it's time to look for answers outside of yourself, to help strengthen your self-discipline. In particular, let's define role models (friends, family, colleagues) that have already accomplished the goal towards which you are working. Tell yourself:

- Who does it right now?
- Who has achieved this goal successfully?
- Who developed the habit successfully?
- Who made this change successfully?
- Who does have the necessary self-discipline in this field?

- What can I learn from this person to help me along my journey?

Allow time to ask these people how they developed their self-discipline. Ask them how they performed specific actions that produced their desired outcome. Use their insight to help you motivate yourself on your own personal journey.

Step 4: Identifying Reasons and Obstacles

By now, you ought to have a clear idea of what it will take to reach the desired result. Of course it becomes more definite with clarification. And it becomes easier, as your confidence grows, to create the self-discipline required to get the work done. Meanwhile, as with all journeys, you will inevitably face various difficulties. These difficulties and obstacles will test and overcome your discipline. When this happens, ask yourself:

- What barriers could stand in my path, despite my objective?
- What unique situations could sidetrack my journey?

The less valid motives we have for accomplishing something, the more likely we are to be sidetracked along the way. So stop being sidetracked. You need to take the time to write down why you want to achieve the desired result. You might ask yourself, for example:

- Why do I want to explicitly achieve this goal?
- Why do I want to explicitly cultivate the habit?
- Why does this matter most to me right now?
- Why do I want this in my life, really?
- What potential rewards will I reap from doing so?

As you answer these questions, it's important you don't just settle for the first answer that comes to your mind. Keep on building the WHYS instead! The more valid reasons that you have to reach your desired result, the easier it will be for you to control yourself along the way.

Step 5: Build Your Action Plan

Now is the time to build a concrete action plan to help you achieve your goal. The effective action plan consists of a time limit to achieve your goal. It also has to be developed on the basis of mini-milestones which break down your target into manageable chunks. Mini-milestones make sure you work in small pieces and short time periods against the desired outcome. This strategy should place you in the driver's seat. This offers you a sense of control over your activities and projects.

What you actually strive to prevent is being frustrated. When you feel overwhelmed, you can easily digress into procrastination and ultimately procrastination can cause stagnation. And obviously, where there is stagnation, there can't be self-discipline. Therefore, given this, it is of paramount importance that you take progressive steps towards your goal of always maintaining control. It is also important to have a specific deadline in place. A clear deadline will help you control yourself, as it will concentrate your mind on a specific deadline for you to achieve your goal.

With an end-date in mind, all of your resources and energy are properly channeled to help you retain the momentum that you need to follow through with your actions. In fact, a deadline gives you a sense of urgency, which helps to keep you focused and vigilant about the tasks at hand.

Step 6: Taking Responsibility For Yourself

The final step in this cycle is responsibility. Not only do you have to hold yourself accountable for your daily choices and decisions, but also have someone else hold you accountable for your actions and results. For example, you might create a support team that will help you stay focused and on track. Heading this support team might be your personal accountability partner (a trusted friend or family member) who checks on you periodically to see how things are going. Finding another positive and motivating voice would help you persevere and persevere longer.

Ideas To Help Strengthen Self-Discipline

Let's expand on what was addressed in the previous part in this section and explain how to strengthen our self-discipline when working to achieve our objectives and goals.

Make A Wholehearted Commitment

Having a wholehearted commitment is one of the keys to self-discipline. We have to be fully committed to doing whatever it takes to get the job done, notwithstanding the difficulties that get in the way. Of course, you can make a personal commitment by developing a contract that lays out the terms and conditions of the agreement you are making to achieve your target.

You can also make a public contribution, as an alternative. Tell several friends, family members, or colleagues about your intentions. This will hold you accountable for your decisions and help you stay more focused and disciplined along the way. Sadly, many individuals will still struggle to uphold their obligations even when using these two types of accountability. They would fail when it comes to the terms of their contract, they are simply not precise enough.

You have this amazing goal you want to reach, for example. Committing to that goal is a wonderful first step. Actually, however, it doesn't mean anything because you've failed to commit to every single step. All the little actions you'll take along the way in search of your target are what you must commit to. For example, your behavior will come in the form of regular behaviors you need to build to see this mission through to the end. Therefore, you are committing not so much to your goal, but rather to creating the behaviors that will help you achieve your goal. Of course all this needs you to devote yourself to self-control, which will benefit you because it will help you avoid getting sidetracked or stuck in the pit of instant gratification. Together these two efforts will help you accumulate the self-discipline you need to see through your mission to the end.

Cultivate A Self-Disciplined Mindset

Cultivating self-discipline is basically cultivating a new state of mind. Nevertheless, it is necessary to cultivate certain qualities in order to obtain this state of mind and practice self-discipline. Excitement, passion, tenacity, bravery, diligence, tolerance, passion, and optimism, for example, are all key attributes that help the self-disciplined mind. It's not just about the qualities that you develop, though, but also about the actions you take. A self-disciplined mind is determined to take consistent action over an extended period of time. A self-disciplined mind is also willing to take the necessary risks in order to complete your work.

Moreover, a self-disciplined mind doesn't take a backseat, but instead keeps on going forward. In fact, it's able to do whatever it takes to see the mission through to the finish. In a lighthearted setting, where things are pleasurable and enjoyable, a self-disciplined mind thrives, too. As such, finding ways to enjoy the process, enjoying every role you play, and enjoying every interaction you participate in are important. With that in mind, ask yourself:

- What do I enjoy about this process?
- How cool is this?
- In what ways do I profit from that?
- How can I enjoy this job/process more?
- How could I make this more fun and exciting?

The more ways you find to enjoy yourself, the easier it is to practice disciplining yourself all day long.

Visualize Your Desired Outcomes

One of the most productive ways to stay focused and inspired is to spend time visualizing your desired outcomes and objectives. Daily visualization exercises will help you achieve your goals by helping you visualize the steps you need to take to reach them. Subsequently, this clarity of mind is likely to give you greater certainty and self-assurance going forward.

Creating A Supportive Environment

Often you may be in the right state of mind, but if your environment does not support this state of mind, then there will be friction and you will struggle to find the self-discipline necessary to achieve your goal. With this in mind, it is absolutely crucial that your work environment fully supports your goal. More precisely, it has to endorse the routines and regular behaviors you are engaging in to help you achieve your goal. Be deliberate about your work environment and ask yourself:

- What routines and rituals do I need to establish to help me achieve my goal?
- What clear actions do I need to take to accomplish this objective?
- How well does my environment help these behaviors?
- What improvements will I need to make to build a more positive working environment?

Basically, the work environment has to support the new behaviors you create and the positive actions you take. At the same time, over the long-term, it needs to keep you focused, motivated, and dedicated.

Prioritize Your Tasks & Activities

Priorities are absolutely paramount when it comes to self-discipline, as they help give the structure and flow required for your day. Once you successfully prioritize, you do not wonder what needs to be done any more. Instead, you are now aware of what's most important, and how you're going to organize your day. A self-disciplined mind always has a structure to work with. Yes, the more structure the better and in the end, the fewer choices you need to make. You are less able to get side-tracked by meaningless tasks and events when you have fewer choices.

Track Your Progress

A self-disciplined mind thrives when noticing the progress toward the goal it is creating. Despite this, creating a process that can help you track your progress using a calendar or journal is important. When you monitor your performance and can accurately assess the progress you are making, this will help to keep you inspired and focused on the tasks at hand immediately. Even in cases where you fail to reach the goals that you set for yourself, monitoring your progress will help you make the necessary changes to stay on track. It's important to control your results when it comes to monitoring your progress along with the temptations that end up sabotaging your progress. Make the necessary changes once you identify them. This way you'll be able to stop those temptations altogether.

Know that stuff will rarely run perfectly, if ever. There will be speed bumps along the way. That is only a part of the process. Nonetheless, you'll manage to maneuver through these challenges effectively if you have self-discipline.

How To Find Self-Discipline When Facing Adversity?

It's easy to assume that all will go smoothly at the start of any journey. All this passion, anticipation, enthusiasm, and energy are there to motivate us to move forward. They dissipate soon, when we face our first big hurdle. What used to seem like a sure thing is clouded in doubt now. We are no longer excited, but rather, perhaps, a bit confused, disappointed, exhausted, and even afraid of what might happen. During such times of adversity, we need to dig even deeper in order to find the self-discipline required to continue plowing along. In this segment, let's look at what it takes to keep self-discipline alive when faced with life's challenges and setbacks.

Make No Excuses Or Complaints

You will throw all of your excuses and complaints out the door when you're faced with setbacks and adversity. Making excuses or moaning about your problems rarely, if ever, helps. It often actually makes things worse. Bad things always happen when you least expect them. But that is really just your view of the situation, isn't it? Life could be a little different to what you expect, for all you know. To change your perspective you only need to move. Leaping to conclusions ahead of time will only undermine your attempts to reach your goals and let your imagination run wild. Instead, make constructive use of your imagination to concentrate your attention on what you need to do to get the job done. If you don't take control of your imagination, you may very well fall prey to rage or frustration. Once in that state of mind, it is easy to engage in excuses and grievances. They make you feel better about yourself and your situation instantly, after all. They don't give you any way to work through the situation, however. Therefore, you must control yourself at all times to keep your emotions in check. You will refocus your attention on what needs to be done to help you achieve your target when your emotions are in check.

Evicting The Perfectination Pit

Perfectination is disguised as the two Ps: perfectionism and procrastination. When you engage in these two self-sabotaging behaviors, you absolutely cannot practice self-discipline. In the face of adversity, it is inevitably trivial to procrastinate. Things aren't going well and you plan, out of fear, to take a backseat and wait for things. Nevertheless, the longer you indulge in the procrastination process, the further you fall into stagnation. A temporary reprieve may be beneficial. Rather, you will focus your efforts once again on what matters most. So, self-discipline can become the grounding force anchoring you toward your target. Tell yourself:

- What's key right now?

- What should I concentrate on, this very moment, to help me move forward?

Focus on small tasks under your control—that will help you move forward in a big way. Then, force yourself slowly to update these tasks as you start to build momentum.

This is where the stuff gets a little tricky when it comes to perfectionism. It's tricky and somewhat frustrating that we often mislead ourselves into thinking that we are making real progress. But of course this is just a lie we are telling ourselves.

When we indulge in perfectionism, we are, in fact, not making much progress at all. Perfectionism is simply a kind of defensive mechanism that we use to avoid dealing with what really needs to be done. Instead, when perfectionism hits, we focus our efforts on trivial tasks, which offer us a certain appearance of control in the face of difficulty.

The big problem with perfectionism is that we often fool ourselves into believing we are actually self-disciplining. That may be valid, for the most part. However, our self-discipline is focused on the wrong things—the things that quickly get us nowhere. It's important to get some clarification to break out of this perfectionist pit. Ask yourself:

- Is this really what I'm concentrating on?
- Is that task important for my goal to be achieved?
- Is there anything more relevant on which I should focus?
- What should I work on that could help me move faster?

The goal here is to channel your self-discipline towards something that matters. At the same time, meanwhile, make sure that you have some semblance of control over this matter. There's something that can help you build the energy you need to get through the hard times.

Simplify, Simplify, & Simplify Even More

It's easy to get upset, irritated, and exhausted when faced with adversity. While it may be difficult to control ourselves in the midst of these crippling emotions, it's hard because it just feels like things are getting out of control. In such situations, the solution is to slowly take back control one step at a time. You'll need to simplify to do this. In the face of adversity, control yourself to start making things easier. Simplify your actions, streamline your routines, and simplify the steps you take to solve a problem. By making things as simple as possible, you start to slowly regain control over your life, goals, and tasks. Only in this way will you start building the momentum you need to attain your target again.

Making Things Pleasurable & Enjoyable

Dealing with adversity is never a lot of fun. Neither is coping with adversity. But what if I were to suggest that if you started taking things so seriously, then you would see adversity in a very different light? Yeah, it may not be fun. But it might very well transform into an extremely valuable opportunity for learning. If we stop taking things so seriously and start approaching them from a different point of view, all of a sudden, it becomes easier to focus our attention on the things that matter most. In fact, adversity is very much like a game that we play with ourselves, rather than a daunting challenge. Keeping this point of view in mind, it becomes significantly easier to control ourselves.

CHAPTER NINETEEN

BUILDING SELF-DISCIPLINE & RESILIENCE AS AN ALPHA MALE

Get Comfortable With Cold Temperatures

ONE OF THE simplest ways to learn how to handle discomfort is by introducing yourself to cold temperatures. Taking a 5-minute cold shower is the fastest, most thorough workout you can do. And no, don't just count in your mind for 5 minutes. Set a stopwatch and don't leave the shower before the 5 minutes pass. Don't cheat, turn the knob to cold the whole way. One of the greatest things I've done to improve my mental toughness was taking two ice-cold 5-minute showers over the span of two months.

The first time I took a cold shower, my whole body went numb. After the first contact with the water I tried hard not to leap out of the tub. Several showers later I got more desensitized to the feeling of discomfort, but the first two minutes were the toughest. After two minutes had passed, things suddenly became much simpler and much effortless. Soon I realized that I could bear the cold.

So, I applied the same principles to other aspects of my life, reminding myself that the first steps always test your self-discipline. You can handle them much better than you think. That is the kind of realization the lessons in this book are intended to help you achieve. Only you can master these on your own. Once you find out exactly how you are tempted to give in and what helps you cope with pressure, you will become able to cope with delayed gratification.

Another practice to measure your mental toughness is to go out in the cold without wearing your jacket. Obviously, when you're sick or trying to explore the wild outdoors, you shouldn't do this. Nevertheless, going for a walk without a jacket once or twice a month, with only a thin jumper on, can be a valuable experience to build mental toughness. Just be reasonable about it. We're talking about suffering a slight discomfort here, not putting yourself in a place where you can get hypothermia or frostbite.

Do Without Something You "Need"

There are some things and habits you need to feel relaxed in your everyday life. You can carry your smartphone everywhere you go, check your email ten times a day, drink coffee first thing in the morning, or sleep in your comfortable bed.

As an example, I chose to sleep on my apartment's balcony a few times, instead of sleeping in my own room. It's a simple, quick thing that most people (at least those with access to balconies and backyards) can do to feel a brief inconvenience and refuse to take the comfort of their bed for granted.

What if you're used to your smartphone and can't leave it at home out of the fear of missing an important message or email?

You know it: leave it at home for a couple of hours and see how you feel without it. Stick with your anxiety and go through it. Nothing bad will happen and you will only feel better for a while by getting rid of one of your "needs." Below are a few more examples of what you can "intend" to do without.

1. Walk to work instead of driving. In many cities it's not feasible to do this, but that's exactly why it's a great self-discipline building exercise.

2. Go hiking, preferably away from any amenities, so you 're forced to shower or do other hygiene-related activities without modern conveniences.

3. Do a 24-hour email fast. Don't check your email during these 24 hours. If you are waiting for an important message or can't afford it because your job requires it, don't do it; that's not the point of this exercise! Do it on your day off or when you're on vacation.

4. Replace your evenings with enjoyable reading instead of sitting in front of the TV (non-fiction books about the skills and ambitions you would like to achieve)

5. Live like a miser for a week or two. Avoid all unnecessary expenses. Don't buy new food. Consume leftovers, canned food, and all the boring items you rarely eat that just sit in your refrigerator or pantry. Don't buy new clothes and don't spend any money on entertainment of any kind. Pretend you don't have any money to spend.

By learning how to live with less, you can take it further. Any time you want to make a purchase, ask yourself whether this is something you really need. If not, you'll probably regret the purchase and it will bring more hassle to your life without any benefits. If you're not absolutely sure that a purchase would add long-term benefit to your life, you need to skip it. That is discipline.

Rejection Therapy

Rejection is a fragment of our everyday lives, yet most people cannot handle it well. For many, it's so difficult that they choose not to ask for anything at all, rather than to ask for something and face rejection. Yet as the old adage goes, if you don't ask, the answer is always no. As an Alpha Male, you need to learn to face and withstand rejection.

Avoiding rejection, which essentially means not having enough control to cope with this kind of pain, has a destructive impact on many parts of your life. All this is only happening because you are not tough enough to handle it.

Consider rejection counseling to help with this issue. To build a thicker skin, you have to get rejected. Do something or ask a question that you know will lead to rejection. For example, take a job in sales. Another way to practice being rejected is flirting with strangers. Haggling or asking for store discounts will also work. By intentionally putting yourself in situations where you are rejected, you will grow a thicker skin that will allow you to take on much more in life. This will help you become more effective in coping with setbacks and adverse circumstances.

Failure Treatment

Well-known baseball player and coach Yogi Berra once said of loss therapy, "Losing is an experience of learning. This imparts modesty to you. They teach you to work harder. Humility, work ethics, and motivation: all three of these are necessary components of personal growth and self-discipline." If you're not careful, you're going to overestimate your ability to withstand temptations. Indeed, a phenomenon called "restraint bias" shows that people overestimate their ability to control impulses and, as a result, over-expose themselves to temptation.

Experiencing disappointment will keep you away from distorted beliefs about impulse-control. When you think you are self-disciplined and are smart enough to know how to resist temptations entirely, you are not really self-disciplined. One of the best ways to get more acquainted with life's disappointments is to strive to achieve difficult goals and set objectives that are potentially outside of our control. Just like a chess player can't continue to advance his game playing against opponents who are worse than him, you can't improve without constantly setting the bar higher.

The increased incidence of disappointment when setting difficult targets and the resulting feelings of discouragement will be a beneficial experience in learning how to stay motivated despite setbacks. When you never suffer defeat, you don't question your self-discipline. It's only when you make mistakes, leap through the hoops, crawl under obstacles, and collapse in defeat that you can test your resolve and grow.

Do the Most Challenging Things

It's an ancient rule in the world of time management that you should do the most significant things first and only after you are done with them are you allowed to move on to less important activities. Yet few individuals obey this advice in their everyday lives. If you have a list of 10 things to do, it is easier to focus on the easiest things first and cross those off your list.

This does nothing to bring you closer to your objectives (in fact, most of these quick tasks are actually unessential). Instead of the difficult tasks, you start with the easy ones. Why? For what? Beating procrastination requires a lot of self-discipline and getting the difficult tasks done first. Change your habits and do the hardest things first. Occasionally, you can do what appears to be a difficult and time-consuming job much faster than you think. The reason you hesitate to do it to begin with is because it seems more complex than it really is, and that makes you hesitant to begin.

The more you let it simmer, the more overwhelming your frustration becomes. If you don't allow yourself plenty of time to think, instead opting to roll the ball and start working on the mission, your hesitation should melt away easily. Repeating the same cycle every time you feel reluctant to do something can help you build a strong habit of self-discipline.

Learn Something Difficult

Learning a foreign language is one of the most difficult, but still realistic, goals you can set for yourself in order to cultivate more self-control in your everyday life. By making it your goal to become a fluent speaker in a new language, not only will you acquire valuable skills, but you will also find out how to learn in general. This also includes mastering how to handle discouragement, which is always lurking nearby somewhere, ready to pounce the moment you are struggling. Studying foreign languages is an uncomfortable experience at all levels, ensuring you will get to know the feeling of discomfort every day (and hopefully learn how to manage it).

You'll be feeling uncomfortable because you are not able to understand anything at first. Later on, what you will see as slow progress will deter you. Even if you're an experienced speaker, sometimes you'll always feel uncomfortable and get angry at yourself when you can't say anything you know how to say in your native language perfectly well. These kinds of emotions are useful when learning a language or working on any challenging task because they help you understand the patterns. What are you doing when you are feeling like giving up? What's driving you to this point? What pops out of you? You will not know the answers until you get going and experience those emotions on your own.

In my case, perfectionism is what triggers my feeling discouraged. I get discouraged each time I know I'm far from a perfect execution of any skills. After I discovered this tendency, though, I transformed it into inspiration, using my frustration as a catalyst to keep working on my abilities until my mind sees them as they are. What do you think? How can you transform your default reply from the urge to give up to more resolve and discipline? Here are several more demanding goals and skills that will help you achieve the same result and develop your own discouragement and/or discomfort coping strategies.

1. Practice a tough sport that requires thorough mastery of technique.

Some sports, such as basketball or football, require certain physical attributes, which give certain players a huge advantage, thus reducing the effectiveness of regular exercise. Few things are more annoying than having an amazing work ethic and still being far behind the inherent physical abilities of other athletes. Such sports won't help you develop confidence and the unfairness of the universe will only leave you angry. Choose demanding sports that reward drills, regular preparation, and going the extra mile to develop more self-discipline by getting comfortable with difficulties. Some of these sports include:

- Golf
- Chess
- Tennis
- Gymnastics
- Wrestling

Any martial arts that do not rely on your size

The simple act of long-term practice, coping with failures on the path to improvement, and achieving success is what you are seeking. What makes this exercise so effective for building self-discipline is the fact that it requires years to become at least average in these sports.

2. Master an ability that requires patience.

If you are not patient enough to trust the process, you are more likely to give up too soon. When you plan and fail to achieve quick results, you are more likely to become frustrated and/or feel bad that you cannot live up to your (unrealistic) standards. Here are few abilities and activities that need a lot of patience, and thus the discipline to remain focused and determined while awaiting the results:

- Cooking, particularly more challenging meals that involve an hour or two of preparation, and over an hour of cooking the food. Since cooking is a complex ability to master (it takes hundreds of attempts to create a "signature" dish), it is ideal as a self-discipline exercise.

- Gardening. Many plants tend to grow for months or years. Some plants, like orchids, may live for months or years without a single flower sprouting out. Talk about exercising persistence.

- Acting creatively. Painting, writing, and any other creative work require a great deal of dedication and persistence to see them through to the end. Even if you create something you're not likely to show others, expressing yourself through art (and becoming used to the long, arduous creation process) can help develop more self-discipline.

- Reading. You know how to read; wouldn't you say that? Okay, when was the last time you completed a full-length novel or non-fiction book without skimming over chapters? It takes patience and courage to read longer books. These are things that will help you develop more self-discipline.

Don't get me wrong, now. The idea is not to choose a sport that is difficult or to develop a skill you hate. If something feels extremely hard in the beginning and you don't like it, there's a high chance you've already subconsciously realized that this isn't a good activity for you. For example, I practiced judo as part of my university curriculum for three months. After the first few sessions, I realized this wasn't for me. I didn't enjoy it, I wasn't good at it, and my back was extremely sore. I started learning tennis several years later. It took me only a few lessons to realize that I loved the sport, despite never having done it before.

3. Master honesty.

It is no understatement to suggest that lying is widespread in society and we meet liars every single day (not to mention our own lies). It's hard to remain honest, particularly when your job, self-worth, or chances of finding a partner in life are at stake. But the best thing you can do to advance the quality of your life and become relaxed with discomfort is to practice authenticity. After all, if it wasn't difficult to tell the truth, no one would lie. It takes time to truly become comfortable with being honest all the time, just like with any other issues that make you uncomfortable. Nevertheless, the regular practice of being honest with people and the rewards that you will receive for it will help you stay the course and meet the minority of people who can be trusted unconditionally.

4. Master communication skills.

In general, improving communication skills starts and ends with a pattern of always putting yourself in the other person's place first. If you have enough patience to tap into empathy before uttering a word, you'll become a better communicator and avoid conflicts. However, it's not simple and is definitely not convenient to resist the temptation to do the complete opposite. Becoming a good communicator requires discipline, so you need to stick to your new ways rather than resorting to the same, counterproductive communication patterns you used before.

Negative behavioral patterns, such as getting angry or fighting, are usually passing reactions that can be manipulated if you make a mindful effort to recognize them before giving in to them. When you control your emotions before making the situation worse, you'll master the ability to communicate with others without resorting to angry arguments. The consequence of this exercise, which is better impulse control, can benefit you in other areas of life, too. It will show you how to benefit from small, instant rewards, and it will help with health issues like headaches and sore throats. How do you stop lying, if you 're used to telling lies on a daily basis? Start by recognizing that your lies hurt people, no matter if they're innocent white lies or more serious ones. This affects your relationships by undermining trust, the cornerstone of any human connection. Moreover, for years to come, lies will haunt you (lying on your resume, lying to your partner), damaging you and others. Lies keep you from obtaining greater, more positive results in the long term.

Being too judgmental can also cause communication problems. Judging others without fully understanding their situation is simple. It's a common tendency to disagree with someone immediately, instead of putting yourself in their shoes.

Understanding how to manage this impulsive behavior is yet another practice you can adopt to learn to control yourself better. The temptation to judge each and everybody you meet is often overwhelming. It's easy to lose yourself and begin a long, pointless tirade that does not help anybody. Try to catch yourself each time someone else judges you and stops you. Saying bad things about others is never of any benefit to anyone. Make it a powerful exercise in self-control by learning how to resist it.

Another detrimental trait of losing contact is being unable to state and/or say no to your needs. It's easier to relent and say you're going to do something rather than refuse and face the consequences of somebody's uncomfortable rejection. That's why learning how to voice your needs is a good idea, so putting yourself in these uncomfortable situations teaches you how to handle them better.

If you are the kind of person who puts others first, it can take years to see an improvement, but even then, you can still feel bad about putting your needs above the needs of others. It's a valuable and insightful practice, though, that will help you deal better with awkward, uncomfortable situations that may arise when you express what you need or want (or when you give a negative response and the other person doesn't take it well). You can't grow your discipline under those circumstances.

5. Learn to trust yourself.

Obsessing over what other people think of you is nothing but setting yourself up for failure. You need to focus on forcing yourself to be consistent. It is easier and more comfortable to ask others for validation than to learn how to feel ok without their approval. It's equally easy to do what others are asking you to do, instead of sitting down and contemplating what you really want.

However, as we have already discussed a few times in this book, choosing comfort never helps you achieve your goals. In the case of caring about what others think about you or doing things to please them, you choose simple comfort (focusing on being liked) over discomfort that would bring more satisfaction (living your own life without worrying about how others view you).

Of course, not caring about what others think has nothing to do with being disrespectful or making yourself stand out with intent. That would be another aspect of the same behavior, which is drawing your self-worth from showing that you don't need approval. The sweet spot, which requires a lot of self-discipline to achieve, is just about being the best version of yourself. Other people's opinion doesn't matter to you, either way. It's not about doing things that are socially accepted or going against the norm, it's about doing what's best for you and staying the course amid doubts and/or other people nagging you to change your direction.

6. Stop complaining.

For most of us, hardly a day goes by without complaining about something. I hate the weather. Traffic is terrible. My friend is running late. How dare he give me a cold meal? None of these complaints give value to our lives, yet we keep making them because it's easier than actually doing something about them (or accepting them, if we can't change them). It's hard and uncomfortable to stop complaining and turn to ideas instead, but eventually it's a positive habit that will help you both grow as a person and become more in control of yourself.

A slip takes you back to day one, making it a daunting task to complete, which will set you back weeks or months. I used to complain about the weather all the time. My life was simpler and healthier as I reduced the number of my grievances and embraced everything I could not control. In turn, this helped me to develop more self-discipline, although I too slip sometimes.

7. Overcome shyness.

There are few things that can hinder the chances of success more than shyness. Lack of trust is a debilitating condition that affects every single area of life, making it hard to reach goals and grow as a person.

It's also one of the most difficult things to tackle, requiring incredible amounts of self-discipline. Only by putting yourself in uncomfortable situations on a daily basis can you tackle shyness. The more reserved you are, the more difficult the circumstances that you have to face before you become comfortable.

Months of continuous exposure to stressors will rattle even the strongest humans. Nevertheless, the ultimate goal you can achieve, a life free from shyness, is one of the most important goals you will ever achieve. Even if you don't suffer from extreme shyness (and you are just not a very confident person), consider working on your self-confidence by introducing yourself to social circumstances that you're normally avoiding (for example, talking to strangers).

These are a few easy exercises that will help you feel more comfortable with social awkwardness, which in turn will help you become a more optimistic person:

Talking to strangers. Chatting with strangers is a great way to get rid of shyness. Start by asking for directions, or the time, something simple and easy (extra points if you ask for the time while holding a phone in your hand or wearing a watch on your wrist) if you lack confidence. If you have more confidence, come up with broader conversation topics.

- Practice eye contact. Initiate and maintain eye contact with strangers for as long as possible (or when catching them staring at you). Just don't forget to blink and keep your smile friendly. Otherwise, you can make people uncomfortable, and that's not the point of this exercise. Bonus points if you establish and maintain eye contact and talk with the person you are looking at.

- To speak openly. If you're a nervous person, little things are more awkward and difficult to describe than standing in front of a group of people with a trembling voice and shaky legs. Yet, this is exactly what you want to do to eliminate your lack of confidence.

These five ideas are only a few different, challenging things you should focus on. They can help you both achieve great personal development as an Alpha Male and improve your self-discipline. In uncomfortable situations, the key is to find something that will push you to expand your comfort zone.

CHAPTER TWENTY

LIVE WITH INTENT

THE OUTER WORLD is moving on from the inner world. If you feel confused, then your outer world will be chaotic. If there is no peace in your mind, it can cause stress to you and everyone around you. If you are not in charge of your inner thoughts, it is unlikely that you will enjoy a lot of self-discipline in your daily life. Few people are bent on actually living their lives. Most are too busy, too rushed, and too overwhelmed to slow down and pay more attention to what's going on in their minds. And their inner life continues beyond them, shaping their outer world without them being aware of it.

It is much more difficult to build self-discipline if you concentrate only on the external side of it and ignore the strength of your mind. When you cultivate a calm mind that can manage your thoughts—filtering meaningless ones, shaping positive ones, and finding justifications for doing the right things, instead of making excuses for not doing them—the act of self-control becomes much easier. How do you start to live with more purpose? It all begins with:

Sharpening Your Focus With Quiet Relaxation

While it is impossible to manage all of our thoughts (according to various estimates, we have close to 70,000 thoughts daily), we can pay attention to those that arise the most often and monitor them if we are conscious of them. An average person does not pay much attention to their thinking. They think that their thoughts and feelings are just there. When they feel nervous, they're worried. When they think they're dumb, they're dumb. They aren't self-disciplined because they feel they can't resist the temptation any longer. They identify with transient emotions and not the other way around. How can you develop on-going self-discipline if you give your thoughts so much weight? Any doubt in your mind is going to destroy your determination and solidify the illusion that you cannot become a more disciplined person.

Realizing that you are not your thoughts and passing stimuli like smells, sights, or sounds will help you understand that you are in charge of what you think. Once you acquire this ability, you will gain the power to shape yourself as you wish. The secret to attaining this state of awareness is to participate in activities of quiet relaxation on a regular basis. However, as much as I want to encourage everyone to cultivate a regular meditation routine, not everyone loves it or finds it worthwhile. It can be too frustrating, or just boring, to sit still with your eyes closed. If after doing it for at least a few weeks, you have tried it and did not find it beneficial, here are a few alternatives worth checking for.

1. Listen carefully to music

No, you're unlikely to have a heavy metal meditative experience. Music that is most conducive to balancing the world around you and discovering your inner world is instrumental music, or music that has harmonious, calming vocals and rhythm. As with meditation, the aim is to allow the world surrounding you to vanish and reduce your being to the humble act of just being there (or just listening, in this case).

2. Practice yoga or tai chi.

Yoga and Tai Chi are one of the few practices that get you as close as you can to meditation without meditation. Maintaining a posture when concentrating on your breath, and letting go of your body's stress is almost the definition of meditation. The only dissimilarity is that you won't be sitting still; instead you will participate in the meditative process with your entire body. It's the only type of meditative experience out of all the seven ideas mentioned here that requires an instructor to perform properly (technically you can learn it from books and videos, but it's not the best way to do it).

3. Journal.

Another meditative practice can be the act of writing down your innermost thoughts. This helps turn off the noise volume in your mind and allows you to explore deeper layers of your inner world. Either write by hand or do it on a device with no internet access (or at least switch off your email and social media notifications) for best results. Otherwise, it is very hard to immerse yourself in the feeling of projecting your thoughts onto a piece of paper or screen.

Embrace Your Tunnel Vision

At any given time, practicing tunnel vision meditation is not just something that you do on its own, as a stand-alone activity. You can also do it on a daily basis to take greater control of disturbances. Each time you slow down, be mindful of what you are doing and concentrate on the feeling that a particular experience gives you. As you do so, you gain more control over your mind.

We skip hundreds if not thousands of special events every day, just because we're distracted by things that are going on elsewhere. Often, these distractions lead us, often unintentionally, to give in to the temptations. You're late for a meeting, so you'll grab the first piece of food you can find (usually something unhealthy) and go on your way. When you slow down and clear your mind of intrusive thoughts, it will be a lot less difficult to conquer the temptations.

That can help if you accept tunnel vision. The first element of this exercise is being able to slow down. If you are in a rush, you can't do it well. If you can set aside at least a couple of minutes (or just use breaks at work) when you can really concentrate on the present moment without thinking about what you're about to do, you can go on to the second step, which is being conscious.

Let's say, as an example, that you're out in the woods enjoying a short walk. Although being alone in nature is conducive to experiencing fewer distractions, you can do something more to reach a meditative state and clear your mind. Pick up a leaf, touch a tree's bark, or look at a bird or a squirrel. Engage all your senses; let the experience consume you. Trace the leaf's contours. Notice its texture. Look at its vivid hue. Touch and smell it.

Use your will to focus all your energy on the leaf on your palm. Fine tune the world around you. Let yourself experience all these strange feelings while being intimate with a leaf. You definitely won't have the ability to do it for longer than a couple of seconds at the start. After all, who in their right mind spends a minute or two looking at a simple leaf (and, actually, who the heck with a sane mind is dreaming about "getting intimate" with a leaf?).

However, not only does the systematic practice of seeing the little things that everyone else misses make the world a much more exciting place, but it also sharpens your perception. As a result, you become more prepared to recognize temptations and deal with them before they become overbearing.

The problem with many self-defeating thoughts and feelings is not just that they come up. It's that you don't care about them and let them influence your actions without paying attention. It is amazing that our minds justify every single action we take. It's only in hindsight, when we can tell our choices were dumb and determined by the way we felt at a particular moment (and it doesn't sound like good decision-making, does it?) that we can recognize what's going on. The reason for this is a short attention span. Through consistently accepting the tunnel vision, you will boost your capacity for concentration, and thereby decrease the risk of making emotionally driven decisions.

Speak to Your Future Self

Any time you choose a smaller reward later instead of a bigger reward, you steal from your future self. We're bad at imagining our future selves and associating who we are now with the person we're going to be in a year. That person sounds like an outsider, not like us. And as it's a stranger now, it's easier to claim small rewards than to wait for better rewards at a later time. We're here now, after all, and not in the future, right?

There is a phenomenon in psychology called temporal discounting. This is the propensity to give greater value to the rewards obtained now or soon compared to the rewards received later in the future. You choose $100 now over $200 a year from now, or a free pizza in two hours over two free pizzas in six months.

Once you apply yourself to self-discipline, you will begin to place more value on fulfilling your immediate desires due to the temporal discount than to reach your perfect physique in six months. After all, the first reward is actually here, at your fingertips, and the second reward (a six month vision) is just an idea, something that is hard to imagine. The exercise which I am about to discuss is intended to solve this problem. We have trouble seeing ourselves in the future because we seldom do it. Through writing a letter to your present self from the viewpoint of your future self, you will solve the problem of the disassociation between your present self and your future self.

Let's say you want to lose 20 pounds and get fit. Nonetheless, you are struggling with this goal. The future reward (a healthy body) can't be given more value than the instant reward (eating the food you love). And instant gratification still wins.

Now imagine yourself as a person who hasn't achieved that goal in the future, who has chosen to rob his or her future self of it. Make the picture even worse than your current situation , let's say you weigh even more than you do now, and your weight continues to rise. What would the (obese) future self-claim to him or herself? Would he or she be satisfied that you have decided to give in to temptation to renounce the long-term goal? How does your self-discipline influence the likelihood of an even worse future today? If you visualize every single detail and make it an emotional visualization exercise, chances are that your future self will cease to be a virtual construct and will become real.

You can try the opposite also, by imagining your future self as a person who has accomplished the weight loss target. What would your (fit) future self say about your goal? How would a person who has already accomplished it look like and comment on the road to achieving the goal?

Often, it's easier to imagine achieving the goal (and the person you're going to become) if you picture the perfect result and then trace every single step you need to complete to achieve it (as opposed to figuring it out where you are now).

Create Your Own Compass

How aware are you of your most important life values and priorities? How do they affect the decision-making process? When asked, most people wouldn't hesitate to say that safety, family, or democracy are their most important values. Yet these values don't represent their daily lives because they don't have clear rules about their beliefs or a personal compass to guide them.

Write down a list of your most significant values every several months and ask yourself if your daily actions suit them. The need for honesty is one of the most powerful powers. When you learn that fitness is of utmost importance to you but you have recently gained a few pounds and stopped exercising as often as before, it can give you the kick that you need to get back on track.

To live with purpose calls for a calm mind and focus. Getting a set of clearly defined principles and the following practices or laws that you must adopt in order to be consistent with them will help you maintain a steady level of self-discipline in life.

CHAPTER TWENTY-ONE

BURNOUT & DISCOURAGEMENT - IT'S NOT ALL ABOUT SELF-DISCIPLINE

Severing Your Attachment To Outcomes

ONE THING TO bear in mind is to relax while you are talking to a woman. To do that, focus on what's going on outside of you right now instead of criticizing and second guessing yourself. When you think too hard, it interferes with the social power of your mind. So, don't evaluate or judge yourself while you are talking to a woman. Be more spontaneous in your social routines.

Concentrate on the here and now. Don't think about the results; they'll happen anyway. Don't hesitate to make fun of yourself too. Relax and don't pay much attention to any of your interactions or behavior.

Remember, you are not bound to a performance. You don't have expectations. What you do is to build the right conditions for an interaction to take place. Once that happens, let go of everything that happens next. If nothing happens, shrug it off. Other opportunities will come up.

There are some things about life that you can't handle, and certain things you can. The trick to achieving happiness is to focus on the things you can manage, while ignoring to the best of your ability those things you have no control over. So, just relax and enjoy. Think of it like browsing online. You don't stress about the content and you're enjoying yourself. This should also apply to your social life.

You shouldn't be relying on getting any results with women, either. Just because you expect a situation to end up in sex doesn't mean that it is always going to happen just because you will it to happen.

Just enjoy yourself, instead! Trust me: when a guy has a particular agenda, women will almost always pick up on it. If, for instance, you have a specific goal of getting married, you'll be subconsciously giving off needy, insecure vibes, which will make you unappealing to any particular partner. Likewise, if she senses that you're going to end up asking or begging for sex, she's going to think of you as a pushy guy. And besides, there's no way to determine what might happen at the end of the day; your best bet is to leave that up to fate. The most important thing is that you're both enjoying yourselves in the present moment.

You'll naturally be much more laid-back when you let go of far-fetched aspirations. If you have any goal at all, it shouldn't be any more ambitious than just having sex. There's nothing wrong with aiming to have sex, but even that isn't always necessary. You may very well find yourself developing a hot and heavy chemistry with a girl even without having been angling for sex during your first interactions.

Remember that talking to a woman, even if she's a total stranger, is completely normal. Women are people, too, and there's no need to be intimidated by them. Focus on being romantic, polite, and non-threatening to the best of your abilities. Let things move naturally and anything that's meant to be is sure to come to pass.

Getting Over Your Insecurities

Do you ever find yourself thinking any of these things?

- "My acne makes me ugly."
- "I'm too fat to be sexy."
- "I'm just not a good person."
- "I'm a failure because I live with my parents."
- "No girl will ever want me--I don't even own a car."

Try to think about any inner beliefs like this that have kept you from thinking that you could possibly be desirable to women. Your truth comes from what you believe--nothing else. If you're full of bad inner values that render you unconfident and unattractive, it's time to demolish them.

I won't pretend that the process is fast because it most definitely isn't. I used to have absolutely distressing levels of anxiety when it came to social interaction. My real issue was my fear of talking to people, especially girls, but I rationalized it by telling myself things like "I respect privacy and want to give everyone plenty of personal space." It wasn't until I sat down to evaluate myself and my life that I realized how shyness was a core problem for me. I found that I was too preoccupied with what other people thought about me. I was so frightened by the prospect of being refused at the end of an interaction that I could never even motivate myself to initiate one.

Once I had this revelation, everything changed. It was an incredible achievement for me--everything happened, quite literally, overnight.

From that point on, when I spoke to people, I tried to concentrate on the external rather than the internal. I paid attention to what the interaction was about rather than my inner insecurities. Furthermore, you may find that you have some positive internal values that can serve to benefit you. If you identify and strengthen these, it can be a massive improvement. In my case, I happen to be genetically gifted when it comes to bodybuilding. Focusing on this can increase my morale level by helping me think of myself as a muscular man.

Easy Alpha Male Exercises

1) Identify the positive, core values that you hold about yourself.

2) Strengthen them by improving what's good for you.

3) Identify the bad faith in your heart and get rid of it.

Again, this cannot happen overnight. It will take a while to be able to get through these three steps, so be patient. Take it slowly. Take baby steps to evaluate your habits and feelings and separate the patterns of thinking that are healthy from those that you want to eliminate. Do yourself a favor and save all your overthinking for later, when you're alone at home, not when you're talking to a woman.

Hold yourself focused outwardly when you are with a woman and just think about the conversation at hand. This will cause you to feel confident and thus more desirable to her as you express confidence, which enhances your chances of having sex.

Handling Your Fears of Rejection

Picture this: you're trying to talk to a hot lady. You see her standing in the supermarket magazine aisle, busy reading an issue of *Cosmopolitan*. Her hair is sleek, silky blonde, her skin is soft and pale, and--that's right--she's rocking some super impressive breasts.

You'll probably start to feel stressed right away. Excuses not to talk to her will pop in your mind: "I'm still in a tired mood," "I didn't dress well today," "I don't even know what to say to her," and so on. This pessimistic self-talk will ruin a potential interaction before it begins, reducing your chances of a sexual opportunity to absolute zero. You finish your shopping, go home, and sleep alone. When this happens, you're the only person to blame--you didn't give the girl a chance to do anything.

The truth is that you didn't hesitate because you were tired or poorly dressed, and you could have always found some conversation opener to break the ice. The real problem was *fear*. You weren't making an approach because you were terrified of rejection. "I wish I could just force myself to get over this ridiculous fear," you might think. But the reality is that, when we enter an unknown environment, we feel frightened. That's just basic human psychology, and there's no way around it.

Since this fear won't go away on its own, the only way to overcome it is to face it head-on. This means that, if you ever want things to change, you need to make the decision to start approaching people.

I used to be so afraid of talking to girls that my vision would start to blur if I so much as offered them a greeting. In every situation, I found another excuse to keep to myself. I kept waiting, and waiting, and waiting--yet my anxiety never ceased. I was immobilized, unable to find out why I was so afraid to speak to women, and spent day after day refusing to even just *try*.

Here's the truth: when it comes to talking to women, almost all guys are nervous because rejection sucks. It hits like a blow to your ego and it can be hard to recover from it. Everyone wants to keep their self-esteem at a high level. For emotionally healthy people, though, that self-worth comes from inside. They don't need to rely on anyone else to supply it.

If you adopt this mindset, rejection stops mattering so much. If a woman likes you, great; if not, you don't need to stress about it. You can't dictate how she feels, and there's not a single Man on earth who's capable of winning over every single woman. Sometimes things work, and sometimes they don't. It's really that simple.

The only way to be less afraid is by exposing yourself. Everyone feels anxiety when they're in an unfamiliar situation and in order to overcome it, you need to make that situation more familiar. At first, you're going to be extremely vulnerable and paranoid, but that's the case for everyone. It's up to you to decide that you're going to overcome it.

Here's the bottom line: everyone is haunted by an invisible specter that will never leave their side. Its name is Fear. If you let it control your life, it'll put you in a straitjacket--but it can also be your faithful friend. As long as you keep trying new things in life, fear will always be with you--but it will only get in your way if you allow it to do so. Fear will be there every time that you try something new and exciting, and that's okay. Even if it may not feel that way, you're the one in control of yourself. Nobody else is.

How To Eliminate Your Fear

You need to do three things to overcome your fear of talking with women:

1. Don't have expectations. Be social if you want to be social. Nothing more.

2. Chat with ladies. Know that doing the thing you fear is the only way to get over your fear. The sooner you commit to chatting for the sake of it, the better the results. When the inevitable rejection happens, you can think, "Been there, done that, it's not a big deal."

3. Identify what exactly scares you. This way, you can eliminate it.

Since fear is common when it comes to chatting with women, it is normal to feel anxiety about approaching a woman. Don't assume that your anxieties are uncommon. However, you need to do what you're scared of anyway. This is what distinguishes a Man like you from all the beta Males out there.

Some people let their fear and anxiety overcome them, not only about women, but other things in life, too, like their career. That's why, unfortunately, some guys never find the success they want. The reason most people never discuss their anxieties is that they don't know where they come from. Anxiety comes from inside. It is your brain that's causing it, not the likelihood that you'll be rejected. If you don't have expectations and open a conversation casually, you're less likely to experience anxiety and fear of rejection.

Since you have no expectations, don't just approach women you find attractive. Since you're looking for easy conversations, try approaching people who usually react best when talking to strangers. These are elderly people, generally, regardless of their sex. This may be because people in certain age groups experience more loneliness than others.

If it helps, set a time limit for interactions, such as speaking to one person for 30 seconds and then bailing out of the conversation. You can say things like, "Well, I'm on my way to meeting a friend. It was a pleasure talking with you" and then you can walk away without making a huge deal out of it. Once you establish a routine and are feeling comfortable approaching people to chat, you can start focusing on women you find attractive.

For instance, if a woman passes you by in a lobby, try saying "Hey--I need a fast female opinion on something," as though the thought had only just occurred to you. Once you have her attention, ask her something that you're genuinely curious about. Another trick from a friend of mine is to think of something hilarious right before you approach a stranger. A little bit of laughter will put you in a much more positive mood, which will heighten the chances of a successful interaction.

Sometimes things will go wrong, and that's okay. Instead of thinking, "Oh my God, this woman must hate me because I'm fumbling my vocabulary," try thinking something like "It's cool that I'm talking to this girl--even if she rejects me, then she's out of the way, and I'm one step closer to finding my dream girl."

If you're nervous, try to identify the parts of your body that are physically reacting to your anxiety. On a physiological level, nervousness is accompanied by muscle tension. In my personal experience, I find that I feel the most tension in my face and jaw. When I make a conscious effort to relax those muscles, it tells my brain that it's time to feel comfortable rather than anxious.

Another way to relieve anxiety requires an exercise in imagination. Before you open your mouth to speak to an unfamiliar woman, envision the scene as though it already happened and she has rejected you. This helps you feel comfortable for a number of reasons. For one, you can be invigorated by the knowledge that you're at least going to give it your best shot-- you're an Alpha Male who goes through life without excusing his needs or apologizing for his desires. Secondly, each rejection is a step closer to success. Every time you're turned down, you'll learn and improve from your mistakes, and your conversational skills will reflect that in the future. Third and lastly, you've made even more progress towards desensitizing yourself, meaning that your next interaction will be that much less intimidating.

Eventually, you'll reach the point where you're so used to talking to women that their negative responses no longer bother you. If you get verbally shot down, your instinct won't be to be embarrassed by it; instead, you'll be thinking something along the lines of "Ha, how original--I've had lots of women give me that exact same rude remark, as if they thought it was clever or something."

Tons of guys, even the ones you would call "ladies' Men," were awkward and insecure at one point or another. They simply got over it. And if they could do it, so can you.

Stretch Yourself, But Don't Break Yourself

It's good to deliberately put yourself in uncomfortable situations, but don't forget that it shouldn't become overwhelming. Any workout in this book is intended to be done regularly, but accept when you can't take any more. Your body will give you obvious signals. The same holds true for your strength of mind.

Although willpower is likely based on whether we believe it is limited or not (and not, as Kelly McGonigal and Roy Baumeister claim, depending on your level of glucose), there is a point where discomfort is too much to handle. The sweet spot is to expand your comfort zone to such an extent that you feel challenged, but not too stressed or threatened.

Going past the bearable level of discomfort will lead to decreased effectiveness, and often to negative outcomes that actually work against you. Hardcore workaholics are proud to work 70 + hours a week, feeling that they are extremely self-disciplined. They expect admiration for their efforts from everyone they know. What they're really doing is the total opposite of self-discipline. Studies have shown that someone who works 70 hours generates nothing more with those additional 15 hours than a person who works 55 hours a week.

Self-discipline is not built overnight. Play the long game and prioritize sustainability over rapid results if you want to become mentally tougher and be more in control of your temptations. If you want to add more pressure in your life, in order to become tougher and more disciplined, note that for the short term, it is not about putting too much stress on yourself. It's about desensitization, which refers to gradual and frequent stressor exposure.

You won't learn new skills easily without proper rest. Give yourself enough time to heal before you try another workout or stick to your routine for more than a couple of months. Do not forget to plan break times each time you set a new daily routine or a target you would like to achieve. Even if you don't exercise, you should still give yourself breaks from your routine and work. This can be done with both your job (through holidays) and a diet (with cheat days).

A Positive Mindset Is Important for Mental Toughness

The purpose of creating self-discipline and mental toughness is to make your life more enjoyable, so that you can manage its temptations, defeats, and failures better.

Such drills can also help you appreciate what you have more in addition to making you stronger. As a result, you become a more grateful person with a positive attitude that helps you take on every day. If you start a 30-day cold shower challenge, you'll develop a newfound appreciation for hot showers from now on. When you start learning a foreign language, you will be more appreciative of the fact that you are already speaking the world's most important language. If you miss food for 24-48 hours, you will be more grateful for the fact that there is always food in your refrigerator and you will also enjoy it more.

As I have already discussed in my book, *Pure and Simple: How to Simplify Your Life, Do Less, and Get More*, gratitude is one of the keys to having a positive attitude. It improves mental and physical health, helps make friends, decreases violence, promotes empathy, and relieves stress and trauma.

Building on your self-discipline and mental toughness will help you to become a person of greater success. Nonetheless, it's your willingness to recognize what you have and maintain a positive attitude that will make you get back to the way things are after a loss or disappointment that is especially difficult. If self-discipline is the only reason you keep going as an alpha, you may find yourself drained of your willpower one day. The second layer of motivation, which is a positive attitude, can keep you going when you don't want to do anything and all your willpower is gone.

Resisting "simple" temptations, such as eating a cake while on a diet, not wanting to put on jogging shoes, or pushing the snooze button instead of waking up early can be tackled using self-discipline alone. Train your willpower, develop better default responses and the majority of these temptations can be overcome.

Difficult, unforeseen temptations and threats to your determination will wreak havoc on your self-discipline. If you've lost a business, there may not be enough determination and resilience alone to get back on track and launch another business within days of the loss.

Tough, self-disciplined people may feel inclined to blame themselves for all they've been through. Worse yet, they may be tempted to continue to work in the same business, feeling that giving up (when it makes sense to do so) would be a sign of weakness.

In such a situation, people who can recognize what they still have (for example, a supportive wife or a learning experience), have something more valuable than pure self-discipline. They have developed psychological endurance and the ability to move forward. If anything fails, it is what it is. Learn the lessons and continue.

Focusing on the positive emotion (gratitude) rather than the negative one (anger) is what helps you escape the long downward spiral. There is a world of difference between a person who cheats and then blames themselves for being weak-minded, and a person who says to themselves, "it's okay to slip up every now and then, now it's just time to get back on the wagon." The first person would keep blaming himself, probably for so long and so seriously that he'll start to think it makes no sense to continue working on whatever target he'd been working on. The second person, although suffering the same loss as the first person, will not make it worse by making themselves feel guilty. They're going to pick up where they left and move on.

Just as I wasn't supposed to be going to the gym because I noticed clear signs of overtraining, you shouldn't always challenge yourself for total endurance and self-discipline. Move with the wind and do not resist.

What to Do When You're Trapped in a Funk or Pessimistic Self-Talk

When working on self-discipline, it's easy to go from one extreme (a lack of self-discipline) to another (being too harsh on yourself) when you're caught in a slump or suffering from negative self-talk. You appear to be harsher on yourself now that you are working on your discipline and judge yourself even more often and stronger than before.

Negative self-talk follows, berating you for every single failure or giving in to any kind of temptation (including those that you might overcome). It is easy to see that building long-term self-discipline isn't the best approach.

How do you deal with this issue and motivate yourself, instead of dragging out your inner criticism? Begin to develop greater self-compassion. There are several ways to build more self-compassion and get out of a funk or avoid negative self-talk as a result.

My favorite thing to do is to put together a list of ways to boost my mood, which will make me feel I care about myself. This is also the simplest thing to do. Each time you feel stuck or grumble about how dumb, frail, worthless or untalented you are, review your list and get your energy levels up. To give you a few examples, the list may include things as simple as listening to a particular genre of music (including different tracks), sitting in the sun, or talking to friends, as well as more creative ways, such as giving a gift to someone, telling someone that you admire them, or coming up with new ideas.

Create your own list. Read it every time you feel down, and choose something to boost your mood. When you feel depressed or irritated, it is hard to come up with ways to raise your spirits. Getting a list of proven ways to feel better ready is self-compassion in action. The lower one's self-compassion level is, the more it aids all those nasty negative thoughts to develop. Self-pity is effective in reminding yourself that there are things that you can do to feel better and it is your choice to stay in an unproductive state of mind.

When manipulating your body language instead of your subconscious, you can get out of a funk, too. When you stand upright, light up your face with a broad smile (it doesn't matter if it's fake), and start jumping up and down while waving your hands, it's impossible to stay down.

This wild advice is supported by science. Research on power posing has shown that maintaining a high-power body language triggers neuroendocrine processes and a simple visualization strategy can also benefit if you suffer from negative self-talk and are harder on yourself than on other people. Imagine you are a friend, family member, or anyone else who loves you, rather than looking at yourself through your own eyes.

How does it change your perception of yourself when you look through the eyes of someone who loves you? The simple understanding that you would not treat someone you love as you treat yourself can help you eradicate the negative self-talk or at least reduce it.

Don't forget that your inner criticism doesn't always have to come from negative self-talk. It can also be the product of a tired body. An example is having been following a strict diet for too long when you've been over-training or when you have not slept well for the past week. It's easy to get in a bad mood if your body is tired, and as a result, you start doubting yourself or feeling you can't put up with anything for a long time. Check your physical condition and make sure you get enough sleep, nutrients (dieting can sometimes cause nutritional deficiencies), sun (the body's lack of vitamin D from sun exposure can potentially cause depression), and quiet time (a hectic schedule can raise stress levels).

CHAPTER TWENTY-TWO

IT'S TIME - LIVING YOUR BEST ALPHA LIFE

Living Like a Legend

THE TERM "ALPHA" isn't only for show. You have to be strong, active, and courageous. Don't act anything less than legendary; wimps need not apply. But, more importantly, be yourself. Always incorporate yourself into everything you do.

Bear in mind that to see the major changes, both mentally and physically, takes time, however. So, sit back and recognize the huge progress that you're making every day.

Keeping Bad Habits Under Control

Controlling your habits is the best way to gain control of your wellbeing in the long term. First, take a look at your habits and decide which ones need to be controlled. You should already have a list of things to fix in your lifestyle. Are you addicted to sedentary pursuits, smoking, drinking, or pornography? These are the roadblocks that can damage your health, both in the short term and the long term. Bear in mind that you cannot remove a habit altogether. You need to develop a new habit that will take its place. In addition to the regular goals you set for yourself way back in the first chapter, consider the following habits as possible alternatives for the bad habits you're trying to break:

Walk: Regardless of your personal situation, where you live, and how healthy you are, you can always allow the time for a brisk walk. Try to incorporate 30 minutes to an hour of fast walking in your day, every day. You can do this on your way home from work, when you go to the grocery store, or for the sake of walking, in a park or nice area of town. Burning up to 300 calories per walking session can relieve stress and help keep weight down to the level you're comfortable with.

Sleep Well: This is vital for your energy levels. Most people don't consider their sleep needs and don't get enough sleep. This is a mistake because your energy levels cannot serve you well when you're sleep deprived. The trick to sleeping well is to regularly schedule your daily routine. Set a daily bedtime and stick to it. Do not consume coffee and other energy drinks later in the day. Only take a nap if your sleep the previous night was poor or you couldn't go to bed early. Taking a walk can do wonders to keep your sleeping patterns regular.

Take a Cold Shower: Cold showers have a variety of proven health benefits. Taking them can help relieve tension, reduce muscle pain, encourage alertness, increase circulation, and help to close pores. Taking a shower is also the best way to avoid body odor. To get used to cold showers, try starting your day with one every day for the next month. This will also show you that you're a true Alpha Male. Beta Males would not be able to maintain a tough routine like this for a month.

Turn Your Body into a Weapon: As the most important asset you'll ever have in life, your body is only second to your mind. You have no excuse for taking control of your body. You can't blame stress or bad genes. Don't get me wrong; you don't need to go to the gym every day to accomplish this. If you do push-ups, sit ups, and squats every day, you've got it covered. Do at least 50 of each or, even better, do sets. These activities can be performed in any order you want.

Take Care of Your Skin: This will make you feel comfortable and desirable besides ensuring that you have healthy skin. Use a facial wash for men. If you have blemishes, like pimples or shaving cuts, try a milder wash. Develop a daily skincare routine. This can be based on making sure that you wash your face daily.

Watch What You Eat: You should also be mindful of what you consume. Avoid foods which are high in sugar, salt, and trans-fats for the next 30 days. Use the guide provided in the next chapter to decide on what to include in your diet.

Boycotting Your Bad Habits

Self-discipline and determination are important if you want to keep your bad habits under control. The hard part is that bad habits are a lot harder to stop than they are to start. This is because the human mind is programmed to prioritize short-term gratification. Long-term rewards, on the other hand, typically require some form of sacrifice like time, energy, and effort before you can enjoy them.

Focusing on the long-term impact of your actions allows your ration and higher mind to control these habits. As an Alpha Male, you are good at being logical and centered. Challenge yourself to make the right decision at all times and decide how to reward yourself after doing so. A simple strategy to help you boycott your bad habits is to present yourself with a choice. As we saw above, there are many good choices that you can replace your bad habits with.

Now that you've accepted the Alpha Male attitude, style, and healthy habits, it's time to move on to the bigger lifestyle changes that you are supposed to live by every single day of your life. The following is a list of the habits and actions that will give you real results over the long term and will significantly improve your life. This list also involves a few financial habits that are not normally used by beta Males.

Take Charge of Your Life

An Alpha Male should always be ready to assume the leader's role. The key to his charisma lies in his perception of the balance between courtesy and assertiveness. In all cases, that acts as an advantage. It may sound simple, but practice can be difficult. You can take charge, as always, one step at a time. And this time, in three simple steps, you can start taking care of your life:

Be a Good Listener

A leader can see the potential in other people and inspire them to use it. This is extremely important in your work, business, and school life. Also, reserving judgment will reflect well on your personality, making you, overall, a more reliable person. Aim to build relationships with your colleagues over the next 30 days by identifying their strengths and encouraging them to take advantage of that.

Be a Financially Sound Person

An Alpha Male knows his way around money. One rule of dating is to always pay for your food. So, make sure you've still got a little extra money left for a rainy day. Save at least $10 per day for the next 30 days by cutting expenses or finding additional revenue opportunities. Invest in your expertise, also, when it comes to investments.

Be a Gentleman

While Alpha Males are supposed to be intimidating, they should always be humorous and chivalrous, not only to women but also to other Men. Being a gentleman can be extended to your daily life activities. All it takes is having a little empathy and being respectful. Pardoning and acknowledging your faults, for example, is not a sign of weakness. Actually, it's the other way around. Practice being courteous to the people around you for the next 30 days and see how appreciative they will be of you.

Eat Right

You should learn by now that Alpha Males keep their weight under control. But this is not just about eating three meals a day. The way you eat depends exclusively on what you need to achieve. Simply put, you need a caloric deficit if you want to lose weight, which can be done by consuming less calories than what your body requires. If you're a skinny guy and need extra pounds, then you need caloric surplus, which is the opposite of caloric deficiency. Both are the core components of a diet and can be calculated by using calculators to classify maintenance calories, such as:

- Calorie King: www.calorieking.com
- Free diet: www.freedieting.com
- A Calorie Counter: www.acaloriecounter.com

Determine whether you need a calorie deficit or surplus and strive for a 500 calorie difference for your meals. Only trust the caloric content of specific foods that can be found on the food labels or online databases. Keep in mind that the main dietary aim is to monitor how much you consume, not how often. You should try spreading your daily calories into 4-5 tiny meals throughout the day to keep your cravings at bay. Doing so will help to keep your appetite subdued all day.

Dominate Your Fears

We are all afraid of something. But the difference between an Alpha Male and a beta male is that alphas know how to believe their fears in an intelligent way. Anxieties can be seen as short-comings or openings to build room for improvement. Do something that you usually hate to do within the next 30 days. It should, of course, be something positive or imaginative, like overcoming your fear of public speaking, rejection, and so forth. Don't pick something insignificant like fear of spiders or heights. Whether it is an opportunity to start a business, approach a girl you're attracted to, or to join a competition that you've never had the guts to compete in, it doesn't matter.

An Alpha Male does not just embrace these opportunities only to win, but also to enrich his life. It may sound cheesy, but believing that you are an Alpha Male and meeting your fears head-on will certainly improve your faith. For example, if you're afraid of public speaking, make engaging in public speaking events a goal and see how comfortable you can be with your newfound confidence.

CONCLUSION

THE INNER ALPHA MALE WRAP UP

Not every guy is an Alpha Male from day one and there's always something that needs working on. For some of us there are many areas to work on! That's exactly what this book is for, to help any Man that has something missing in his life to figure out what that is and drive home a solution for the long term. Of course we all have bad days, weeks, even months. However, if you're aware of these things and you are actively working to improve yourself, including staying sharp, keeping control, and remaining fit and healthy, then you'll be putting your best foot forward each day, no matter what the level. We must always endeavor to move forward and be better Men.

This kind of attitude and approach to each day is what makes great Men, leaders, partners, friends, and regular Alpha Males. That's how you'll create and live a great life and how you'll inspire and help others to do the same. You might be saying to yourself that getting in shape and eating well doesn't really seem like world changing stuff. However, that's exactly what it is. What this world needs is a new breed of Man, a combination of the great parts of a modern Man with all the primal (and largely missing) parts of our ancestors.

Training and eating well are two of the very foundations that make a great Man. These things help you develop your strength and confidence and become able to go on to do great things, regardless of the scale. As we've seen, for this to happen, your head must be in the right place, and you have to think about the things you need. Putting time and effort into who you are, what you want out of each day, and how you want to be perceived by others is critical. Asking yourself what your ultimate motivation is and what ultimately makes you happy is vital for a Man that wants to be a real alpha. Remember, it's the thoughts that lead to actions, and these actions become habits, and soon this is who you are. It's really quite simple when you set it out, so go back through the key points of this book and start using your head.

Next comes the biggest factor – your nutrition. Getting this wrong can be a health, waistline, and libido killer. Having a big gut and finding it hard to walk up a few flights of stairs is really only the start of a number of issues affecting health, including low sex drive, diabetes, heart disease, depression, and low confidence. It's easy to see how so many can get it wrong. Mass advertising, lax government policies, celebrity fads, and know-it-all nutritionists present conflicting messages. It can be too much to even contemplate, let alone master. However, it's really quite simple. When performed on a regular basis, healthy nutrition can be your best form of medicine that helps to create the awesome body that your mirror will reflect. Not to mention, healthy nutrition will shape a healthy, confident, and vibrant guy who loves waking up each day.

Once you understand healthy nutrition, you should write your own weekly meal plan. After that, check the plans we provided, as well as the included bonus material for more details and information. For the most part, you can follow the plans laid out in this book. Pay attention to the food you eat and how your body reacts to it and let this be your guide. Once you've followed the guidelines and you're feeling awesome and starting to look like the kind of Man you want to be, then you can start getting specific. In this instance, turn to the back of the book to see how you can contact Mike if you have questions or would like guidance.

It's easy to see how exercise and training can become confusing for some people. While this part of your daily life is not affected by the same level of propaganda as food is, there are still mixed messages. However, exercise (and getting to a point where you look good) involves hard work, people commonly look for an easy option or a quick fix. This can lead to stagnation, frustration, injury, weight gain, and a feeling of losing heart about training entirely. This often results in giving up until you reach the breaking point again and feel you need to do something or you'll keep getting worse.

Perhaps you're in danger of not having that realization. That's where the good news comes in. Training isn't that complicated; in fact it's really basic. You just have to work hard. There are many programs and approaches, but if you stick to these principles and combine staying active with the other steps in this process, you'll be well on your way to becoming a ripped and athletic Alpha Male. Again, go through your key points. Check the information in your bonus material if you want to learn more and then start using the available programs. Too many guys over-think training and try to get everything a certain way, constantly searching for the "perfect" program that will finally get them in shape. Don't fall for this. Keep it simple and train as if you're an athlete and your paycheck depends on it. Do keep in mind that, no matter who you are, where you live, or how old you are, you can train hard and get in shape.

Living a balanced life sometimes seems impossible. Some people say they'll get a more balanced life when they retire. However, this approach will always prevent you from reaching it. Many Men today struggle with the concept of balance. We spend too many hours at the office and not enough doing the things we enjoy with the people we enjoy. What's worse, we don't get nearly enough quality sleep. The week can't go fast enough and the weekend comes and goes. This pattern of high stress, little enjoyment, and poor sleep results in a hormonal imbalance that, left to its own devices, can give rise to metabolic diseases or worse. Living like this means that you're heading to a bad place.

One of the best tools for feeling amazing every day is managing stress by getting enough quality sleep. Many people miss this point and this is why there are so many stressed out, fat, and hormonally disbalanced Men everywhere. Like everything else, it doesn't have to be that way. It's easy to put some actions in place to ensure that you get enough sleep, less stress, and more enjoyment out of your day. Start by always enforcing a positive frame of mind in yourself. Once you set goals that are based on your core values, you'll start heading in the right direction each day. From there, focus on sleep and nutrition and ensure that you are always balanced in all that you do. If this seems like a nice idea, but you feel that it isn't practical, you need to sit down and get a hold of your priorities. Go back to your core values and find out what matters most to you. If all you care about is to make lots of money and die rich, so be it. However, if you want to be healthy, well-adjusted, and able to spend time with your loved ones doing things that give life meaning and make you smile, reconsider your priorities and take control of your life. After all, this is what we're talking about: Alpha Males have control of their lives and they love how they live.

The final step in your journey to unleash your inner alpha is to master the finer points, the icing on the cake and the polish that makes the shoe shine. This is an area that is lost on a lot of Men. If you don't understand the consequences of your choices and how you come across to others as a Man, you'll miss out on many moments in life that matter. No doubt, confidence will come from getting in shape but it also comes from your actions. You have to actively seek activities that improve your confidence levels and exude confidence. We're not talking about arrogance, self-importance, or selfishness. We're talking about subtle confidence that includes self-worth and looking after yourself. We're also talking about being able to do the things that a Man should do. There's a missing link in our development as Men because of a lack of traditional rite of passage; this can arguably cause a women-dominated world without the proper tools to function as a Man. Conversely, we can have far too much masculine energy that causes us to act based on ego and macho bravado. Our primal and animal instincts are to garner respect and be desirable to encourage potential mates who want to mate with us. These instincts can be defeated as a result of our lifestyles. It is up to you to walk proudly and assert your confidence and dominance. This is what being an Alpha Man means and it is exactly where the finer points of being an Alpha Male are relevant.

Once you've started to initiate some of these steps, you'll see your confidence grow, your situation improve, and your life change for the better. This isn't due to the universe aligning for you, but because you're starting to develop a clear view about yourself and becoming a better Man. You'll be doing things for yourself. You'll be doing things for others. You'll be hustling all the time to improve and be an awesome guy and become an alpha legend. Once you nail this stuff, you can begin fine-tuning your progress with the help of a life coach.

To become an alpha legend, a leader, and a magnet for people and good luck, you have to be dedicated to these changes. Don't wait or deviate from the path or you'll miss opportunities. Get to a point where you're happy and stay the course. If need be, you can always iron out wrinkles as you go. If you're staying the course, you're staying productive, which means that you're moving forward. This is the hustle you need to get into. To improve any part of your life, from sleep to weight loss to attracting the right mate, you have to hustle and work your butt off. No one will do this for you. You have to take ownership of your own life and your own fate. You're now actively working to build your muscles and become strong. Similarly, train your hustle muscles. Always look to increase your hustle. Stop obsessing over the things that don't matter and just get going.

Get out of your comfort zone, stretch yourself, and evolve. You should always make your own luck, remember?

This whole process is about recognizing the potential within you. This is about patience, practice, progress, and being dedicated. This is about having maturity when it's needed and the power of laughter when it's not. This is about your mission to become a better Man and positively affect the world and the people around you every day. This is about hustle and hard work. This is about building a better version of yourself, a great body, a great character, and a great life.

SELF-WORTH AFFIRMATIONS FOR ALPHA MALES

- I am unique. I feel good about being alive and being me.
- Life is fun and rewarding.
- Amazing opportunities exist for me in every aspect of my life.
- There are no such things as problems, only opportunities.
- I love challenges; they bring out the best in me.
- I replace "I must", "I should" and "I have to" with "I choose". (try it with something you think you have to do, and replace must with choose... notice the difference?)
- I choose to be happy right now. I love my life.
- I appreciate everything I have. I live in joy.
- I am courageous. I am willing to act in spite of any fear.
- I am positive and optimistic. I believe things will always work out for the best.
- It's easy to make friends. I attract positive and kind people into my life.

- It's easy to meet people. I create positive and supportive relationships.
- v I am a powerful creator. I create the life I want.
- I am OK as I am. I accept and love myself.
- I am confident. I trust myself.
- I am successful right now.
- I am passionate. I am outrageously enthusiastic and inspire others.
- I am calm and peaceful.
- I have unlimited power at my disposal.
- I am optimistic. I believe things will always work out for the best.
- I am kind and loving. I am compassionate and truly care for others.
- I am focused and persistent. I will never quit.
- I am energetic and enthusiastic. Confidence is my second nature.
- I treat everyone with kindness and respect.
- I inhale confidence and exhale fear.
- I am flexible. I adapt to change quickly.
- I have integrity. I am totally reliable. I do what I say.
- I am competent, smart and able.
- I believe in myself,
- I recognize the many good qualities I have.
- I see the best in other people.
- I surround myself with people who bring out the best in me.
- I let go of negative thoughts and feelings about myself.
- I love who I have become.
- I am always growing and developing.
- My opinions resonate with who I am.
- I am congruent in everything I say and do.
- I deserve to be happy and successful

- I have the power to change myself
- I can forgive and understand others and their motives
- I can make my own choices and decisions
- I am free to choose to live as I wish and to give priority to my desires
- I can choose happiness whenever I wish no matter what my circumstances
- I am flexible and open to change in every aspect of my life
- I act with confidence having a general plan and accept plans are open to alteration
- It is enough to have done my best
- I deserve to be loved
- I have high self-esteem
- I love and respect myself.
- I am a great person.
- I respect myself deeply.
- My thoughts and opinions are valuable.
- I am confident that I can achieve anything.
- I have something special to offer the world.
- Others like and respect me.
- I am a wonderful human being I feel great about myself and my life.
- I am worthy of having high self-esteem.
- I believe in myself.
- I deserve to feel good about myself.
- I know I can achieve anything.
- Having respect for myself helps others to like and respect me.
- Feeling good about myself is normal for me.
- Improving my self-esteem is very important.
- Being confident in myself comes naturally to me.
- Liking and respecting myself is easy.

- Speaking my mind with confidence is something I just naturally do.
- Each day I notice I am more self-discipline.
- I enjoy being self-disciplined.
- I am doing the best I can with the knowledge and experience I have obtained so far.
- It's OK to make mistakes. They are opportunities to learn.
- I always follow through on my promises.
- I treat others with kindness and respect.
- I see myself with kind eyes.
- I am a unique and a very special person.
- I love myself more each day.
- I am willing to change.
- I approve of myself.
- I care about myself.
- I am a child of God.
- My work gives me pleasure.
- I give praise freely.
- I am respected by others.
- I rejoice in my uniqueness.
- I attract praise.
- I deserve good in my life.
- I appreciate myself.
- Each day I am becoming more self-confident.

201 POSITIVE AFFIRMATIONS
FOR ALPHA MALES

DESCRIPTION

These affirmations are designed to improve your personal magnetism, harmonize your brain's abilities, and help your subconscious mind to change your unconscious beliefs.

Read these powerful affirmations for 21 days in a row and watch your life and how you think of yourself begin to transform around you.

Your dominant thoughts create your reality.

The brain is made up of the conscious and the subconscious mind. 90-95% of our everyday life is the result of our subconscious mind being programmed. It controls everything from breathing to cell repair, hair growth, to our heartbeat. We all have subconscious beliefs and habits that prevent us from living out our true potential. To change old beliefs, we must replace them with new ones.

Use these affirmations to reprogram your subconscious mind. Read them for at least 21 days/nights in a row as you're in bed falling asleep. When reading, try to imagine yourself as your ideal version, and feel the emotions of how it would be if you were already that ideal version.

50 Positive Affirmations For Success

1. I am focused and never quit

2. I am committed to maximizing my success

3. A challenge brings out the best in me

4. If I am to fail, I will fail forward

5. My dreams are there to achieve

6. My confidence has no limit

7. I will do what it takes to achieve my goals

8. I will seize every opportunity presented to me

9. I am prepared to go the extra mile

10. Hard work fulfills me

11. Success comes naturally to me

12. Success is my driving force

13. I love what I do

14. I believe in myself

15. I'm worthy of success

16. I choose what I become

17. I deserve success

18. I excel in all that I do

19. I set high standards for myself

20. I am focused

21. I am patient

22. I trust the universe

23. I respect myself

24. I will be great

25. I have limitless potential

26. I have an opportunity

27. I will do whatever it takes

28. Nothing can stop me

29. I will achieve my goals

30. I see my goal clearly

31. I am determined

32. I see challenges as opportunities for growth

33. I am the architect of my life

34. I'm a magnet for success

35. I'm right where I need to be

36. I live my life without fear

37. I feel things falling into place

38. I like myself

39. Success is second nature to me

40. Mistakes are a stepping stone to success

41. I am proud of my success

42. I think only of success

43. All problems have a solution

44. I am in charge of my life

45. My power comes from within me

46. I find inspiration easily

47. Consistency is key to my success

48. Everything I touch is a success

49. I am persistent

50. Life is full of choices. I choose success

51 Positive Affirmations For Wealth

1. Money comes to me easily

2. I attract money

3. My mind is focused on wealth

4. Every day, I am becoming richer

5. My actions lead to prosperity

6. Prosperity is my birthright

7. I enjoy the rewards of working

8. I appreciate the value of things

9. I radiate positivity

10. My attitude attracts wealth

11. I can provide for my family

12. Money allows me to help people

13. Fortune favors me

14. I will become financially abundant

15. I am receptive to wealth and success

16. My life is filled with riches

17. I will achieve my financial desires

18. I am grateful for my wealth

19. My success is predetermined

20. I am abundant

21. Success leads to wealth and I am successful

22. I am a wealth magnet

23. I attract people who will help me in achieving wealth

24. I am highly driven

25. I will become financially free

26. I choose to be wealthy

27. My energy is aligned with wealth

28. I am wealth

29. Money comes to me in expected and unexpected ways

30. I deserve wealth

31. Money always finds its way to me

32. The universe serves my best interests

33. I always have enough

34. I am worth the money

35. I love luxury

36. I am blessed with money

37. I deserve to live a life of luxury

38. My wallet is overflowing with money

39. I feel rich

40. My prosperity is unlimited

41. Money is great

42. I am financially secure

43. I attract wealth and prosperity

44. I am happy, healthy, and wealthy

45. I always have opportunities to make more money

46. I attract money, love, and happiness wherever I go

47. I welcome unlimited income into my life

48. I am destined to be wealthy

49. It's my choice as to how much money I make

50. I have an endless supply of cash

51. Today is a day of amazing good fortune

25 Positive Affirmations For Alpha Male Mindset

1. I embrace my masculinity

2. I view myself as a strong and capable Man

3. I feel strong and confident, regardless of the situation

4. I become stronger and more beautiful every day

5. I am a natural leader and easily accomplish my goals

6. My greatest weapon is my optimism

7. I have the courage to wear whatever I want

8. Women naturally gravitate towards me

9. I am in love with my true self

10. I deserve the love of a strong woman/Man

11. Confidence comes naturally to me

12. I am dominant

13. I am totally secure in myself

14. When I speak, I carry authority

15. I can take the lead in any social situation

16. I was born to be an Alpha Male

17. Assertiveness and dominance come naturally to me

18. I enjoy being a leader

19. I am highly respected

20. It's OK to be strong, both mentally and physically

21. I am proud to be a Man

22. Today, I will start loving myself more

23. I will surround myself with other positive, confident Men

24. I will continue to strengthen my Alpha traits

25. Others look up to my strength of character

25 Positive Affirmations For Dealing With Depression

1. Life is beautiful

2. I feel grateful to be alive

3. I am in charge of how I feel, and today I will feel happy

4. I forgive myself for my past mistakes. Every new day is an opportunity to start over

5. I will overcome and get through any feelings of sadness

6. My mind is powerful. When I fill it with positive thoughts, my life will begin to change.

7. I am brave

8. I have enthusiasm for life

9. I will not focus on what hurts me. I will focus on what brings me joy

10. I will keep going, and I will grow stronger

11. It is in my power to be happy

12. This, too, shall pass

13. I deserve to be happy

14. I am grateful for the good things in my life

15. I love myself

16. More and more, I can see the beauty of my own being

17. I am worthy of love and happiness

18. I will not let myself become discouraged

19. I can find beauty in even the smallest things

20. I'm OK with where I am right now

21. I love myself

22. Hard times oRer me opportunities to grow

23. I find and enjoy the simple pleasures life has to offer

24. Life wants the best for me

25. I will not judge myself negatively

25 Positive Affirmations for Men: Anxiety

1. I am safe and loved

2. I have faith that everything will work out in the end

3. What I want is already here or on its way

4. I appreciate everything I have

5. As I let go of things, the better I feel

6. I breathe in relaxation, I breathe out the tension

7. I am free of anything that will weigh me down

8. Life is beautiful, wonderful, and peaceful

9. I am mentally strong and don't take things personally

10. I attract positive energy into my mind and body

11. I attract positive and confident people into my life

12. I accept myself for who I am

13. I am cool, calm, and collected

14. Worry and anxiety will not change my circumstances. Only positive actions and thoughts can

15. Happiness and joy flow easily to me

16. I have confidence in myself and my abilities

17. Success will be the force that drives me

18. I will speak with confidence

19. I do not fear to be wrong

20. When I put my mind to something, I am unstoppable

21. Happiness is within my grasp

22. I accept and love myself for who I am

23. I am ready to take on any challenge

24. I become stronger and more confident every day

25. I am in complete control of my anxiety

25 Positive Affirmations To Start Off Your Day

1. Every time I wake up, I am grateful to be alive

2. Today, I will focus only on positive thoughts and energy

3. Today, I will finish all my tasks with joy

4. Each day is filled with abundance and joy

5. I will go to sleep a better person than I am at this moment

6. Good energy flows through me

7. Today, I will manifest new opportunities

8. I am full of ideas

9. I will make the most out of today

10. Today could be one of the best days in my life

11. My happiness grows stronger every day

12. I am calm and at peace

13. I choose to do great things today

14. I will enjoy everything today has to offer

15. I am ready to take on the day

16. Today, I will be smarter, kinder, and wiser

17. I honor all my responsibilities

18. I trust the process that is life

19. I manifest abundance easily

20. I will become a better version of myself today

21. I will start each day with a grateful heart

22. The world needs my energy and ideas

23. No matter what happened the day before, I will get up, show up, and never give up

24. I am positive and will attract good things in my direction

25. Today, I will worry less and smile more

"ALL THAT WE ARE IS THE RESULT OF WHAT WE HAVE THOUGHT."

BUDDHA

ALPHA MALE BIBLE

Charisma, Psychology of Attraction, Charm.

Art of Confidence, Self-Hypnosis, Meditation.

Art of Body Language, Eye Contact, Small Talk.

Habits & Self-Discipline of a Real Alpha Man.

ALPHA MALE DATING
THE ESSENTIAL PLAYBOOK

Single → Engaged → Married (If You Want).

Love Hypnosis, Law of Attraction,

Art of Seduction, Intimacy in Bed.

Attract Women as an Irresistible Alpha Man.

ALPHA MALE
THE 7 LAWS OF POWER

Mindset & Psychology of Success.

Manipulation, Persuasion, NLP Secrets. Analyze & Influence Anyone.

Hypnosis Mastery ● Emotional Intelligence.

Win as a Real Alpha Man.

★★★

**I Would Appreciate It if You Left a Review,
It's Very Important.**

★★★

 SEAN WAYNE

 **mr.sean.wayne.author@gmail.com**

Printed in the USA
CPSIA information can be obtained
at www.ICGtesting.com
LVHW020013101123
763156LV00032B/10

9 781739 622923